THE UNITED NATIONS AND THE QUEST
FOR NUCLEAR DISARMAMENT

The United Nations and the Quest for Nuclear Disarmament

DIMITRIS BOURANTONIS
Athens University of Economics and Business

Dartmouth

Aldershot · Brookfield USA · Hong Kong · Singapore · Sydney

Published by
Dartmouth Publishing Company Limited
Gower House
Croft Road
Aldershot
Hants GU11 3HR
England

Dartmouth Publishing Company
Old Post Road
Brookfield
Vermont 05036
USA

British Library Cataloguing in Publication Data
Bourantonis, Dimitris
  United Nations and the Quest for Nuclear
  Disarmament
  I. Title
  327.1

Library of Congress Cataloging-in-Publication Data
Bourantonis, Dimitris
    The United Nations and the quest for nuclear disarmament /
  Dimitris Bourantonis.
      p. cm.
    ISBN 1-85521-344-3 : $59.95 (approx.)
    1. Nuclear disarmament–History.   2. United Nations–History.
  I. Title.
  JX1974.7.B655   1993
  327.1′74′09–dc20   93-20001
                                                                          CIP

ISBN 1 85521 344 3

Printed in Great Britain at the University Press, Cambridge

Contents

Acknowledgements

I would like to express my appreciation to Dr. R. J. Barry Jones and Peter M. Jones for their encouragement and valuable advice throughout the various stages of my research. I am also very grateful for the helpful criticisms of portions of the manuscript to John Edmonds and Professor Keith Dill Nunes. My thanks are due, too, to Sydney Bailey with whom I discussed various aspects of this work. None of these can be held to blame, however, for any errors of fact or failings of judgement. Finally, I am grateful to the staffs of all the libraries in which I have worked, in particular for the assistance, patience and kindly interest of the Librarians and staffs at the Royal Institute of International Affairs, the Public Record Office and the UN Office in London, on whom I depended a great deal.

Abbreviations

AEC	Atomic Energy Commission
CCA	Commission for Conventional Armaments
CCD	Conference of the Committee on Disarmament (1969-1978)
CD	Committee on Disarmament (1979-84)
	Conference on Disarmament (1984-)
CTBT	Comprehensive Test Ban Treaty
DC	Disarmament Commission
ECOSOC	Economic and Social Council
ENDC	Eighteen Nation Disarmament Committee (1962-1968)
ENMOD	environmental modification: in particular, the 1977 Convention on the Prohibition of Military or Any Other Hostile Use of Environmental Modification Techniques
FO	Foreign Office (UK)
GA	General Assembly
GCD	general and complete disarmament
IADA	International Atomic Development Agency
IAEA	International Atomic Energy Agency
ICJ	International Court of Justice
INF	Intermediate-Range Nuclear Forces

NATO	North Atlantic Treaty Organization
NIEO	New International Economic Order
NPT	Non-Proliferation Treaty
PTBT	Partial Test Ban Treaty
SC	Security Council
SALT	Strategic Arms Limitation Talks
SIPRI	Stockholm International Peace Research Institute
SSOD-I	The first special session on disarmament (1978)
SSOD-II	The second special session on disarmament (1982)
SSOD-III	The third special session on disarmament (1988)
START	Strategic Arms Reduction Talks (US title)
	Arms Limitation and Reduction Talks (Soviet title)
UN	United Nations
UNGA	United Nations General Assembly
WDC	World Disarmament Conference

Introduction

The study of the role of the United Nations (UN) in one of the most sensitive areas of international peace and security, that of disarmament, was one of the prime concerns of the academic and other research institutions in the early life of the world organization. Valuable contributions concerning the performance of the UN in the field of disarmament were made during this period. However, the subject as a focus point of research began to decline in the 1950s during the long-lasting Cold War era which was accompanied by a lack of success in the actions of the UN. The subject assumed much more prominence in the sixties mainly due to the UN's substantial involvement in the making of certain breakthroughs in the realm of arms control measures.

Since the superpowers, in the era of detente, were more concerned with the stabilization of the arms race than with disarmament as an objective of their policy, the latter was relegated to the margins of public interest. This had its own consequences on the course of the academic debate. It was diverted more than ever within the limits of the narrow intellectual framework of strategic analysis. Thus, the analysis of the UN's performance was disregarded, and still remains so, by a large part of the academic family in spite of the fact that disarmament has been established as a permanent item on the agenda of the UN. Nowadays the astonishing scope of changes in the world and the looming trend towards more democratic international relations open up a prospect of commitment of the states to the services of the UN and, consequently, a refocusing on the UN as a centre of academic reference.

The lack of systematic analysis of the UN's work on disarmament created a cleavage in the study of this subject and has prevented the attainment of a complete insight into the whole picture of the UN as it has evolved in more than forty years of activity in the field of disarmament. The UN has developed since its inception a life and a political ethos of its own; it has built up its own environment which, changing from time to time, embraces decision-making, means of negotiation, approaches to disarmament, norms and values sometimes relevant and sometimes not to the outside world. This means that a failure to keep a constant and close watch on the UN proceedings in relation to disarmament makes it difficult to identify the weaknesses, the difficulties and the problems spawned by the imperfections which characterize from time to time the world organization's functioning.

The focus of this book is on the role the United Nations (UN) has played in the negotiating process of nuclear disarmament. This book is intended to provoke thought and discussion about the past, present and future involvement of the UN in the disarmament negotiations. It is thus hoped that the book may be of interest to the general reader interested in international organizations, as well as to students having a more specialized concern with disarmament and arms control. For the purpose of this study, nuclear disarmament should be understood as the actual reduction or the renunciation of nuclear weapons; whereas arms control or arms limitation denotes any measure of restraint, not involving actual reduction of nuclear weapons, on testing, manufacture, possession, deployment or use of weapons. The notion of arms control also includes all the measures which can promote confidence among states.

The essential starting point for a discussion concerning the performance of the UN in the past and future should be an understanding of certain key political and normative assumptions upon which the UN was founded. That is to say, clarify what is the UN about. Failure to do this and be seized of the goals of the UN could lead to contradictory analysis and bad outcomes in the near and long term.

The UN was designed to be an entity of sovereign states, not a prototype of world government. The Charter of the UN in its declaratory principles, in the preamble, appropriately makes a reference to 'We the Peoples of the United Nations'. But this is far from being misleading, as it goes on to clarify in the preambular culmination that 'our respective Governments, through representatives assembled in the city of San Francisco have agreed to the present Charter of the United Nations and do hereby establish an international organization to be known as the United Nations'. The governments represent their states and peoples amongst equals.

The attribute of the UN as a non-supranational authority means that its potential for the attainment of its goals to afford a more or less comprehensive regime depends exclusively on its member-states. The member-states not only determine what UN action or policy should be adopted at any given time but also the means by which to accomplish this policy. The UN Charter, by appealing in Article 2 paragraph 5 to all members 'to give the UN every assistance in any action it takes', realizes that the success of the UN efforts is primarily based on the extent to which they arouse and engage the active support of its membership. Hence, Article 2 paragraph 5 mandates such support for action the UN 'takes in accordance with the present Charter' and, furthermore, prohibits its members 'from giving assistance to any state against which the United Nations is taking preventive or enforcement action'.

Relying basically on the assumption that the decision structure of the UN preserves its member-states as centres of authority, this study departs to evaluate the measure of agreement among the member-states and the political groups on particular policies of the UN *vis-à-vis* nuclear disarmament throughout the life of the organization. The crucial questions are: what was the particular policy or approach of the UN to nuclear disarmament at any given time and to what extent was there a broad consensus among its membership? Behind these questions lies an important and general one: was the UN afforded with a primary or secondary role in dealing with nuclear disarmament negotiations?

In writing about the UN and its role in relation to nuclear disarmament this study has restricted itself to the UN and its bodies: deliberative and negotiating ones. It is an analysis which is based on a view from within the UN. It is an attempt to assess the UN's performance, failures and successes in its dealings with nuclear disarmament. A detailed examination of each act or policy in the UN or a vast array of facts and historical data would not satisfy the real purposes of this study. As a consequence, the best approach would be to consider the most important facts and discuss their connection with the specific developments and trend which produced them or followed them.

The context and framework of the analysis is not conventional but deliberately divided into coherent sections which carry varying degrees of importance. Chronological periods relate the changing scope of consensus, co-operation, and conflict between the member-states on policies, approaches, and decision structures of the UN which have given the UN a distinct role at different times. There were also other important parameters used to divide this study into parts dealing with specific periods of time. They are the basic elements of which the disarmament and arms control negotiations consisted; the different trends in the ways the UN approached the question of nuclear disarmament; the evolution of the disarmament institutions; the relationships between the political groups of the UN, the procedures, the outcomes in terms of tradeoffs; the topic of primary concern; the duration of the negotiation on a specific issue; and contextually the state of international relations.

Accordingly, the whole work is divided into six chapters. Each of them built around all the parameters mentioned above. Chapter one focuses on the prospect which was opened up for the UN to become the repository of nuclear energy with far-reaching powers of control, development and inspection. 1950 is the starting point of chapter two. This year marked the breakdown of previous negotiations and the coming of a new round of negotiations in a broader context wherein for the first time nuclear disarmament and conventional reductions were dealt together as one inseparable question. 1950 also marked the commencement of the Korean war, the adoption of the 'Uniting of Peace' Resolution and a crisis of international interest. This marked the point at which the issue of disarmament became one of the facets of the Cold War. It is within this context that disarmament is examined in this chapter. The concluding date of chapter two, 1960 is also the beginning of chapter three. It was chosen because at that time there was a significant change in the UN's framework for disarmament negotiations. The multilateral negotiations were taken away from the UN's supervision and were put under the control of the superpowers. At the same time a new political force, the group of Non-Aligned states, made its first political appearance in the UN disarmament negotiations. Another main feature of the period was the remarkable change in the policy of the UN towards arms control measures rather than disarmament which remained the predominant negotiating course with the concurrence of the entire UN membership until 1968, when successful negotiations on the Treaty for the Non-Proliferation of nuclear weapons were completed.

The period from the accomplishment of the Non-Proliferation Treaty to 1978, date the first special session of the General Assembly devoted exclusively to disarmament was convened, is discussed in chapter four. Important developments made this period of time of particular interest. A crisis erupted in the UN which was the result of the appearance of different perceptions of the political groups over the role of the UN in the global disarmament process. The superpowers took the substantive talks outside the multilateral purview while the Non-Aligned group emerging as the dominant arithmetical power demanded reforms of the existing disarmament machinery with the view to placing the UN at the centre of the global negotiating process.

Chapter five covers the period from the convening of the first special session on disarmament to the present. It deserves special consideration because it provides a critical evaluation of the restructuring of the UN framework of negotiations. This restructuring coupled with new more universal approaches to disarmament in the pursuit of a redefined concept of security, had had far-reaching consequences for the UN and its involvement in the negotiations on nuclear disarmament.

The critical assessment of the past and especially of the most recent period is of particular relevance to the last part of this study which occupies chapter six. This chapter presents concluding remarks for the entire work and assessment of the performance of the UN and the nature of the factors which affected this performance, in both a positive and negative way, with a view to making suggestions for more efficient use of the UN institutions in the future.

During the period of this study three main sources of information were sought. The first was the search of primary source which included documents of the UN. The official documents of the UN allowed the keeping a close watch on the proceedings of the General Assembly, the debate in its Plenary sessions and its First Committee dealing with security matters as well as discussions in the Security Council and the details of the talks in the various negotiating forums. The UN sources are further supplemented by other publications of the Department for Disarmament Affairs, such as the Disarmament Yearbooks (annual since 1976); the Disarmament Study series; the Journals of the UN; the Disarmament Fact Sheets; and the Disarmament Newsletters. Research papers produced by the UN Institute for Disarmament Research (UNIDIR) and UN reports and background papers supplement the whole package of UN materials.

The second category of primary sources employed in this study were the official documents of the Governments of the United States and the United Kingdom released by the Department of State and the Foreign Office respectively. One difficulty encountered here was that documents of this category have not generally been made public by Governments other than the United States and the United Kingdom. This made essential the recourse either to the first category of sources, the UN materials, or to secondary sources which form the vast body of materials enlisted in the third category.

Thirdly, a discretionary choice was made to take into account published books, newspapers, periodicals and other publications which covered or contained sections dealing with the UN in general and disarmament in particular. The criterion for this selected use of those materials was their relevance to the scope of this research. As it was above mentioned these three sources were correlated to insure the greatest accuracy in the analysis which is attempted in this study.

1 The first years: A missed opportunity for the UN

Disarmament and the Charter

The Charter of the UN contains no disarmament provisions analogous to those of the constitutional document of the League of Nations. Disarmament has not had a prominent place in the Charter. The constitution of the UN by no means echoes the disarmament provisions of the Covenant of the League with specific responsibilities for developing plans for the limitation and reduction of armaments (Article 8) and a permanent Commission to advise the League Council on military questions and disarmament (Article 9). The basic reason for the relatively little attention to disarmament and arms limitation in the Charter is due to historical fact. The Allies that fought against aggressions, war crimes, and genocide of Hitler were determined to approach the problem of war through the adoption of a collective security system that was called to maintain and restore, in cases of threats or breaches of the peace, international peace and security rather than through disarmament or arms limitation.

During the discussion on the draft Charter it was agreed that the Security Council was to set the maximum-minimum levels for armaments for all states and that any state violating such limitations imposed on it should be held to be a threat to the peace. Subsequently, disarmament even in its more limited sense as a limitation of armament was not discussed in detail either at the Dumbarton Oaks or San Francisco conferences, from 21 August to 7 October 1944, by the joint discussions of the four powers and from 25 April to 26 June 1945 by the fifty nations, due to the fact that the central issue that received more attention was the collective security provisions of the Charter. Nor was it an issue in the extensive six-month public discussion prior to San Francisco. These events undoubtedly demonstrate the grip the notion of collective measures had as means for achieving the maintenance of international peace and security on the participants' thought, on their perspectives. The four allied powers saw the security functions of the world organization as central, and they provided that major responsibility for the maintenance of peace would be borne by the major powers.

What was finally agreed by the founders of the UN at San Francisco was to give authority to the General Assembly, as part of the general political powers with which this organ was entrusted, to 'consider principles governing disarmament and the regulation of armaments, and make recommendations with regard to such principles to the members or to the Security Council or to both' (Article 11). Authority was given to the Security Council to 'formulate, with the assistance of the Military Staff Committee referred to in Article 47, plans to be submitted to the members of the United Nations for the establishment of a system for the regulation of armaments' (Article 26) and 'possible disarmament' (Article 47). The underlying reason for this Security Council peace and security planning action is to minimize withdrawals from 'the world's human and economic resources' for armaments (Article 26).

The nuclear question in the UN

The Charter of the UN and nuclear weapons date their existence from the same year. However, the first atomic bomb was exploded three weeks after the signing of the Charter and six weeks later, on 6 August 1945, Hiroshima gave a grim warning that the age of atomic weapons had arrived. Immediately the newborn organization entrusted, as the preamble of its Charter provides, with the primary responsibility 'to save succeeding generations from the scourge of war', was confronted with unexpected military and political challenges coming from the development which had taken place secretly in the field of atomic energy. The UN had to deal with situations and problems which either did not exist or were not foreseen or as a matter of fact were not discussed during the drafting of the Charter.

It soon became apparent that there was no agreement among the member-states on the ways and means of getting rid of nuclear weapons. As the

Charter specified no exact procedures for dealing with the problem of atomic energy and the bomb, there was scepticism about which procedures within the UN would be capable of dealing with this urgent problem. Would the member-states prefer to pass the responsibility to the Security Council or the General Assembly? The former had been given primary but not exclusive competence for the maintenance and promotion of international peace and security, while the latter enjoyed a secondary competence to consider 'principles governing disarmament'.

The United States, as the result of the public pressure[1] and demands for the elimination of the new weapon, took the initiative in holding meetings with its former partners in atomic energy work, namely Britain and Canada. At their meeting in Washington in November 1945, this group adopted the so-called 'three nation agreed declaration on atomic energy' which included a recommendation for the establishment of a UN Commission:

> In order to obtain the most effective means of entirely eliminating the use of the atomic energy for destructive purposes, we are of the opinion that at the earliest practical date, a Commission should be set up under the UN to prepare recommendations to the organization. The Commission should be instructed to proceed with the outmost dispatch and should be authorized to submit recommendations dealing with separate phases of its work.[2]

However, at the Washington meeting there was no agreement on how to involve the UN machinery. President Truman subsequently clarified, at a press conference, that the General Assembly of the UN should hold the rein on the nuclear problem and that the General Assembly and not the Security Council alone would be asked at its first meeting to set up a Commission.[3] Shortly after, the American Government requested that the question of the nuclear bomb should be put on the agenda of a conference which was to be held in Moscow in December 1945 between foreign ministers of the three 'big powers' (United States, United Kingdom, Soviet Union) to discuss pending matters of outstanding importance. The Soviet Union agreed without demur.

The impending conference and the eagerness to adopt in advance an agreed common line of action to be followed in Moscow prompted an extensive exchange of views between the signatories of the Washington declaration. The discussion centred on what was the most suitable procedure for bringing the proposals in the tripartite statement before the General Assembly of the UN.[4] There was complete agreement that the Washington declaration should be channelled through the General Assembly.[5] However, the three governments were divided over the tactics to be employed. The British Government assented to the American position that 'the atomic energy matter should be discussed with the Russians before it is presented to the UN, otherwise the Russians may not agree to it'.[6] The basic reason for accepting this view was that 'the decision between the competing claims of the General Assembly and the Security Council will be a delicate one involving a real risk of friction among the UN, (and) in particular that Russia might refuse to co-operate'.[7] Because of these risks cautious steps had to be taken and this necessitated the holding of consultations with the Soviet Union before the UN took up the nuclear question. The Canadians on the other hand, were less certain. They argued that 'past experience indicates that Soviet Government would be unlikely to associate themselves in sponsoring a statement about which they were not consulted, and might also complicate the whole procedure at this stage'.[8] The Canadians thus lined up with the view that the matter should be presented directly in the UN and that the General Assembly should take early charge of the nuclear question.

At this point there was no indication of the likely Soviet reaction to such a proposed course of action. The Soviet Union had so far maintained a stony silence on its attitude towards the joint tripartite statement on the atomic bomb. However, a report by the British Ambassador in Moscow about the present state in mind in the Soviet capital weakened the Canadian position. 'If we are to secure Russians' co-operation', the Ambassador reported, 'we must go about things in a different way. I mean that, before the Assembly gathers, we and the Americans must have preliminary and private talks with Molotov'.[9]

The chief Anglo-American objective in Moscow was to get the Soviets formally into the UN and to induce them to play a significant role from within the General Assembly under the terms of reference of the Washington declaration.[10] To open up procedures in the General Assembly would cause far reaching consequences for the Charter which was itself the outcome of long discussions with compromises to all points of view. That is why the handling of the atomic issue had to be treated with extreme care if Soviet confidence in the UN was not to be destroyed and wither its hopes at the start. It had to be such that it would not lead them 'to fall out with the Soviets at this stage'.[11] To approach the Soviets seemed to be the best way of proceeding. It was intended to serve two purposes. Firstly, to exhort the Soviets not to introduce the atomic issue into the discussions of the Preparatory Commission which was to be held before the Moscow meeting but to make them wait until the meeting of the 'big three'. According to a

San Francisco agreement - signed by all signatories of the Charter - the Preparatory Commission was not authorized to interfere with political problems which must await action by the UN itself. Its task was to make the first procedural arrangements for the opening sessions of the various organs of the UN so that the world organization would be properly organized and deal promptly with world problems. One of the most significant powers entrusted to the Preparatory Commission was the drawing up of the provisional agenda for the first meeting of the Security Council. As top officials of the British Foreign Office put it 'it was quite on the cards that, even if it is not the Anglo-American intention to raise the matter (i.e., the nuclear issue) in the Preparatory Commission, some other delegations may raise it there'.[12] If the matter was to be raised for discussion in the Preparatory Commission, 'it might be difficult to argue convincingly that the question of the control of the atomic bomb is not an appropriate subject for inclusion in the agenda of the first meeting of the Security Council'.[13] Secondly, to secure Soviet co-operation would give broader legitimacy to their task of entrusting primary competence to the General Assembly. The Anglo-American side could easily obtain the acquiescence of the other permanent members of the Security Council because they were pro-western. If they could convey this point of view to the Soviets and gain acceptance of their proposals in Moscow, it would amount to an agreement for an immediate shift of responsibility from the Security Council to the General Assembly with the concurrence of all the five permanent members of the Security Council even before the UN had really begun to function.

Thus, the Anglo-American side arrived in Moscow with a definite proposal. They wished to obtain the co-operation of the Soviets in an effort whereby the five permanent members of the Security Council, together with Canada, would join in the sponsoring of a proposal which would incorporate the principles of the Washington declaration. This would provide for the formation of a Commission the work of which would come within the province of the General Assembly. As the Americans said, in confidence, to the British delegation in Moscow 'it was out of question for the United States Administration to take the lead in proposing that the Commission should be under the Security Council'.[14] If the three powers would fall in with the Anglo-American proposal they would join in recommending it to the Governments of China, France and Canada.

During the Moscow talks there was no discussion of the political, military or scientific aspects involved raised by the problem of nuclear weapons, nor did the Soviets attempted to examine in detail the terms of reference suggested by the United States. On the contrary, the Soviet Union agreed that all the five permanent members of the Security Council together with Canada should sponsor a resolution at the UN in January 1946 to put the proposals into effect. The only fundamental divergence between the two sides concerned the body to which the proposed Commission should be responsible: the General Assembly or the Security Council. A long discussion took place on this issue. The Americans wanted the Commission to be under the control of the General Assembly, whereas the Soviets insisted that it 'should be put squarely under the Security Council'.[15] The difficult political question of the relationship of the Commission to the two branches of the UN threatened to produce deadlock. In the end, the United States made certain revisions to their initial draft resolution which constituted an essential compromise to buy Soviet co-operation.[16] In consequence, a final draft resolution, which was mostly in line with the American original proposal, sponsored by all the five permanent members of the Security Council plus Canada, was deposited with the Secretariat in the first days of January 1946 and was immediately placed upon the agenda of the General Assembly.[17]

The General Assembly, after brief deliberations on 24 January 1946 unanimously adopted, as Resolution I, the draft agreed in Moscow and established the Atomic Energy Commission (AEC) composed of the eleven members of the Security Council plus Canada. The General Assembly entrusted the AEC with the task of making specific proposals to secure the control of atomic energy; the elimination of atomic weapons; the exchange of basic scientific information; and effective safeguards against the hazards of any violations and evasions.

The nuclear weapon and its dynamics were of such revolutionary nature that it made necessary the exploration through the UN of innovative methods of atomic energy control. The bridgeable gap between the Charter and its applicability to the question of nuclear disarmament and control of atomic energy did not create any political impediments but, on the contrary, increased the flexibility of the Charter and gave the UN and its component parts, the member-states, much more freedom to act. In addition, it gave the UN the chance, much more than a Charter of restrictive and specific powers would have given, to provide in the first years of its life for management intervention which could open up long-term prospects not only for the solution of the problem of nuclear disarmament and control but also for the world organization itself. This would have required an increasing transfer of state sovereignty to the UN by its members, and especially the superpowers, which would have to agree to make the UN the repository of atomic energy by allocating to it far-reaching powers so as to take the world organization beyond the limits set out in the original constitution. It was possible that the world organization could be changed in decision structure to achieve some of the attributes of supranational authority. If the UN had been transformed into something nearer to a supranational authority it could have taken decisions which could have interfered with the decision of any member-state. The world organization could then have handled the nuclear disarmament issue more efficiently.

The earliest proposal for control of atomic energy, the Baruch plan of 14 June 1946 to the newly created AEC, came very close to securing this change in image and reality of the UN. This constructive American plan proposed that there should be exclusive international control over all phases of atomic energy production and use, including aspects suitable for weapons of war wherever situated, before any measure of nuclear disarmament. As the free inspection of UN members and the process of control became effective, the United States promised to destroy its atomic bomb stockpile. The plan called for a new security system to come into existence, whereby international atomic control and discretionary power would be vested in an international agency, the International Atomic Development Authority (IADA). The IADA would be a new non-political organ of the UN, the composition, functional powers and procedures of which would be determined by the basic atomic control treaty. Furthermore, the IADA would act by a majority vote so that action could not be prevented by the exercise of the veto by the states which would be parties to the treaty. 'There must be no veto', the United States explained, 'to protect those who violate their solemn agreements not to develop or use atomic energy for destructive purposes'.[18] The enforcement of the decisions of the IADA and the punishment of wilful violators would be ineffectual if, in any cases of breaches of treaty violation, they could be rendered nugatory by the use of a veto of a member-state.

Defining the relations between the IADA and the various organs of the UN, the United States made it clear that it considered the Charter to be incomplete and therefore unable to deal with the technicalities of the problem. The radical changes in the international situation would necessitate a deep cut in the Charter commensurate with and dictated by the advent of the atomic era. In a memorandum submitted by the Americans, in which they attempted to define the functions and powers of the proposed IADA, it was argued that:

> none of the existing organs of the United Nations possesses the managerial, proprietary, and licensing powers necessary to effective

international control and development of atomic energy. A new agency therefore is necessary. Moreover, even if the Charter could be construed to provide for a subsidiary organ created by collective action of several of the existing organs and possessing an aggregate of powers delegated by each of them such a subsidiary organ would not have adequate powers under the Charter.[19]

As the United States perceived the Charter to be incomplete and the existing organs of the UN to lack adequate powers to face a problem which for them was most technical, they were of the opinion that, if the Charter was to survive, it needed to be carried further or supplemented. Even before the convening of the AEC, the Anglo-American side had agreed that 'if the atomic bomb is in some way to be put under the control of the UN, this, in order to be effective, must be accompanied by an amendment of the San Francisco Charter so as to abolish the so called Great-power veto'.[20] The American proposal implied a very profound modification of the veto system of the Charter and that explains the American insistence in the Moscow meeting of 1945 on opening up proceedings before the General Assembly.

However, looking behind such a proposition and taking into account the whole framework of the UN at that moment, there are certain implications as to the role the General Assembly could play in the whole process despite the declared 'autonomous' and 'non-political' nature of the proposed IADA.[21] Although the new control authority was not to be established under the auspices of either the General Assembly or the Security Council, its 'non-political' character would have come into question due to the very fact that its establishment would not have led, according to the American proposal, to the formation of an international agency independent of the UN but to one fashioned in relationship to it. The only feasible form to be adopted for the organization of the IADA would have been the constitutional form of the UN, the organization of which relies upon the acceptance of the state as the basic unit of its legal and political system. Consequently, its composition would have been analogous to that of the UN where all the states are represented in the General Assembly, which from its inception had overwhelmingly favoured American leadership. This, in turn, was to make the role of the General Assembly predominant, as admission of any state to membership could be effected under the Charter provisions by that body's decision upon the recommendation of the Security Council. Consequently, the composition of the international control authority could remain substantially unchanged and thus favourable to United States' leadership.

This fact raised the question of whether the Soviet Union could have been expected to entrust its security in the nuclear age to an international authority dominated by states with a predisposition to accept American leadership. The Soviet Union rejected forcefully such an optimistic view. The Soviets claimed that 'it is easy to understand that the granting of such rights to control organs would mean a complete arbitrariness of these organs and, first of all, of those who would be in a position to command a majority in these organs'.[22]

The Baruch plan received majority approval. However, since the project necessitated a considerable sacrifice of national sovereignty, the Soviet Union and its satellites were not ready to accept it. The Soviets were in a small minority in the UN and if any international system of UN control over atomic energy was to be established under a veto-less authority and reflect UN membership, it would have put them at the mercy of the Anglo-American pro-Western majority of the world organization. They demanded prohibition of the production and use of the atomic bomb as well as destruction of atomic stockpiles before any international control system of atomic energy be established and put into operation. The Soviets forcefully rejected the idea of handing over control of their atomic energy to the UN, and of unlimited inspections, and in making their counter-proposal to the Baruch plan entrenched themselves behind the letter of the Charter of the UN. They saw the Baruch plan as a device designed to circumvent or alter the provisions of the Charter: 'the appeals to perfect the UN Charter recently adopted at the San Francisco conference boil down in the main to a demand to renounce the Charter's principles of unanimity of the Great powers constituting the permanent members of the Security Council.[23] The Soviet representative in the UN, commenting on the American proposal, stated that 'we cannot accept proposals that would undermine in any degree the principle of unanimity of the permanent members of the Security Council in the maintenance of peace and security'. [24] According to the Soviet press

> the principle of unanimity or its version, the right of veto, is being subjected to attack. However, in contradistinction to the earlier assaults which were undertaken under the guise of protecting small nations from the dictatorship of the Great powers, the present attacks are being conducted in so frank a form that their principal argument is the atomic bomb.[25]

The Soviets took a static approach to the Charter of the United Nations which was designed to facilitate the unrestricted invocation of the sovereign power of the state. The central idea of the Soviet proposal was that there was a constitutional limitation from which there should be no departure, namely the provisions of the Charter dealing with the maintenance of peace and security under which the primary responsibility of the Security Council is fully recognized. They argued that 'the atomic bomb was to be viewed exactly as any other weapon and that it could be handled entirely within the existing framework of the UN Charter'.[26]

By adopting such an approach to the Charter the Soviet Union advocated a system of international control and inspection which was fundamentally different to that proposed by the United States. The International Control Authority suggested by the Soviet Union was built upon a recognition of the necessity to preserve the dominant status of the Security Council. The Soviet view was that 'the power, authority and prestige of the Security Council would not undermined in connection with the problem of atomic energy'.[27] Accordingly, the control authority would be composed of states which were members of the Security Council. The control authority would undertake control based on the assumption of national ownership and management of materials and facilities including inspection and verification; accounting; and the preparation of rules of technological control and the observance of their operation. Furthermore, it was recognized that inspection, as the most crucial control measure, was to be of a periodic character and might be carried out by the decision of the international control authority in cases of necessity. However, what would constitute necessity was a matter for the judgement of the authority, which would function in subordination to the Security Council where the veto prevailed. The Soviet proposal was, therefore, consistent with the expressed provisions of the Charter, which permit penalization only with the concurrence of each of the five permanent members of the Security Council.[28]

With the two sides insisting on their fundamental different positions the UN which might, by a process of evolution through pragmatic law-making decision, have become something different from what it was, remained substantially unaltered. The pervasive onset of the Cold War among the former allies against Hitler's war rendered nugatory of commanding wider acceptance in the UN calculation of proposals to regulate atomic energy - with more authority over development and control of nuclear activities than the currently operating International Atomic Energy Agency in Vienna which has been unable to assure that fissionable material is not waylaid to bomb programmes from commercial or experimental nuclear reactors. The AEC terminated its work in 1949 shortly after the Soviet Union had exploded an atomic bomb, thus making it the second nuclear power.

Notes

1. See letter from Atlee to Truman, 16 October 1945, cited in United States, Department of State (1967), *Foreign Relations of the United States, 1945,* vol. ii, United States, Government Printing Office: Washington, pp. 36-7; see also John Gaddis (1972), *The United States and the Origins of the Cold War, 1941-1947,* Columbia University Press: New York, p. 269.
2. For the actions taken before the Washington meeting see J.P.G Freeman (1986), *Britain's Nuclear Arms Control Policy in the Context of Anglo-American Relations,* Macmillan: London, pp. 5-11; see also Herbert Feis (1970), *From Trust to Terror, The Onset of the Cold War: 1945-1950,* Norton and Co: New York, pp. 91-100.
3. United States (1945), *Public Papers of the President of the United States: Harry Truman,* United States, Government Printing Office: Washington, pp. 504-514; see also Telegram No 8230, from Washington to FO, 9 December 1945, cited in FO 371/44539/AN 3744.
4. Memorandum of FO: Proposed Discussions at Moscow on Atomic Energy, 12 December 1945, cited in FO 371/50937.
5. Telegram No 8283, from Washington to FO, 11 December 1945, cited in FO 371/50937; see also Memorandum of FO, Minutes from Sir Cadogan, 21 November 1945, p. 1, cited in FO 371/50936/U 9356.
6. Memorandum of Conversation by the Secretary of State, 29 November 1945, cited in United States, Department of State, op. cit., p. 590.
7. Memorandum of FO: The Next Step in Control of Atomic Energy, 21 November 1945, para. 6, cited in FO 371/50735.
8. Memorandum of FO, 3 December 1945, cited in FO 371/50937; see also Telegram No 7995, from Canada to FO, 30 November 1945, cited in FO 371/50735. See also Aide-Memoire submitted by Pearson (Canadian Ambassador) to Byrnes, cited in United States, Department of State, op.cit., pp. 78-80.
9. Telegram No 5192, from British Ambassador in Moscow to FO, 3 December 1945, cited in FO 371/50735; see also Telegram No 12234, from FO (Lord Halifax) to Washington, 16 December 1945, cited in the same file; see Telegram No 8378, from Washington to FO, 15 December 1945, cited in FO 371/44539/AN 3804.
10. Gaddis, op.cit., pp. 270-1.
11. Memorandum of FO: Notes for United Kingdom Delegation on Committee I of the General Assembly, 19 January 1946, para. 5, cited in FO 371/57095/U 2162.

12. Memorandum of FO, 21 November 1945, para. 6, cited in FO 371/50936/U 9356.
13. Ibid.
14. Telegram No 60, from Moscow (British Delegation) to FO, 21 December 1945, cited in FO 371/50938/U 273; see also Telegram No 14, from Moscow (British Delegation) to FO, 17 December 1945, cited in FO 371/50938/U1020; Telegram No 24, FO to Moscow (British Delegation), 19 December 1945, cited in FO 371/50938/U146. For differences between the American draft resolution as it was presented in Moscow and the suggestions the British Secretary of State had made to the Prime Minister see Memorandum of FO: Russia and the Proposed Atomic Conference, cited in FO 371/50937.
15. FO 371/50939/U 10485, p. 4; for the Soviet suggestions see Telegram No 88, from Moscow (British Delegation) to FO, 22 December 1945, cited in FO 371/50938/U 294; see also Records of the Informal Meetings Held in Kremlin, cited in FO 371/50939/U 10485; see also Leland Goodrich, Edvard Hambro and Anne Simmons (eds) (1969), *The Charter of the UN: Commentary and Documents*, Columbia University Press: New York, p. 213.
16. Telegram No 60, from Moscow (British Delegation) to FO, 21 December 1945, para. 3, cited in FO 371/50938/U 273; see also Telegram No 8665, from Washington to FO, 30 December 1945, para. 3, cited in FO 371/44539/AN 3921. See also Feis, op.cit., p. 105.
17. Records of the Informal Meetings, Annex B, in FO 371/50939/U10485; see also Telegram No 100, from Moscow (British Delegation) to FO, 23 December 1945, cited in FO 371/50938/U10311.
18. Official Records of the Atomic Energy Commission, Special Supplement, Report to the Security Council, 1946, pp. 92-102 and 106-111; see also Gregg Herken (1980), *The Winning Weapon, The Atomic Bomb in the Cold War*, Alfred Knoph: New York, p. 173.
19. (1946) *Department of State Bulletin*, vol. xi, no 308, 21 July.
20. Memorandum of FO: Atomic Energy and the UNO, 6 December 1946, cited in FO 371/50936/U 9719; see also Parliamentary Debates, House of Commons, vol. 426, no 190, 2 August 1946, pp.1377-1394. See also Address delivered by Pearson, Canadian Ambassador to the United States, cited in FO 371/57107/U 5700.
21. For a discussion whether the Charter preclude establishment of autonomous agency to exercise nuclear control see USSR statement in UN Document AEC/C.1/PV. 4, p. 7.
22. Security Council, Official Records, Second Year, No 22, 115 meeting, 5

March 1947, pp. 445 and 453; see also Telegram No 70, from British Delegation in the UN (Paris) to FO, 1 October 1948, p. 3 cited in FO 371/72657; see also Feis, op.cit., p. 399.

23. UN Document AEC/C.2/PV. 4, 5 August 46, para. 3; see also speech of Gromyko at the meeting of the Security Council on 14 February 1947, in UN Press Release PM/298, pp.10-12; see also *Economist*, 12 July 1947, pp. 60-1.

24. (1946), 'The Control of the Atomic Energy', *International Conciliation*, no 423, p. 378.

25. *Soviet Monitor*, issued by Tass Agency, 2 December 1945.

26. United States, Department of State (1972), *The Foreign Relations of the United States,1946,* vol.i, United States, Government Printing Office:Washington, p. 923.

27. Statement by Mr. Gromyko at the second meeting of Committee No 2 of the AEC, 29 July 1946; see also *The New York Times*, 25 July 1946.

28. For the Soviet policy concerning the control of atomic energy see Joseph Nogee (1961), *Soviet Policy Towards International Control of Atomic Energy*, University of Notre Dame Press: South Bend, 1961.

2 Disarmament as a Cold-War issue (1950-1959)

The way the UN dealt with nuclear disarmament in the 1950s differed substantially from that which was examined in the previous chapter. The scope and the subject matter of disarmament also changed significantly. The certainty that there was no long-lasting monopoly of nuclear weaponry had by now been established. The most striking change, however, was what happened to the international environment. This change was much the most significant in terms of its differentiating the UN's position as regards the question of nuclear disarmament from the position it had occupied before. The difference became visible in the light of the general climate which prevailed in the consideration of the nuclear problem and in the light of the possibilities of negotiation, as well as in terms of the UN's potentialities for a real rapprochement among its membership in order to achieve common policies towards disarmament.

The 'honeymoon' period of the first post-war years definitely expired and the Cold War began in earnest as East-West relations had been perceptibly aggravated. The taking of Romania and Czechoslovakia into the economic and political orbit of the Soviet Union, the division of Germany and the Berlin crisis as well as other sporadic crises all over the world had made the wartime coalition rapidly collapse. The limited confidence which had existed in the first post-war years had been completely destroyed. The bipolar division of the world was carried further by the establishment of two military blocs: in 1949 the North Atlantic Treaty Organization (NATO) was formed, while bilateral defence arrangements between the Soviet Union and each one of its satellites and between the satellites themselves had already produced a well coordinated network equivalent to the multilateral defence system of NATO. When the Warsaw pact was finally signed in 1955, it was merely the bringing of this network under a more cohesive centralized Soviet supervision.

The rapid development of the Cold War led to the inclusion of the superpowers rivalry into the activity of the world organization. Nuclear disarmament had been growing as an issue in the Cold War during the previous years. It was, however, during the 1950s that the manner with which the UN treated disarmament demonstrated its character as an issue of the Cold War. The existence of disarmament as a Cold War issue spilt over into the work of the UN, negatively affecting its potential. Disarmament was introduced into the realm of the UN in successive but interrelated stages and its existence as a Cold War issue was manifested in two broad ways. Firstly, the UN failed to mobilize its membership and especially the superpowers to use its apparatus for negotiations on disarmament despite persistent efforts to do so. Secondly, when the UN finally succeeded in sponsoring negotiations, it was converted into an instrument of American policy and afterwards as an arena for gamesmanship between the two chief antagonists.

Disarmament negotiations in a divided world organization

For three years after the negotiations broke off in 1949 the UN was unable to get to grips with the question of nuclear disarmament. This was due mainly to its failure to stimulate common action by the superpowers and its changed character after action was taken under its mantle in Korea with the blessing of the Security Council, thanks to an earlier Soviet walkout. This image of the UN was further changed following the adoption by the General Assembly of the American-initiated 'Uniting for Peace' Resolution in the autumn of 1950.[1]

The 'Uniting for Peace' Resolution was a consequence of the intense hostility which followed the transfer of the Cold War struggle into the UN's purview. The Resolution was adopted at a time when the efforts of the United States to use the UN as an appendage to its foreign policy machinery reached their climax. The Resolution was a turning point for the UN itself which might now be used as a basis for the development of an anti-communist machine. A new collective security edifice, never contemplated in the UN

Charter, was devised under which the General Assembly was cast in the role of an organ of action quite separate from its original role of exhortation through recommendations. In contrast to the collective security system envisaged in the Charter, which required unanimous decision among the five permanent members of the Security Council, the new 'collective security system' might be easily mobilized at any time by the pro-American majority. Great-power unanimity as the cornerstone of the collective security system under Chapter VII of the Charter had completely disintegrated. In the eyes of the Americans, the UN had become, after the adoption of the 'Uniting for Peace' Resolution, a cornerstone of their policy. Since it provided for a new and more effective machinery of collective action it was seen by them as 'a suitable body for the overall political and military organization of the non-Soviet world against the Soviet threat'.[2] For the Soviets, the UN, on the occurrence of the most severe attack on the unanimity rule, had overstepped 'its narrowly defined competence beyond the range of the veto'. Because of this, the world organization was regarded as 'a hostile coalition which dances to the tune of its fascist-capitalist paymasters'.[3]

The implications of the 'Uniting for Peace' Resolution were sufficient to disrupt completely the UN and cause considerable disunity among its membership. It even brought discord into the united Anglo-American family. In a Foreign Office memorandum, British policy-makers admitted that they were now faced

> with all the consequence of serious divergence of view between the United States Government and H. M. Government on the proper role of the UN in the present world situation. Whereas H. M. Government consider that the UN should be maintained as a cohesive world organization where international disputes can be discussed and adjusted by peaceful means, the United States Government seems to be intent on turning the organization into a coercive instrument of collective security against communist aggression.[4]

As far as nuclear disarmament is concerned, the question at issue is whether the UN, in the light of all these circumstances and in the midst of a most fluid revolution in the technological situation, was able to embark on a serious disarmament policy. It should be pointed out that following the failure of the UN, in its first years, to find a way to bring atomic energy under its control and to ensure that atomic energy would never be used for warlike purposes, the world organization remained an agency without any intrinsic power to affect the process of nuclear disarmament on its own account and, therefore, powerless. In light of the unfeasibility of a more forceful UN role on the question of nuclear disarmament, its role as a body for as a service institution which would provide the states and especially the superpowers with services which would facilitate and encourage the search for disarmament and the process of negotiation had taken on an increasing importance. The UN had to develop itself as a body for potential conciliation. Effective disarmament policy on the part of the UN presupposed that its machinery would be a forum of peaceful co-existence and that it would be used with scrupulous moderation. In turn, this would mean that the UN could act as a third party, as a kind of an impartial actor.

It was the fact that it was already in the service of American policy - which was orientated towards increasing the might of the military sector of the UN, with a view to waging war in potential cases of aggressive Communist acts - that severely limited the scope of the UN for possible exploration of common avenues, itself essential for disarmament negotiations. There was a basic incompatibility between the functions of the UN as a place for conciliation and peaceful co-existence and its use as an agency for military organization by one side against the other. The two superpowers, far from acting in concert with each other, had been in a state of Cold War and this fact had been reflected in every aspect of the UN. The UN could hardly be utilized as an instrument to achieve world solidarity directed towards the superpowers taking joint initiatives and approaches in the field of disarmament. Disarmament is not a problem existing on its own. It is eminently political and as such it is intimately intertwined with problems of great power relations which had, by this time, converted the UN into a divided world. The barriers to disarmament are primarily political and psychological. No other question depends on the state of international relations as much as this question of disarmament. As Bennet put it 'disarmament is primarily a political problem linked to the whole range of problems of nations in a competitive world. The obstacles to disarmament are the obstacles for international co-operation generally'.[5] This lack of political co-operation became even more apparent in the work of the UN in the field of disarmament as both superpowers leading their allies changed the character of disarmament as a negotiating issue and converted it into an issue of Cold War.

The first steps to bring nuclear disarmament into the realm of the UN as a negotiating issue at the centre of the Cold War came from the United States. The United States abandoned its previous scruples which were essentially fears that bringing the issue of disarmament before the UN 'might be represented as a sign of weakness and have a depressing effect on the non-communist countries'[6] and decided to sponsor disarmament negotiations in the world organization. Thus, the United States proceeded to the UN with a draft resolution which, although also sponsored by United Kingdom and France, was mainly the production of the State Department. Attempts to go through all the work involved in trying to reach an agreement prior to the submission of the draft resolution to the General Assembly, so that it would represent the highest common factor of consensus, were excluded by the United States from the outset. The United States intention was to make its own 'sensational' peace proposals, to take the UN by surprise, and to place upon the UN record a *fait accompli*, that is a new disarmament policy along American lines. Thus, the United States selected its own ground ignoring the points in which the Soviet Union might be interested. This was a decision of the State Department based on the view that 'as a matter of general policy, we have on the whole tended to look upon the UN as a democratic organization, where world opinion is reflected in and shaped by, the votes of the majority'. In dealing with Cold War issues like disarmament in the UN they 'particularly desired to be surrounded by sizable majorities'.[7] To achieve this surprise in the UN, the United States refused even wider Western sponsorship of the resolution. They informed the British delegation in the General Assembly, that they excluded any consultation which would be necessary to achieve a wider sponsorship although they did agree that the draft resolution should be shown, just before its submission to the General Assembly, to friendly delegations.

The draft resolution recommended that the Atomic Energy Commission (AEC) and the Commission for Conventional Armaments (CCA), which had been pursuing their courses independently, should now be merged and placed under a new and consolidated negotiating body, the Disarmament Commission. Furthermore, the draft resolution called for full-scale disarmament programmes for both nuclear and conventional weapons.

The United States had now come close to the Soviet position according to which the nuclear question and the question of conventional weapons should not be split. Part of the explanation for this concession to the Soviets seems to be the realization of the fact that, as the Korean experience showed, even in the nuclear age wars can be conducted or won by the use of large conventional weapons and, thus, the whole problem of armaments should be seen in a wider context.[8] The underlying reason, however, for the change in the American attitude was their search for wider fronts for conducting propaganda warfare which would give them much more room for manoeuvre. The merger of the two Commissions into one single body meant that the scope of disarmament would be wider.

The British Foreign Office and State Department confidential papers provide abundant evidence of the real intentions behind the American public attitude. It is worth going to some lengths to describe them. Firstly, the mobilization of the UN apparatus by the Americans was dictated by the need they felt to counter Soviet peace propaganda and to outmanoeuvre the Soviets.[9] The Soviet Union, as long as disarmament was not being brought to the foreground of the UN actions, had been skilfully campaigning for peace and disarmament outside the UN's purview in a way which had impressed world opinion. This propaganda exercise had been intensified after 1950, when a Communist-sponsored 'World Congress of Partisans of Peace' was convened in Stockholm and launched huge campaign for disarmament. The main contention of this 'peace campaign' was that Western rearmament was responsible for international tension and that it was being carried out despite the Soviet manifestations of will to negotiate the reduction of armaments. 'Like Trotsky at Brest-Litovsk in 1918', Howard noted, 'the Soviet Union was shouting over the heads of governments to the peoples they represented'.[10] Furthermore, according to Bechhoefer, the so called movement of 'partisans of peace' began to align a significant part of the world public which was horrified by some of the Communist excesses which accompanied the campaign.[11] The accusations were concerned with the destructive power of the nuclear weapons which, according to Soviet propaganda, the United States was preparing to exercise.

The second objective of the American proposal was to rectify what was felt to be disadvantage under which the Western countries laboured from the propaganda point of view, since by separating discussions of the two types of weapon in the talks which had been held in the UN before 1950, attention has been concentrated on the atomic weapons in which the United States had complete superiority. By merging the two bodies it was hoped to draw attention equally to the vast Russian preponderance in conventional weapons.[12] Thirdly, by taking the initiative the United States calculated it would put the Soviet Union on the defensive and thus kill undesirable initiatives on its part in the UN.[13] In one of the official papers prepared as guidance to the American mission in the UN, the State Department argued that 'our national interest is served by the use we make of the instrument (i.e., the UN), and by our effectiveness in preventing its misuse by others'.[14] Fourthly, as the result of the initiative of the Western bloc to come to the UN and table their own proposal for an immediate resumption of the negotiations, it was possible to satisfy public opinion in America and other countries that the question of eventual disarmament had not been dismissed from consideration. This would make it appear to the world that it was the

United States which was coming forward as the champion of peace and that it was only they who genuinely wanted disarmament and had constructive proposals to make. From the American viewpoint, disarmament at that time 'was a political device for convincing our friends and the neutrals (as well as the Russians within limitations) of our interest in ending the arms race and of our peaceful intentions'.[15] Finally, in the eyes of the world, the reassociation of the Soviet Union with the negotiation process would simultaneously offer both legitimacy and credibility to the UN in a period when it was seen systematically as an organization under American political domination.

The idea of using disarmament policy for propaganda purposes was not new. As a commentator, Frye, wrote

> from time immemorial the idea of disarmament has been one of the most favoured forms of diplomatic dissimulation of the true motives and plans of those governments which have been seized by a sudden 'love of peace'. Any proposal for the reduction of armaments could invariably count upon broad popularity and support from public opinion.[16]

In the circumstances of the Cold War neither of the superpowers could afford to have it appear to world opinion that, in the UN debate or any other debates, the cause of disarmament was impeded or obstructed by its words, positions or deeds. Another fundamental reason which motivated both states to resort to a propaganda disarmament campaign despite paying lip service to disarmament was to mitigate the pessimism of world public opinion which, especially during the long-lasting Cold War, feared that weapons and, most of all nuclear weapons, held an even darker future in store for mankind. It should be pointed out that the propaganda game is not one played as a last resort or choice; it is a phenomenon which usually appears in almost all the cases of public debate and negotiation on disarmament, sometimes in extreme and sometimes in toned-down form, according to the international circumstances prevailing at the moment.

The history of the disarmament question in the Cold War context reveals a constant relationship between public opinion and the conduct of the foreign policy of the states and particularly the superpowers in the public forum of the UN. As a consequence, it is necessary to ask whether there were any specific reasons which decided the United States and shortly after the Soviet Union to come to the UN and use it as a kind of theatrical board. The UN was working on disarmament which, as a matter in which public interest is very great, put it under the spotlight of publicity. The UN's efforts occupied enormous public attention and in that sense the world organization was unique in moulding world opinion. Those people in the State Department who were responsible for mapping out the strategic direction for the conduct of United States participation in the UN had no doubts about it. For them, bringing the issue of disarmament before the UN was an advantageous course of action for propaganda purposes because 'the UN itself constitutes a special audience'.[17] The UN, by virtue of its wide membership, open meetings and multiple news media coverage was the favourite location for running a propaganda exercise. An official United States Government report argued that 'frequent appeals to public opinion not only by speeches and resolutions but also by substantive policies have come to constitute one of our main objectives in order to maintain the level of support for us in the General Assembly, and through it, in the world at large'.[18]

Public support for the UN's activities in the field of disarmament derived particularly from the fact that 'its actions (i.e., UN actions) come nearer to representing world consensus than any other institution that exists'.[19] In fact, the UN represents the collective judgement of the world community. The General Assembly's resolutions calling for disarmament crystallize a trend in public opinion in favour of such activity. At this point, one can identify the reasons upon which the advocacy of the UN for negotiations on disarmament is founded, in spite of the failures and disillusion which have from time to time accompanied its efforts. As a reflector of world opinion the UN exhorts its membership to use its chamber for the business of disarmament. States cannot ignore the UN which is voice of the desires of the world community and it is difficult for them not to respond. Thus, whilst the foreign policy of states, as far as disarmament is concerned, may appear to be more or less formed by what the international community desires, most of the time this is manifested in a way which in reality reflects a lack of political support for actual disarmament.

The UN concern for a resumption of the negotiations and the underlying public sentiment was something which could not be defied by individual states. However, this concern merely provoked the use of the UN for Cold War purposes. This opportunity was exploited mainly by the Western side as the UN was an organization which provided this side with a host of services and was a real asset for it. The UN still remained a family of select states with the door closed to new members and, therefore, the loyalty of the majority of the UN to the American position could guarantee that the organization would support initiatives which that country took.

The UN misled: Its disarmament policy in the wrong direction

The proceedings of the UN vindicated the American position in the form of a Resolution adopted by the General Assembly in 1952. By promoting this Resolution, the United States had acted as the real and exclusive agenda-setter. In essence, the UN had authorized the United States to speak for the organisation on the question of disarmament. No doubt, the atmosphere of restrained optimism at this time had little in common with the enthusiasm generated by the unanimous decision of the General Assembly when it set up the AEC to deal with the nuclear problem. The deterioration of international relations had made the superpowers lose sight of the magnitude of the enterprise they had embarked upon. This becomes more obvious if attention is drawn to the disarmament policy the UN chose to support. The pertinent and operative part of General Assembly Resolution 502 (VI) reads as follows:

> The General Assembly,
> Believing that a necessary means to this end (i.e., the maintenance of peace through disarmament) is the development by the UN of comprehensive and co-ordinated plans,
> 1. Establishes under the Security Council a Disarmament Commission.This Commission should have the same membership as the Atomic Energy Commission and the Commission for Conventional Armaments, and shall function under the rules of procedure of the AEC with such modifications as the Commission shall deem necessary.
> 2. Directs the Disarmament Commission to prepare proposals to be embodied in a draft treaty (or treaties) for the regulation, limitation and balanced reduction of all armed forces and all armaments, for the elimination of all major weapons to be adaptable to mass destruction, and for effective international control of atomic energy to ensure the prohibition of atomic weapons, and the use of atomic energy for peaceful purposes only.[20]

The UN, by its Resolution 502, called on its whole membership to develop plans for full-scale disarmament. The question arises as to whether the call for comprehensive programmes of disarmament was a suitable method of approach. Furthermore, could the members of the UN make such an ambitious effort to collaborate in an undertaking based on the uncertain premise that disarmament could be discussed and achieved before any progress had been made towards political understanding between the major powers? The problem of disarmament gave rise to a dilemma which had been faced in the days of the League of Nations and had again reached the surface in the UN. The hard choice was centred on the question of what is established first, perspectives of mutual confidence or actual disarmament ?

That an agreement on disarmament would lessen political tension would be difficult to refute; but the crucial question is whether it was politically feasible that any such agreement could be reached at a time when tensions had made states and especially the superpowers extremely distrustful of each other. The solution seemed to lie in an endeavour first to diminish tensions through the pursuit of confidence-building measures of perception and then to embark on negotiations. A change in the present state of tension and distrust, a change in the state of world, would be advantageous out of all proportion to the actual path of disarmament negotiations itself. However, it was an outright deceit to think that this change could be brought about by disarmament. Misleading positions like that of the United States which argued that 'disarmament, by relaxing tensions and fears, should facilitate peaceful settlement of political differences'[21] had been responsible for the wrong approach by the UN to disarmament. In reality, this position was equally shared by the Eastern bloc which publicly agreed with the Americans that 'the common sense way to reduce tension was to reduce armaments'.[22] The Soviet delegation in the UN argued that 'it was quite plain that to make disarmament contingent on the solution of international political problems was tantamount to abandoning all hope of an agreement on disarmament'.[23]

The approach which was now adopted by the UN departed from the assumption of the interdependence of existing disputes and disarmament and in a way proclaimed that the realization of disarmament constituted the prime condition for the solution of political disputes. The reasoning was defective since it implied, by analogy, that in the event of a world war there could be disarmament of the parties involved without a prior end to the conflict. The armaments race is not the consequence but rather a symptom of international tensions arising out of conflict. Armaments were at first a reflection and later, together with the changing nature of technology, a contributory agent of world tension. It is interesting to note that the General Assembly of the UN in the preamble of Resolution 502 acknowledged this when it explicitly provided that 'the general lack of confidence plaguing the world leads to the burden of increasing armaments and the fear of war'. Moreover, the present efforts were undertaken by the UN under the misleading belief that it was feasible to relax the general tension by an agreed system of drastic reduction of both nuclear and conventional weapons. Such a system, however, would itself depend on the state of international relations.

Disarmament negotiations can lead nowhere if it is not realized that in practice any progress must be proportional to the degree of international perspectives of confidence prevailing. The major determinants of the level of perspectives are not armaments. Rather, international tension is conditioned by the politics, or more precisely the policies, in whose services the armouries may be employed. Perspectives that were shared by the superpowers were not enough to uproot the habit of armed peace. It can be said that the approach taken by the UN was not fitted to its task in a time of a world convulsed by cross-currents of great intensity, like the German problem; the Indochina crisis and the continuing Korean war, during which the mobilization of one camp against the other could have set off World War III. International work on disarmament was undertaken from a hopeless position as it was approached on the basis of ignoring the complete absence of confidence. In these circumstances, it may be argued that the UN put the cart before the horse and was led up the garden path on the quest for unrealistic plans for full-scale disarmament.

Disarmament as an issue for propaganda warfare

A study of the role of the UN during the Cold War should focus attention upon the crucial question of who brings what issues to the UN and why? Yeselson and Gaglione, writers on UN, convincingly argue that 'behind this question is the need to know the relationship between the initiator (i.e., the state which brings an issue in the UN) and the defendant'.[24] This can be carried further by saying that the relationship between the initiator and the defendant largely determines the role of the UN either as an instrument of one-sided policy (usually of the initiator) or as an arena for a battle between the two. In the case of disarmament, the UN was called into service by the United States which was in this case the initiator. Since the UN adopted American policies in the form of resolutions and later Western plans of disarmament, it became an advocate of a particular viewpoint, that is an instrument of American policy.

However, 'just as bringing an issue (in our case disarmament) to the UN is a hostile act calculated to maximize national advantage',[25] whatever this advantage might be, the choice of the Soviet Union to defend its position within the ambit of the UN was an unavoidable tactical response. As a consequence, the UN assumed an additional role distinct from that of being solely an international forum at American disposal; it turned into an arena of battle between the two blocs. The Soviet Union was dragged unwillingly before the UN to participate in its drama in the role of defendant. Soviet policy in the UN became a kind of reaction to that of the United States. Just as a law of physics says every action is followed by reaction, so any American initiative provoked a Soviet response of similar kind. The Soviet Union came to the UN to play the game of disarmament on America's own terms. Thus, the UN was rendered the battleground in the political struggle for the opinion of the uninformed world. In the following years of work on disarmament, activities at the UN took the form of an endless propaganda contest. Both superpowers rallied behind the disarmament policy of the UN because the way the UN approached the problem, that is the search for full-scale disarmament programmes, suited them best. It left them with the maximum freedom for manoeuvre, gave them the possibility to devise a variety of plans in the service of their propaganda and inexhaustible opportunity for argument. In short, the call for comprehensive programmes of disarmament imposed as a disarmament policy in the UN provided the two sides with more than sufficient ammunition in their propaganda warfare.

To have a clear-cut picture of the negotiating posture which, from the outset of disarmament activities in the Disarmament Commission, converted the negotiations into a free-for-all propaganda tournament, attention should be drawn to certain assumptions upon which the policy-makers of the major powers relied to form their policy in the UN *vis-à-vis* disarmament. The most important of these was their knowledge that disarmament was not practical politics at the present time: 'it must be recognized that in the existing state of the world, it is impossible to devise disarmament proposals which would be acceptable to the Russians and at the same time compatible with the minimum national security requirements of the United Kingdom, France and the United States'.[26]

In view of this position, the Western side and especially the United States appeared to have no scruples in abandoning any hope of evolving realistic disarmament plans since it would be clearly impossible to secure Soviet agreement to any scheme that was acceptable to the Western bloc. They acted upon the expectation, which was subsequently verified, that 'the basic Soviet attitude will be uncooperative and the chance of making real progress towards disarmament will therefore be remote' and that the Disarmament Commission's work would be resolved into 'a struggle between the Western powers and the Soviet Union to gain the most favourable propaganda position'.[27] The degeneration of the discussion into a propaganda exercise was what the State Department expected. They were, therefore, not prepared to commit themselves either to any actual measures of disarmament or to any real discussion with the Soviet Union in the UN. The Department of State and the British Foreign Office were converted into machines for preparing plans to be put forward in the UN 'which would be very reasonable, but which the Soviet Union would almost certainly have to reject. Even in the unlikely event of Soviet acceptance, the proposals could be carried out without the disadvantage to the Western powers'.[28] This was the political assumption on which Western attitudes relating to disarmament negotiations were based. They presaged what actually appeared with surprising consistency in the negotiations as the Soviet strategy in the UN was built up on similar assumption. The two sides could not come within negotiating distance of one another since the narrowly defined national advantage being the main feature of any disarmament plan left no margin for negotiations. An attitude of stony immobility was maintained without any desire to find avenues for compromises.

The two sides were both more than a little cynical in making their offers and in contemptuously dismissing the counter offers of the other side. Both sides stored up disarmament surprises in order to counter any proposal which was likely to come from the other side. They invented alternatives to any plans presented and when the other side agreed to push a proposal, the side which espoused that alternative reverted to its previous position. The appropriate yardstick for prejudging the value of any disarmament plan to be submitted in the UN was the potential it carried to rally public opinion behind it. To prepare and submit plans which the other side 'would almost certainly have to reject' was dominant in the mind of the policy-makers and implied the inclusion in every plan of features 'that the other side could not possibly accept, thus forcing a rejection'.[29] They were deliberately looking for something which the other side would strain at accepting it so that, in the case of an anticipated breakdown of the talks, the breaking point would be an issue not accepted by the other side. This would allow the side which submitted the proposals 'to claim that the rejector is opposed to the idea of disarmament in toto'.[30] The features inserted in every plan submitted during this period, with a view to making it difficult for the opposite side to accept it, may be considered, as Nogee originally called them, the 'jokers'. For example, a joker systematically used by the Western powers was the making of their disarmament plans conditional upon the acceptance of systems of international control and verification which, as the Soviet Union remained a closed society, were unlikely to be accepted. Even concessions made by one side to the other constituted artificial gestures of good will designed to demonstrate to the public its moderate attitude in contrast to the hard-line policy of the other side. For example, a governing rule for the Western side in the negotiations was 'to find some way of making concessions to the Russians since further gestures were needed to convince public opinion that we were being reasonable and the Russians obstructive'.[31]

The negotiations turned out to be a public debate of controverted theses and there was the paradox of major powers proposing disarmament at a time when armaments were increasing on a bigger scale than ever before in time of peace. Not only do the public papers provide ample evidence but also President Truman himself in his address before the General Assembly admitted that a policy founded on an intensive rearmament programme was considered by the major states to be a necessary course to be followed as a measure of security in the present circumstances. According to Truman

> disarmament is the course which the United States would prefer to take. It is the course which most nations would like to adopt. But, until an effective system of disarmament is established, let us be clear about the task ahead. The only course the peace-loving nations can take in the present situation is to create the armaments needed to make the world secure against aggression. That is the course to which the United States is now firmly committed. That is the course we will continue to follow as long as it is necessary. The United States has embarked upon the course of increasing its armed strength only for the purpose of helping to keep the peace.[32]

To plough through the plethora of disarmament proposals engendered by all these propaganda ploys is a depressing experience. However, the point when the talks ceased to be solely a propaganda exercise turned out to be fascinating in terms of the means by which the two sides handled the discussions and used certain tactics never previously employed. The practice adopted by both sides boiled down to 'take it or leave it' without leaving scope for real negotiations or modifications of the proposals made.

The interplay started in April 1952 with the submission by the Western powers of their own proposals which advocated a comprehensive programme for the regulation, limitation and balanced reduction of all types of armaments and armed forces. These proposals envisaged as a first and indispensable step the establishment of a system of progressive and continuing disclosure and verification of all armaments. This process would begin with conventional weapons (disclosure of information whose accuracy should be effectively verified) and would be completed with nuclear weapons. The sponsors stated that verification should be based on continuous inspection and that, until a better plan was presented, the Baruch plan for the control of atomic energy should continue to serve as the basis for negotiation. The whole system would have been provided with an effective system of safeguards for the detection of any violations. Furthermore, the proposals provided for reductions in all types of armaments and armed forces which were defined to include 'para-military security and police forces'. Finally, according to these proposals a programme of disarmament should include 'criteria according to which the size of all armed forces would be limited; the portion of national production which could be used for military purposes would be restricted and mutually agreed military programmes would be arrived at within the prescribed limits and restrictions'.[33]

The priority and the emphasis given to the thorny question of international inspection and verification in the Western proposals served the means by which the United States chose to conduct its propaganda warfare. As one United States official noted, 'since there is not one chance in a thousand that the Soviet Union will accept the proposals, their chief purpose is certainly their propaganda value'.[34] According to British officials, the main strand in the American thinking was that

> the discussion would begin with an aspect which we have chosen an aspect of the armament problem on which the Soviet Union is at a clear disadvantage from the propaganda point of view, and where the West would have a clear advantage. It would give us the opportunity to focus on the lifting of the Iron Curtain on armaments matters as the prerequisite to further progress on the problem.[35]

The State Department appreciated that the question of disclosure of armaments, inspection and verification, which was given priority in General Assembly's Resolution 502 itself, was one which not only would put the Soviets on the defensive but also would force them into a position of rejecting the degree of inspection required under the Western proposals. The way the British Foreign Office interpreted the American intentions leaves no doubt that the object was 'to score a propaganda success over the Russians by demonstrating that it is the obstructiveness of the Soviet Union which is blocking progress towards disarmament and that this obstructiveness is rooted in the whole Soviet system'.[36]

The British Government, being involved in the process of planning the American-inspired proposals, showed up what it considered to be the weak points in them before their submission. However, their differences with the Americans at that time were less in the particular content of the proposals and much more in style of presentation and points of emphasis. The British policy-makers now believed that the Americans were proposing to make agreement on the principle of a phased system of inspection and verification an essential preliminary condition to the introduction of any scheme towards limitation of armaments, while we preferred that the initial emphasis should be on positive proposals for the reduction of armed forces and armaments.[37]

Since for the Americans, the whole operation was an propaganda exercise, this would lead to an early controversy and quite possibly to a breakdown. If they were to concentrate on a phased system of disclosure and verification, as the Americans proposed, then the reasons for such a breakdown would not be well understood by public opinion. The British argued that 'breakdown on this point might not be very easy to explain publicly'[38] adding that

the danger is that we shall get bogged down in discussions which may appear to the general public to be remote from the question of concrete disarmament and play into the hands of Soviet propaganda which has always maintained that we were side-tracking the real problem of reducing armaments with irrelevant issues. The question of safeguarded verification and inspection is important. But we ought not to allow ourselves to get bogged down in arguments against us. People will say it is no use asking the Russians to open their frontiers.[39]

Therefore, the British Foreign Office was of the opinion that without retreating from the basic theses, it would make the position all the stronger if the main weight of the discussion could be diverted from the outset onto concrete proposals about conventional armaments which would have greater appeal for the public. It appeared that the two allies had approached the same plan from different angles because they made different estimates of what constituted a striking popular appeal. But the British appear to have had one more profound reason for believing that their position would work more effectively. They foresaw, with accuracy, that 'the Russians will, at the UN, revive their proposal for a cut of one third in the arms and armed forces of the five Great powers which Vysinsky (the Soviet chief negotiator in the UN) made with some éclat in 1948 (in the CCA)'.[40] Thus, if the Soviets were to accompany this proposal with a suggestion for the abolition of nuclear weapons, 'the American proposals will look tame by comparison'.[41] Finally the British Foreign Office argued that 'for the effect on public opinion, some proposal would be required at least as striking as the Soviet percentage proposal. This proposal would appear reasonable and easy to grasp, and we feel it would cut the ground from under the Soviet proposal. If it were rejected (as of course it well might be) our propaganda position would be strong'.[42] The British remained convinced that their position would make better headlines but soon realized that there was no prospect of persuading the United States to depart from its position. Thus, they decided to fall in with the Americans because 'the most unfortunate impression would be created if it became clear that we and the Americans disagreed over a subject of such major political significance'.[43]

During the negotiations in the Disarmament Commission, the Western powers under the guidance of the United States tried to impose their own terms. Their position was that work in the Disarmament Commission should start with the disclosure of armaments, based on submission by states of data as to how many armed forces and armaments each had at its disposal, and what imbalances existed at the moment. This data was to be officially disclosed and verified. Once the Disarmament Commission had this data and agreed on an effective system for verification and inspection, it could pass on to other problems such as the consideration of means of regulation, limitation and reduction of all arms including nuclear weapons.

The Soviet Union would not tie its hands and refused the course of negotiations the Western powers tried to impose on the Disarmament Commission. It chose to go about it the other way around and proposed, first, the unconditional prohibition of all nuclear weapons before the establishment of a system of control, and second, a one-third reduction in the conventional armaments and armed forces of the five great powers prior to the formulation of plans for verification of these reductions.[44]

That the Soviet proposals did not constitute practical plans but high sounding and in fact empty slogans becomes more obvious if one checks their conformity with the general principles and prerequisites which should be followed or satisfied to obtain their objective of disarmament. The Soviet proposals called for the destruction of existing stocks of nuclear weapons before any organ capable of ensuring that their destruction was real and complete had been established. The question still remained as to what would happen if all the nuclear weapons were destroyed while the possibility to make new ones secretly was left intact. The problem could not be solved even when the Soviets subsequently agreed that the prohibition of nuclear weapons should be put into effect simultaneously with the establishment of an international control organ. The Soviets were strongly opposed to a control organ being empowered to conduct effective inspection on a continuous basis on the ground of the principle of sovereignty; the control organ according to their view was not to be entitled to interfere in the domestic affairs of states. Assuming that the nuclear weapons would be destroyed, the one-third cut in conventional armaments, which the Soviets proposed, would have ensured the maintenance of their supremacy in conventional weapons thus reinforcing the existing state of disequilibrium and accentuating insecurity. As it was well known the Soviet Union enjoyed at the time superiority in conventional weapons, whereas the United States retained a commanding lead in nuclear weaponry. What seems to be natural for the West is that the Soviet proposals should be rejected since their adoption would eliminate United States superiority, while enhancing that of the Soviet Union. As a matter of fact, the impracticability of the Soviet proposal stood as the hidden joker forcing their rejection by the West. Furthermore, the one-third cut in conventional armaments of the five big powers was arbitrary so long as it was not known from what levels of strength these powers were reducing their armaments and to what levels the reduction would be effected. This proposal was a mathematical formula which made it apparent that, for the implementation of a comprehensive programme like that of the Soviet Union, a thorough study of all elements of armaments and an inventory of the quantities possessed by everyone would be necessary. Armaments comprised many elements of a diversified nature; any attempt to deal with all of them simultaneously under comprehensive plans seemed likely to result in failure. These complicated plans posed serious and perhaps insuperable obstacles in the way of the speedy attainment of their goal.

Although the Soviet proposals were in essence impracticable, it was sufficient to gain publicity and to put the Soviets in a privileged position in terms of propaganda. Their formula was simple and direct and therefore had a popular appeal. Their proposal for the total prohibition of nuclear weapons was a catchword designed to impress the world because the nuclear weapon was what the man in the street was most concerned about. By putting also concrete proposals for a one-third cut in conventional weapons they had shown to the people around the world that they were trying to do something special about armaments on which they enjoyed superiority. The Soviets at this stage of the proceedings had made a lot out of the fact that, whereas they had put concrete disarmament proposals and thus had come straight to the heart of the matter, the West had made suggestions which were no more than a rehash of the old ideas of the Baruch plan extended to apply to conventional armaments. Indicative of the positive effect the Soviet proposals had on public opinion were the assertions made by the Western mass media that 'the Soviets have none the less made great propaganda gains, in their attempt to portray themselves as real peace-lovers and us as the true war-mongers'.[45]

The tactics of the Western powers to put emphasis on disclosure, inspection and verification turned out to be self-defeating. The Western powers realized that they had come badly out of the debate and this made them to review their policies. The Soviet success in propaganda began to make the Western powers realize their vulnerability on this flank and prompted them to re-examine their attitude in the negotiations. In light of the fact that 'public opinion has shown itself remarkably sympathetic to the Soviet proposals',[46] they now agreed that the set of proposals on which they should throw their emphasis should be something similar to the Soviet proposals. They were convinced that 'one of our great disadvantages *vis-à -vis* the Russians is that we have never been able to take the initiative with concrete proposals for an actual cut while they have done so and continually repeat their proposal'.[47] To do so and satisfy public opinion that 'they were not neglecting any genuine possibility of reducing armaments' they decided to put forward new proposals in May 1952. These proposals called for the reduction of the size of the armed forces of the five big powers as a part of their comprehensive programme for the regulation, limitation and balanced reduction of armed forces. They provided that the maximum strength of the armed forces of these states should be fixed at between 1 million and 1.5 million men for the United States, the Soviet Union and China and between 700,000 and 800,000 for the United Kingdom and France.[48] One may reasonably argue that these absolute figures were chosen because they offered to the Western powers a reasonable and safe basis for discussion in the event of their proposal being unexpectedly accepted by the Soviets. The test of reasonableness was one to which the Western powers constantly subjected all their proposals before they submitted them to the UN; for a proposal which would not appear reasonable could not be effective from a propaganda point of view. What seemed to the Western powers to make these figures sound attractive was the introduction of the idea of parity or equality between Eastern and Western forces. The employment of the equilibrium criterion added, according to the Western viewpoint, credibility to their proposal. A letter sent by the British delegation in the UN to the Foreign Office admitted that

> the idea that some sort of balance should be struck between the armed strength of the Soviet Union and the Western democracies is one which should be fairly easy to put across in public and what might have a wide appeal. At the same time it would not be wholly unrealistic since if there is ever to be some agreement on disarmament, the basis for agreement must presumably be that the armed strength of the two opposing camps would be about equal.[49]

The proposed figures provided for an overall parity between (i) the East (USSR and China) and the West (United States, United Kingdom and France), (ii) the United States and Soviet Union, (iii) China and the Soviet Union, and more significantly (iv) between the armed forces of the United Kingdom and France on the one hand and the Soviet Union on the other. In reality, the target of this proposal was to focus on the superior Soviet armed forces *vis-à-vis* the inferior strength of the British and French armed forces in Europe. The figures in the Western proposal were specified in such a way as to virtually require, if implemented, heavy cuts in the Soviet armed forces; while at the same time there would be little scope for adjustment in the strength of the British and French forces. Taking into account the British Foreign Office calculations, the British forces were barely above the suggested figure (British forces were stated by the Foreign Office to have reached the figure of 865,000 in mid-1952) while French forces were just below it.[50] However, as details of actual armed strength on both sides had not been revealed, the suggested numerical limitations of the ceilings of armed forces were as arbitrary as the Soviet proposals for a percentage cut. As the Soviets were extremely reluctant to accept the formation of an international system to verify the adequacy and accuracy of the information about the existing numbers of armed forces, the talks could not but reach an impasse. The Soviet tried to get off the hook by complaining that the Western powers had attempted to separate the question of armed forces from the whole Soviet package which contained also calls for the prohibition of nuclear weapons about which there were no provisions in the new Western proposals.[62] As a matter of fact, the negotiations in the Disarmament Commission were now in a maze from which there was no way out.

Shortly after the death of Stalin, in 1953, the UN by its General Assembly Resolution 715 (VIII) mandated that the negotiations should be taken up in a new disarmament Sub-Committee of the Disarmament Commission - the first negotiating body limited to those powers 'principally involved'.[63] This Sub-Committee consisted of five states, namely the United States, the United Kingdom, France, Canada and Soviet Union.

The first phases of the talks in the Sub-Committee were devoted to the review of the general principles which must govern any disarmament programme. This was occasioned by the Western attempt to ascertain whether there had been any modification in the Soviet attitude concerning especially the aspect of international control;[52] and above all to cover up the fact that they had not yet made up their minds about the strategy to follow in this round of negotiations. This was actually reflected in the content of

Resolution 715. It is well known that any resolution passed at the end of each year's talks used to contain an endorsement of the Western proposals and pattern the subsequent negotiations on Western lines. On this occasion, however, Resolution 715 did not lay down one side terms of reference for the Sub-Committee but made only a detailed reference to the general principles which would be paramount for the implementation of a disarmament scheme. It also set the objective of reaching agreement on a comprehensive and coordinated plan as the course along which work on disarmament was to continue.

Several months after the adoption of Resolution 715 and while the first stage of talks in the Sub-Committee was still going on, the whole situation appeared to change. The sensation aroused by the Hydrogen bomb experiments in the Pacific served to stimulate the Western powers towards submitting new proposals. The Western powers perceived that

> the propaganda value of the Russian proposal (for the total prohibition of the nuclear weapons) might well have been considerably enhanced as the result of the effect of recent H-bomb experiments on some segments of world opinion, and that this has to be taken into account in any presentation of the Western position on disarmament.[65]

They were perturbed by the prospect of losing the initiative in the negotiations, if the Soviets, prompted by the impact the H-bomb had made in the world, were to re-table their proposals for a prohibition of nuclear weapons.[54] Holding on to the initiative became the paramount concern in their thinking. To this end, they felt that the general discussion on principles of disarmament should be dropped. Dixon, chief negotiator of the United Kingdom at the UN, in a personal letter send to the British Foreign Secretary explained the situation which the Western powers were now facing:

> I am frankly dismayed at the prospect of the Western powers approaching discussions in the Disarmament Commission unless they have something constructive to offer. The idea would be to produce a striking and simple plan which would show that we are live to public anxiety about weapons of mass destruction. Since it is unlikely that the Russians would agree to such a plan, it may be regarded as a cold-war exercise.[55]

Thus, the Western powers invented a plan, run off in a hurry, to serve their own purposes (its preparation took two months). Because it brought out the principal points which the British Government had emphasized, its drafting should be credited to the British Foreign Office. The United Kingdom, being already the third nuclear power in the world, had undertaken more responsibility in the handling of the disarmament affair in the UN on behalf of the Western powers and, in fact, made most of the running during the negotiations.

The Western powers plan was submitted by the United Kingdom and France in June 1954.[56] It was the most comprehensive disarmament programme in the post-war negotiations to date. It outlined a disarmament programme which was to take place in three progressive stages. The plan provided as stage one, an overall freeze of military manpower and budgets. In stage two, one half of the agreed reductions in conventional armaments and armed forces to be concurrent with a cessation of the production of all kinds of nuclear weapons. The final stage would include the second half of the agreed reductions in conventional armaments and armed forces and, on the completion of it, the total prohibition and elimination of all nuclear and other weapons (for example, biological weapons) would be carried out and the existing stocks of atomic materials be converted to peaceful uses. All these stages would be carried out after the formation and stationing of an international control organ with sufficiently wide powers of inspection, verification and enforcement to ensure its effective operation. Each stage would begin when the states were satisfied that this organ was ready to verify effectively the measures of that stage and the measures of the preceding stage. Thus, it was for the international control organ to decide when the next step was to be taken.

By placing greater emphasis on nuclear weapons the Western powers tried to meet the most serious of the Soviet concerns. Their main target was to call the Soviet Union's bluff of campaigning for the elimination of the nuclear weapons. They thought that their scheme, which began with conventional weapons and ended with nuclear weapons, would surely be unacceptable to the Soviets.[57] As a consequence, they decided not to be engaged at an early stage, in a detailed discussion of any one aspect of disarmament, before agreement had been sought on the basic principles of the plan. There were two reasons for this. Firstly, they calculated that talks on these principles (i.e., disarmament in successive stages and reductions of conventional weapons before the elimination of nuclear weapons) would not go very far because the Soviets would not agree with the essential principles of the Anglo-French plan and, therefore, it would be possible 'to establish that lack of progress in the Sub-Committee is due to Soviet inability to accept any of these principles'.[58] Secondly, if by any chance the Soviets did accept them, they could still preserve their freedom of manoeuvre.[59]

In September 1954, the Soviet Union astonished the world and, most of all, astonished the Western powers by accepting the Anglo-French plan as the basis for discussion on disarmament.[60] Viewed against the background of nine years of unyielding obduracy with which the Soviets had spurned all Western proposals, the sudden announcement that they were willing to consider the Anglo-French plan as a basis for negotiations was like a flash of light in an impenetrable gloom. The Soviet acceptance was accompanied by concessions which marked substantial progress on certain major points in the direction of the Western point of view. The Soviets appeared to accept the general principle of phased disarmament both in regard to conventional and nuclear weapons; they dropped their demand for a one-third cut in the armaments of the five big powers and accepted instead the principle of reductions to agreed levels coupled with a total prohibition of all the weapons of mass destruction; and they also accepted that reductions and the introduction of controls of the disarmament programme should take place simultaneously.

The Soviets had now come to play the game with the cards the Western side had chosen. It was the smartest propaganda move ever seen in the disarmament negotiations. It shocked the Western powers and aroused great uneasiness among them.[61] The first short term advantage the Soviets gained from their unexpected move was that they stole the thunder of the Western powers who had anticipated coming to the General Assembly and pressing for a so called substantive resolution which, remitting the disarmament question to the Disarmament Commission and its Sub-Committee, would include an endorsement of the Anglo-French plan. The acceptance of the Anglo-French plan by the Soviets had been intentionally made at an opportune time, just as the discussion of the subject in the current session of the General Assembly began. However, the Western powers did not feel that 'such an endorsement, though desirable on general grounds was essential, because the Russians may have represented this as a rebuff to their efforts to meet us half way'.[62] As a consequence, they were deprived of the approval of their plan by the world community of the UN; instead they agreed to the adoption of a 'procedural' resolution (Resolution 808 of 4 November 1954) which requested the Disarmament Commission to seek 'an acceptable solution'.[63]

However, what caused real trouble to the Western powers in the long term, was their difficulty in finding out the real intentions which lay behind what appeared to be a Soviet *volte-face*. There were a number of unanswered questions. Firstly, had the Soviet Union really accepted the basic principles of the Anglo-French plan? Secondly, in what way and to what extent did the

Soviets accept or reject the proposals and ideas embodied in the plan? Finally, was the Soviet Union seriously interested in making progress on disarmament or was it mainly offering some horse trade against the plans for remilitarization and the drawing of West Germany into the North Atlantic bloc and the Western European Union at that time being attempted within the framework of the London and Paris agreements of 1954? One possible interpretation of the modification in the Soviet attitude could be that they were interested in holding out the prospect of disarmament as a means to persuade the Western side not to go ahead with its policy of rearming West Germany and bringing it under the NATO umbrella and/or to demonstrate to the world that this policy was, in effect, undermining or inconsistent with, the efforts now being made to achieve disarmament. The contradictory way the Western powers tended to analyse the 'new-look' Soviet policy was manifested in a letter sent by the Foreign Office to the British Ambassador in Moscow which stated that 'it looks as though we may not know whether the Soviet attitude was solely directed at Western plans for German rearmament or is also intended as a genuine attempt to reach agreement on disarmament'.[64] In their desperate effort to discover where the Soviets stood, the Western powers approached Hammarskjold, the Secretary-General of the UN and others but they were unable to draw any definite conclusions.[65]

Guessing what the Soviets were up to became their main preoccupation, but the way the Soviets had conducted disarmament policy in the past convinced them not to read too much into the Soviet positive reaction to the Western proposals. Additionally, there were still differences between the two sides which had not yet been investigated. For instance, there was nothing in the Soviet proposals for a preliminary freeze of all military manpower and expenditures. The Soviet proposals also provided for the prohibition of nuclear weapons to be carried out concurrently with the second stage of the reduction of conventional armaments and not on its completion as the Anglo-French plan suggested. There were also two crucial issues which had not been explored at all, the levels of the reduction of the armed forces and armaments and certainly the international control of the disarmament programme for which there was obscurity in the Soviet proposals as far as the constitution and function of the control organ was concerned. It was not at all clear whether the Soviets were ready to forego enough of their sovereignty and accept a kind of control activity on their soil which was utterly alien to their traditions.

All this allowed the Western powers to return to the negotiations with a reasonable degree of confidence. In the meantime, they considered it wiser for them not to appear anything but conciliatory. They had hailed the new

Soviet position as an important advance in their direction and, therefore, had to convince the public that they were taking the Soviets seriously. It was now their tactical position not to be engaged in any controversial correspondence with the Soviets but to wait for them to show their hand considerably more than they had done so far.[66] The posture of waiting for the Soviets to become clearer in their positions had no luck as the Soviets evaded debate on the real issues. Their negative attitude prompted the Western powers to alter their posture. They agreed now that the next tactic should be 'an exercise in probing and smoking out the true Soviet position'[67] and therefore their new attempt would be purely exploratory to bring the Soviets out into the open. This could be done with the submission of a 'searching proposal' dealing with an aspect which had not yet been explored.[68] The question of international control was automatically excluded because of its controversial nature. It did not fit the 'interrogative character' they wanted to give to this stage of talks. An additional reason which inspired them to keep it off the current negotiations was their suspicion, arising from past experience, that the Soviets would come forward with their old claim that what mattered was to start talking about disarmament rather than about control and verification.

The 'searching proposal' which was invented for the sole purpose of testing Soviet sincerity, was concerned with the levels of the armed forces which might emerge from their comprehensive disarmament programme. The Western proposal, which was introduced in March 1955, called for the reduction of the armed forces of the United States, the Soviet Union and China to one million and a half men and of the United Kingdom and France to 650,000 men each.[69] To highlight the fact that they approached the new talks in a conciliatory mood, the Western nations backed up this proposal with an offer that the elimination of nuclear weapons should take place after 75 per cent of the reductions in conventional armed forces and armaments had been completed instead of waiting until all the reductions had been achieved as their original plan suggested. What they desired to discover by this 'gesture' was whether the Soviets were really prepared to accept the phasing of the disarmament programme in the concrete stages which the Anglo-French plan recommended. The Western efforts to elucidate the Soviet intentions met with no success. The Soviets refused to be interrogated and did not take any position as far as the new proposal were concerned. As a matter of fact, the Soviets were deliberately stalling since they realized that worldwide attention was turned on and that world opinion felt that agreement on the disarmament programme as envisaged in the Anglo-French plan was now dependent primarily on them.

This realization made the interplay even more dramatic than ever. In May

1955, the Soviet Union submitted its own plan which brought them closer than ever to the positions of the West.[70] The Soviets accepted the most recent supplementary proposals of the Western powers with regard to the specific ceilings for armed forces and the elimination of nuclear weapons after the 75 per cent reductions in conventional forces. It accepted almost all the major principles of the Anglo-French plan and moved ever closer towards the Western positions with regard to international control. Their plan anticipated in the first stage the creation of an international control organ, which would be allowed to install in the territories of all states concerned, on a basis of reciprocity, permanent control posts at major ports, at railway junctions, on main highways and airfields. The functions of the agency would be extended in the second stage and would include inspection on a permanent basis. It would be entrusted with the power to require states to provide information about their armaments, and unimpeded access to 'all objects of control' and to budgetary records. These constituted significant concessions. This proposal was described by Baker as 'the moment of hope', because of the fact that the Soviets approximated so closely the Western positions that it appeared now feasible for the two sides to move directly for a comprehensive disarmament programme along the lines of the Anglo-French plan.[71]

The Western powers were quite bewildered by the big surprise the Soviets had delivered. Just a few days before May 10, 1955, the British Foreign Office evaluation of the negative Soviet attitude in the UN to their most recent proposals had amounted to shouts of triumph over the poor propaganda skills of the Soviet Union. The response of the Western powers made it evident that the Soviet plan came as a complete surprise to them and, it is fair to say, this development caused deep divisions within the ranks of Western policy. The British Government acting on the advice of the head of the British delegation in the UN (Nutting), perceived that it was necessary, from the point of view of public opinion, not at this stage to break off the talks but to produce a counter move as an alternative to the Soviet plan.[72] The Soviets had now called the Western bluff and the British Foreign Office appeared to share Nutting's conviction that any cessation of the talks 'would still leave the Soviet proposals as the latest and most comprehensive word on the subject, and this alone would be bound to impress other members of the UN.[73] It would be seen very much in our interests to re-formulate our disarmament proposals, so as to regain the initiative'.[74]

The British Government tried to undermine the State Department's decision for an adjournment of the Disarmament Commission arguing that 'it is not a matter for State Department but High Government policy'.[75] The implication was that the decision of the State Department, shaped by one individual, Governor Stassen, did not reflect the policy of the American Government. Stassen had been appointed as Special Assistant to the President of the United States 'with responsibility for developing, on behalf of the President, the broad studies, investigations and conclusions which, when concurred in by the National Security Council and approved by the President, will become basic policy toward disarmament'.[76] He was given the position of Cabinet rank which was quite unusual practice.[77] When, shortly after his appointment as a Special Assistant, he became the head of the American delegation to the disarmament negotiations, the Office of the Special Assistant to the President was transferred to the Department of State. His appointment resulted from the suggestion which had been made within the American Government that 'the lack of progress made in the review of its disarmament policies warranted the appointment of a high ranking individual with sole responsibility for co-ordinating the work'.[78]

The British Government hoped that its reaction would prevent the Americans from forcing an adjournment of the negotiations for the time being. In his book 'Disarmament', which was published a few years later, Nutting was highly critical of the decision to recess the Sub-Committee's session immediately after the presentation of the Soviet plan although he did concede that the United States had important reasons for asking for one.[79] These were the impending Summit Conference in Geneva, the appointment of a new chief disarmament negotiator for the United States (Stassen); the necessity of this person familiarizing with past negotiations; and, as Stassen himself telegraphed to Dulles, the United States Secretary of State, 'to give the United States Government themselves an opportunity to clear their minds on the issues raised by the Russian proposals'.[80]

It may be argued, however, in the light of the contemporary public documents, that none of these reasons was the real determining factor which made the United States favour a recess. The United States was now in the process of re-evaluating its policy with regard to future negotiations. This should be considered in conjunction with the appointment of Stassen as a high rank official.

If Stassen's appointment indicated the fluidity of the American stand *vis-à -vis* the disarmament negotiations, the next step, taken by him personally after the adjournment of the Disarmament Commission, made it plain that the United States was looking for changes in its public disarmament policy. This also provides sufficient evidence of what purposes the appointment of Stassen came to serve. The United States, in the person of Stassen, entered reservations on all previously offered disarmament proposals:

The United States does now place a reservation upon all of its pre-Geneva substantive positions taken in the Sub-Committee or in the Disarmament Commission or in the UN. In placing this reservation upon our pre-Geneva positions, may I make it perfectly clear that we are not withdrawing any of these positions, we are not disavowing any of them.[81]

Admittedly, the placing of all past commitments of the United States on a reserve status brought to light the emptiness of the Anglo-American plan. Nutting, therefore, had good reasons, reflecting the views of his government, to criticize this statement considering it 'unnecessary' and damaging 'to the whole Western position, because it 'exposed the West to charges of backsliding and handed the initiative to the Soviets'.[82] While this argument is absolutely true as the West appeared to confirm publicly its retreat from its previous positions, the American position can be defended on the basis of utility. It carried with it the implication that continuation of the discussion along past lines should be rendered obsolete.[83] It reflected United States determination to change the locus of the proceedings in the Disarmament Commission from disarmament per se to arms control measures. As such, it was a kind of public pronouncement of the change in American intention and this, for the Americans, superseded the short-term detrimental effects on public opinion in the West which their reservation statement caused.

The evolution of the UN policy

The fact that the UN showed poor political judgement in attempting to pursue a policy of disarmament at time when such a policy was inconsistent with the conditions of international life does not mean that its role was detrimental to the conduct of the negotiations on disarmament. To have been so, it would have had to impair the implementation of a clearly expressed desire on the part of the major powers to go ahead with disarmament. Although the events did not vindicate the UN's chosen course, it should be recalled that no a genuine desire for disarmament was in the air.

Would the contribution of the world organization have been greater if it had been involved in wide-ranging activities which affected general political conditions and relations between states rather from being committed to the sponsorship of negotiations on disarmament? This is a question which is difficult to answer. It may be said, however, that if the discouraging record of negotiations was caused by the wrong directions and directives of the UN which had given to the Disarmament Commission insoluble tasks, these

47

wrong approaches and directives should be attributed to the general discord which characterized the normal part of international behaviour during the worst years of Cold War. States and especially the major powers could not overcome their fundamental disagreements on the issue of disarmament because disagreement was a significant part of the Cold War which was also reflected in the UN and its policies. Nevertheless, the UN played a very valuable role in the most intense period of Cold War. It is most gratifying that the frustrating situation the world witnessed during these years did not provoke a break in the long and depressing series of discussions, thanks to the UN's consistent support of the negotiations. Thus, the UN stood for the study of the disarmament problem though not for its consideration as a negotiating issue. Continuous work while tedious and frustrating was immensely important and did, at least, help to uncover hardcore problems and sometimes narrowed the debate to the real issues.

However, what was the most important service in the cause of disarmament was that, at long last, the right questions could be asked as to the approaches and directions of the disarmament policies and wrong answers and approaches were exposed. If failure came in the negotiations, the reasons for it could be investigated and become known so that a new attempt could be made under approaches which had not been tried before. This began to take place when a gradual change in world political conditions occurred after the mid-fifties which offered the UN's membership the possibility of using a more rational approach to disarmament than before. The Indo-China war had ended while the post-Stalinist period had just begun with a markedly more moderate Soviet policy in world affairs the first step of which was the withdrawal of the Soviets from Austria. The Korean war, the most critical and explosive local conflict confronting the UN itself, was over as well. The guns had been silenced everywhere, after thundering incessantly for a half a century in various parts of the globe. The changing atmosphere enabled the major powers (United States, United Kingdom, France and Soviet Union), for the first time in a long time, to meet at Geneva for high-level talks about the major political problems dividing East and West including disarmament. The Geneva Conference of 1955 was the beginning of a change of mood. It signified the establishment of a sort of a working relationship between the superpowers with a view to ending the tensions of the Cold War days and creating an overall improvement in the climate of world affairs despite the fact that the outstanding political differences between the two sides still remained unsolved.[84]

The change in the attitude of the major powers became a part of the new picture at the UN. Tensions never ceased to exist, but as they commenced their downward swing they provided the essential ingredient for, at least, a more flexible approach of the membership of the UN to multilateral negotiations. The menacing events of the past years which had strained relations between the superpowers almost to breaking point had fortunately brought a sense of realism in dealing with and approaching disarmament. However, this realism had not given rise to an analysis in order to find a remedy and ensure a more productive future in the field. A major contributing factor in the making-up of the new picture at the UN was the fact that its use as a monopolistic instrument of United States policy began rapidly to decline when in 1955 sixteen new members were admitted. By virtue of this mass admission, the UN began to develop qualities of a third party, standing between and sometimes above the two blocs, as an arena for debate on and approaches to the political issue of disarmament which exceeded the narrow concerns of one bloc. This had a positive impact on the negotiating process which was much improved as an element of objectivity was added to it.

The first practical inference which can be drawn is the conclusion that the way to call a halt to the armaments race and to achieve disarmament was to solve the problem of mistrust and to reduce the hostile atmosphere which weighed heavily upon the world. The membership of the UN had now started reappraising and actually revizing its earlier attitudes to the disarmament problem. It was now more likely to refuse measures for the reduction of armaments and the prohibition of nuclear weapons and to recognize that at that time comprehensive disarmament programmes could not be implemented. It was now accepted that 'the political difficulties in the way of progress towards a comprehensive plan of disarmament had been correctly identified as essentially the lack of mutual confidence';[85] that 'it was absurd to ask states to do something which presupposed confidence when confidence did not exist'.[86] Thus, it was now admitted that the lack of international confidence haunted them at every turn in the search for comprehensive disarmament.

In consequence, there now seemed to be a more flexible approach and there was considerably less tendency to advance plans such as those for full-scale comprehensive disarmament proposals, which were recognized as unacceptable even by their advocates. The United States declaration of reservation on all their previous positions was designed to undermine the significance of comprehensive disarmament proposals and the Soviet decision not to press their plan of 10 May 1955, underscored the fact that the UN membership would do well not to attach importance to proposals of this kind. There was further evidence of a weakening of the old view which the advocates of these proposals had held as governments were now coming to recognize that 'comprehensive measures of disarmament are dependent upon progress in the resolution of major international political issues'.[87] It is interesting, at this point, to record the words of Marshal Bulganin, the Soviet Prime Minister: 'A broad disarmament programme can be carried out only if the Cold War is brought to an end and the necessary confidence in relations between states, which unfortunately is now lacking, is established'.[88]

At this time, states as well as the superpowers, made observations concerning the lack of a suitable political climate which would not allow them to negotiate and began to reappraise what ought to be attempted. There had been a clear move towards a redefinition of the approaches and the issues. As a consequence, a new and encouraging approach which represented an important advance on previous approaches was being gradually visualized. This was the need for a study of plans and agreements on the implementation of limited objectives of disarmament designed to build up mutual confidence on the basis of which it would be feasible to proceed to larger areas of agreement. This was the result of the acceptance that the basis on which the UN had proceeded so far had been wrong and unreal. States had at least broken the deadlock searching for a new, more promising UN policy; a new avenue was opened up.

However, the movement forward appeared to be slow and cautious. The past was very much alive in the sense that states and mainly the superpowers had been led into such extreme positions that they had difficultly in retreating from them immediately thereafter. The emphasis on building up confidence through limited measures of arms control as a precursor to disarmament appeared to be common to both superpowers but the problem was how to disengage themselves, in the eyes of the world public, from their earlier commitments. As a matter of fact, the new course on which they now wished to embark undermined the logic of their previous positions which were based on out of date assumptions. They had in the past created the false optimism that genuine disarmament was just around the corner and they had led public opinion to have great expectations that this would happen. Now, public opinion might take the view that the superpowers were ganging up to take retrograde steps away from the actual process of disarmament.

To find a way out of their present difficulty the superpowers began to use the UN to educate and prepare public opinion for a new approach, that of the search for limited measures. Very helpful in this respect was the voice of the Non-Aligned states which, in line with what they had agreed in their Conference in Bandung in May 1955, appealed to all powers in the UN, pending total prohibition of the manufacture of nuclear weapons, to reach agreements on arms control measures.[89] The Premier of India, Nehru, was personally leading the campaign for a 'standstill' agreement for the suspension of nuclear experiments. To make the switch and to get onto the track of such a limited but forward-looking project the superpowers, playing a game not only with one another but also both of them against the others, deliberately prolonged the discussions in the UN with the aim of influencing public opinion. As a matter of fact, much of the subsequent activity in the UN was affected by this practical necessity and tactics.

At the initial stage of their delaying tactics the superpowers continued talking about disarmament because they did not want to give the impression that they had abandoned all hope of finding a practical scheme of disarmament; while at the same time they were signalling to the world that they were not thinking solely in terms of disarmament schemes. The position was at this time governed by Resolution 914 of December 1955 which was passed by the General Assembly and gave equal priority between agreement on 'confidence-building measures' on the one hand, and agreements 'on all such measures of adequately safeguarded disarmament' on the other.[90]

To show that if any progress was to be made it must be in the direction of agreement on limited measures, the major powers even thought of establishing scientific ad hoc committees for the study of technical aspects of disarmament. They argued that 'if the scientists were to say that control of the nuclear weapons is impossible at the present stage, it would help to prepare public opinion' in favour of these measures.[91]

The search for limited objectives was still far from being the dominant approach in the UN but at least the UN had already claimed that there is not just one way to disarmament and had put its membership for the first time for a long time into a real negotiating frame of mind. The balance between the two approaches shifted further in favour of concentration on limited measures in November 1957 when the General Assembly passed Resolution 1148. Moreover, while it was expected that the UN's institutions would turn their energies to the new approach in the negotiations, dramatic developments suddenly took place. By virtue of these developments the adoption by the UN of the arms control policy seemed now to be in jeopardy.

Unlike previous periods of negotiations, new talks at a technical level were held at conferences outside the UN in which a parity of representation between East and West blocs was well established. What seems to be interesting is that the means by which these talks were taken outside the UN made it plain that the main reason why the superpowers did so was to establish a new institutional pattern into which, at a later stage, political talks on disarmament could be introduced. That is to say that a changing role for the UN was foreshadowed.

The first moves towards shaping a new institutional pattern were made by the Soviet Union which sprung a surprise on the UN by its decision no longer to participate in the work of the negotiating bodies of the UN either the Disarmament Commission or its Sub-Committee. It had previously asked for an enlargement of the Disarmament Commission to consist of all members of the UN and equal participation in the Sub-Committee with the Western bloc but its request was not satisfied.[92] From the Soviet point of view, the composition of the Sub-Committee, consisting of the United States, United Kingdom, France, Canada and USSR, 'did not do justice to its position as a nuclear power'.[93] The West had found in the unchanged composition Disarmament Commission and its Sub-Committee a place of negotiations in which its numerical superiority was still maintained. By virtue of the Soviet boycott, the Disarmament Commission and its Sub-Committee fell into a state of suspension from which it never recovered, as there was not much sense in holding meetings so long as the Soviets were absent. When the Soviet Union left the Disarmament Commission, the Western powers were automatically exposed within the General Assembly to strong pressure from the Non-Aligned states to make concessions in order to bring the Soviets back. By this pressure the Non-Aligned states also exerted influence on the Western powers for concessions which would, inter alia, satisfy their own request for participation in the negotiations.[94] The Soviet Union had thus been able to capitalize upon the pressure of the Non-Aligned states, inspired by their own self-interest. The outcome of this pressure was that the Western states accepted an increase in the membership of the Disarmament Commission by adding fourteen states. However, the Soviet Union did not remove its objections and continued boycotting the negotiations. The Soviets were calculating that the United States could not tolerate negotiations in a body in which a majority of Eastern and Non-Aligned states could weigh against it, or could it co-operate in the Sub-Committee which, even under terms of parity between East and West, would be accountable for its work to the Disarmament Commission. The United States had already publicly said that a further enlargement of the Disarmament Commission would render this body 'useless for negotiations'.[95]

By making the Disarmament Commission unacceptable to the United States, the Soviet Union was trying to provoke the Americans into taking practical initiatives leading to the removal of the talks from the UN's regime. It is revealing that at the same time the Soviets were hardening their position, they were also making it known to the Americans that they would not oppose the placing of the negotiations into a bilateral setting. This was welcomed by the Anglo-American side which, 'because of the depressing state of the UN discussions'[96] in which the Non-Aligned states had already made their political influence felt, had not ruled out the possibility of discussion outside the UN disarmament forums.[97] The common perception of the UN forums was that 'it would give us a worse time with neutrals at the meetings of the Disarmament Commission of which Russians will want to make all use they can'.[98] Thus, in response to the Soviet challenge, the Anglo-American side went a stage further by offering the Soviets technical talks outside the UN with a view to produce, as they said, assessments of the technical problems of disarmament between East and West and the differences thereof. The Soviet Union 'considering that the principle of equal representation has been set up as the basis for carrying out the Conferences', immediately agreed. Thus, the Non-Aligned states were excluded as the talks were to be held between those who had 'scientific claims' for participation. In addition, two other issues which looked at measures of potential agreement were the subjects of two Conferences held in Geneva. The first was the 'Conference of Experts for the study of possible measures which might be helpful in preventing surprise attack' which was established to assess the effectiveness of various measures aimed at reducing the danger of surprise attack, and the technical inspection or observation requirements for assuring effective implementation of various methods. The second was the 'Conference of Experts on detection of nuclear tests' which was established to study the possibility of detecting violations of a possible agreement on the suspension of nuclear tests.

A specific significance should be attached to the 'technical services' which bodies like these two Conferences can provide and which can be related to a risk which runs systematically through disarmament negotiations. It is certain that even a technical understanding between the major powers on particular aspects of disarmament, apart from the fact that is necessary, creates a kind of commitment between them. However, the technical talks are of such nature that the outsider, who has no scientific knowledge, is apt to become lost due to unfamiliarity with the technical surroundings; while on the other hand the expert may go astray and lose sight of the political implications of these actions. However it could be pointed out that the diversion of the negotiations towards technical bodies can be to the advantage of the sides which may be determined to avoid agreement. In fact, when a body is entrusted with the task of discussing technical questions, it is possible for the participants by means of technical discussions to frustrate or obstruct any possibility of agreement and conveniently to cover up political lines running counter to the adoption of disarmament measures with the use of technical smoke screens. This can be done by finding grounds for refusing to reach an agreement under the pretext of the existence of differences of views on technical matters. This is the method of subverting the political substance of the matter in question by raising technical doubts.

The question which might now be put is whether the major powers by entangling questions of arms control in technical trammels were to block the path towards agreements. In other words, were they willing to make use of the capacity with which these technical Conferences provided them to oppose the search for limited objectives of arms control by the raising of artificial technical objections? A second question which might now be asked is whether the superpowers were intended to use these Conferences not only for exploring the technical bases for future agreements on arms control but also as vehicles for bringing to pass a change in the institutional framework of the future negotiations and taking them outside the UN. One could argue that the eagerness the superpowers now showed to avoid a breakdown in the first stages of the life of the Conferences because 'if either Conference breaks down we shall almost certainly have to face renewed general discussion in the 81-member Disarmament Commission' [99] was a sort of evidence of their intentions. Likewise, the preference of the United States and the Soviet Union to avoid the risk of renewed talks in the sessions of the General Assembly indicated a trend in their attitude towards minimizing its role in the negotiations.

Conclusions

During the fifties the Cold War seriously invaded the negotiating environment of disarmament at the UN which was led onto the false path of the quest for plans for full-scale disarmament which, given the immense hostility which ran through international relations, was not feasible. Its call for such full-scale disarmament was based on the erroneous assumption that agreement on disarmament would make the world community get rid of its political tensions. The superpowers in shaping up against each other began to request the UN to be in the service of such an unattainable goal. They sought to rally the UN behind their conflicting world policies on account of the arena it gave them for playing ideological strategies under the full glare of publicity under which the UN was working and scoring debating points off each other at the expense of any compromising attitude towards common action. Presenting a variety of disarmament proposals, each side used the debate on disarmament so as to make it appear that in reality its policy was all for disarmament and that if disarmament did not come about it was not its fault, and that the blame for the failure should fall upon the other side. In that sense, the UN was used not in the service of the world community but in the service of the two most powerful states eager to get the UN as a forum for reinforcement of their policies.

A change in the international environment in the late fifties led the membership of the UN to reappraise its attitude towards disarmament. It began to think of a new but more limited approach by the UN to disarmament, that of the quest for arms control measures. The period between 1949-1959 saw American monopoly cease with the transfer to the hands of two more major powers (Soviet Union and United Kingdom) as well as their proliferation in quantity and type. Disarmament negotiations now shifted from the atomic/hydrogen bomb emphasis to interrelation of all weapons systems with extension of nuclear power to tactical battlefield weapons. The Atomic Energy Commission was merged with the Commission for Conventional Armaments by the UN on January 1952, to form the Disarmament Commission, consisting again of all members of the Security Council plus Canada with augmented authority over this whole problem. However, the withdrawal of the Soviets from the UN negotiating bodies in 1957 raised the question whether the UN membership would attribute sufficient authority to the UN in the coming years for it to pursue a policy of arms control.

Notes

1. UNGA Resolution 377 (V), 3 November 1950.
2. Paper prepared by the UN Planning Staff, Bureau of UN Affairs, cited in United States, Department of State (1979), *Foreign Relations of the United States 1952-4*, vol. iii, United States Government Printing Office:Washington, p. 95.
3. Rupert Emerson and Inis Claude (1950), 'The Soviet Union and the UN: An Essay in Interpretation', *International Organization,* Spring, p. 4; see also Soviet Monitor, issued by Tass Agency, 3 March 1951.
4. Memorandum of FO: Proposed Anglo-American Talks on the Future of the UN, para. 1, cited in FO 371/95612/UP 133/2; see also FO Document: American Opinion and Attitude Towards the UN, cited in FO 371/95612/UP 133/2.
5. A. LeRoy Bennet (1977), *International Organizations,* Prentice Hall: New Jersey, p. 203.
6. Draft Minute to Prime Minister cited in FO 371/95673/UP 237/92.
7. Memorandum Prepared in the Department of State for the White House,

in United States, Department of State, op.cit., p. 86.

8. J.P.G. Freeman (1986), *Britain's Nuclear Arms Control Policy in the Context of Anglo-American Relations 1957-1968*, Macmillan: London, 1986, p. 17.

9. Memorandum of FO: Disarmament, cited in FO 371/95671/UP 237/45; see also Memorandum of FO: Manners of Advancing Disarmament Proposals, Annex II, cited in FO 371/95671.

10. Michael Howard (1989), 'The UN and International Security', in Adam Roberts and Benedict Kingsbury (eds), *United Nations, Divided World: The UN's Roles in International Relations*, Clarendon Press: Oxford, p. 41.

11. Benhard Bechhoefer (1961), *Postwar Negotiations for Arms Control*, Brookings Institution: Washington, pp. 145-147.

12. Letter from UK Delegation to the UNGA, Paris, to FO (Mr. Mason), 12 January 1952, cited in FO 371/101343/UP 237/27.

13. Telegram No 4553, from FO to Washington, 5 September 1951, cited in FO 371/95671/UP 237/45; see also Minutes of FO: Disarmament, Draft Note for the Secretary of State cited in FO 371/95675/UP 237/132.

14. United States, Department of State, op.cit., p. 70.

15. Ibid., p. 109.

16. William Frye (1959), 'K's Disarmament Plan: Pie in-Sky ?' *Foreign Policy Bulletin,* vol. 39, no 3, October, p. 17.

17. United States, Department of State, op.cit., p. 107.

18. Ibid., p. 86.

19. Joseph Nogee (1960), 'The Diplomacy of Disarmament', *International Conciliation*, no 526, January, p. 280.

20. United Nations (1970), *The UN and Disarmament 1945-70*, United Nations: New York, p. 41; see also Bechhoefer, op.cit., p. 166; see also UN Document A/6/PV. 358,11 January 1952, pp. 294-313.

21. Disarmament Commission, Official Records, Third Meeting, 24 April 1952, p. 6.

22. UN Document A/C.1/8/PV. 661, 10 November 1955, p. 192, Czechoslovakia.

23. UN Document A /C.1/11/PV.823, 11 January 1957, p. 44.

24. Abraham Yeselson and Anthony Gaglione (1974), *A Dangerous Place, The UN as a Weapon in World Politics*, Grossman: New York, p. 3.

25. Ibid., p. 173.

26. Disarmament: Draft Memorandum for the Defence Committee, p. 7, cited in FO 371/95673/UP 237/91.

27. Letter from UK Delegation to UNGA, Paris, to FO (Mr. Mason), 12 January 1952, para. 4, cited in FO 371/101343/UP 233/27.

28. Letter from British Embassy, Washington to FO, 30 July 1951, para. 5, cited in FO 371/95667/UP 232/26; see also Minutes of FO: Brief For Defence Committee, cited in FO 371/95670/UP 237/32.

29. Nogee, op.cit., p. 282.

30. Ibid.

31. Telegram No 265, from New York (UK Delegation to UN) to FO, 7 May 1952, cited in FO 371/101347/UP 233/157.

32. UN Document A/5/PV. 295, 24 October 1950, p. 247; see also John Morray (1962), *From Yalta to Disarmament*, Merlin Press: London, pp. 170-171.

33. (1951) *United States Department of State Bulletin* , vol. xxv, no 647, 19 November, p. 802.

34. United States, Department of State (1979), *Foreign Relations of the United States, 1951*, vol. i, United States Government Printing Office:Washington, p. 499.

35. Memorandum of FO: Manner of Advancing Disarmament Proposals, Annex II, p. 5, para. 7, cited in FO 371/95671.

36. Memorandum of FO: Disarmament Commission, para. 2, cited in FO 371/101344/UP 233/51.

37. Telegram No 3191, from Washington to FO, 3 October 1953, cited in FO 371/95671/UP 237/54.

38. Telegram No 4553, from FO to Washington, 5 September 1951, cited in FO 371/95671/UP 237/45; see also Memorandum by Mr. Meyers of the Office of the UN Political and Security Affairs, cited in United States, Department of State (1979), *Foreign Relations of the United States, 1951*, vol. i, op.cit., p. 524.

39. Memorandum of FO: Disarmament Commission, para. 7 (a), cited in FO 371/101344/UP 233/51.

40. Draft Minute to Prime Minister: Disarmament, para. 5, cited in FO 371/95673/UP 237/92.

41. Ibid., para. 6.

42. Telegram No 4553, from FO to Washington, 5 September 1951, cited in FO 371/95671/UP 237/45.

43. Letter from UK Delegation to the UNGA, Paris to FO, 31 January 1952, p. 1, cited in FO 371/101343/UP 233/39.

44. UN Document A/7/PV. 363, 19 January 1952.

45. New York Herald Tribune cited in FO 371/101349/UP 233.

46. Draft Minute to Prime Minister: Disarmament, para. 7, cited in FO 371/95673/UP 237/92.

47. Letter from UK Delegation to UNGA, Paris to FO (Mr. Mason), 18

January 1952, cited in FO 371/101343/UP 233/27.

48. Anthony Nutting (1959), *Disarmament*, Oxford University Press: London, pp. 8-9.

49. Letter from UK Delegation in the UN to the FO, cited in FO 371/95670/UP 237/21.

50. Memorandum of FO: Notes for the Secretary of State's speech in the House of Commons Debate, cited in FO 371/95667/UP 232/49.

51. UNGA Resolution 715 (VIII) was adopted with 54 votes to none, with 5 abstentions.

52. Memorandum of FO: National Peace Council, cited in FO 371/112377/UP 232/28.

53. Incoming Message from the Acting Secretary of State for External Affairs, Ottawa, to the High Commissioner for Canada, London, 22 April 1954, para. 6, cited in FO 371/112383/UP 232/202.

54. See Minutes of FO: FO 371/112381/UP 232/119; see also Telegram No 560, from Washington to FO, 1 April 1954, cited in FO 371/112379/UP 232/88.

55. Letter from UK Delegation to the UN, New York (Sir Dixon) to FO (Sir Lloyd), 2 April 1954, cited in FO 371/112380/UP 232/101.

56. UN Document DC/SC.1/PV. 17, 14 June 1954.

57. Letter from UK Delegation to the UN, New York, to FO (Mr. Mason), 6 April 1954, cited in FO 371/112380/UP 232/112.

58. FO Minute from M.Williams, para. 4, cited in FO 371/112383/UP 232/213.

59. Telegram No 1713, From FO to Washington, 20 April 1954, cited in FO 371/112382/UP 232/158.

60. UN Document A/9/PV. 424, 30 September 1954.

61. In a memorandum, the FO admitted that 'we never thought that they (the proposals) would prove attractive to the Russians, cited in FO 371/112391/UP 232/446b.

62. Telegram No 1422, from FO to New York (UK Delegation to the UN), 15 October 1954, para. 2, cited in FO 371/112393/UP 232/500.

63. United Nations, op.cit., pp. 54-55.

64. Letter from FO to British Ambassador in Moscow (Sir Hayter), 23 October, 1954, cited in FO 371/112392/UP 232/490; see also FO Minute (Mr. Cope): Analysis of the Soviet Proposals on Disarmament, para. 1, cited in FO 371/112392/UP 232/486. See also Cabinet, Official Committee on Disarmament, cited in FO 371/117370/UN 1152/70; see also Evan Luard (1982), *A History of the United Nations*, vol.i, St. Martin Press: London, p. 331.

65. Letter from New York (UK Delegation to the UN) to FO, 15 September 1954, cited in FO 371/112391/UP 232/447.

66. Tactical Plan for Disarmament Talks, para. 6(b), cited in FO 371/117370/1192/74.

67. Letter from FO to the UK Delegation to UN (Sir Dixon), 10 February 1950, cited in FO 371/117371/UP 1192/97. The fact that it was an exercise to test the Soviet sincerity makes plain that the assumption of Cavers that 'the West made some concessions in the interest of agreement' was wrong; see David Cavers (1956), 'Arms Control in the UN: A Decade of Disagreement', *Bulletin of Atomic Scientists*, vol xii, no 4, April, p. 109.

68. Memorandum of FO: Disarmament, para. 4(c), cited in FO 371/117368/UN 1192/25.

69. UN Document DC/SC.1/PV. 35, 29 March 1955.

70. UN Document DC/SC.1/PV. 47, 10 May 1955.

71. Philip-Noel Baker (1958), *The Arms Race*, John Calder: London, pp. 12-22.

72. Telegram No 250, from Vienna to FO, 14 May 1955, cited in FO 371/117381/UN 1192/341.

73. Letter from UK Delegation to the UN (New York) to FO (Mr. Pink), 28 May 1955, cited in FO 371/117383/UN 1192/386.

74. Ibid.

75. Memorandum of FO: Disarmament, cited in FO 371/117380/UN 1192/303 (a).

76. Cited in Bechhoefer, op.cit., p. 259.

77. As the British diplomats telegraphed from Washington 'his announcement came as a complete surprise to officials in the State Department dealing with disarmament', see Telegram No 623, from Washington to FO, 19 May 1955, cited in FO 371/117377/UP 1192/246.

78. Telegram No 623, from Washington to FO, 19 March 1955, cited in FO 371/117377/UN 1192/240.

79. See also Telegram No 403, from New York (UK Delegation to the UN) to FO, 25 May 1955, cited in FO 371/117383/UN 1192/374.

80. Telegram from Vienna to FO, No 250, 14 May 1955, cited in FO 371/117381/UN 1192/341.

81. UN Document DC/SC.1/PV. 55, 6 September 1955.

82. Nutting, op.cit., p.19.

83. Letter from New York (UK Delegation to UN) to FO, 2 September 1955, para. 8, cited in FO 371/117393/UN 1192/611; see also William Frye (1961), Characteristics of Recent Arms Control Proposals and Agreements', in Donald Brennan (ed.) *Arms Control, Disarmament and*

National Security, George Braziller: New York, p. 76.

84. See Pravda, 18 August 1955.
85. UN Document A/C.1/10/PV. 806, 7 December 1955, p. 266.
86. UN Document A/C.1/10/PV. 807, 8 December 1955, p. 268.
87. Telegram No 1841, from Washington to FO, 13 September 1957, cited in FO 371/129844/UN 1192/1041.
88. This statement was made during his talks with the Western States in the Summit Conference at Geneva on 21 July 1955; see also UN Document A/C.1/10/PV. 803, 5 December 1955, p. 238.
89. UN Document A/C.1/10/PV. 806, 7 December 1955, p. 263.
90. UNGA Resolution 914 (X) was adopted on 16 December 1955 by 56 votes to 7.
91. Letter from Nutting to the FO, 13 September 1955, cited in FO 371/117595/UN 1192/659.
92. UN Document DC/PV. 51, 23 April 1954.
93. Nogee, op.cit., p. 109.
94. Letter from New York (UK Delegation to UN) to FO, 19 November 1956, cited in FO 371/ 123708/UN 1192/691.
95. Conversation with two Members of the French Delegation, 8 November 1957, cited in FO 371/129854/UN 1192/1271.
96. Telegram No 510, from Commonwealth Relations Office to UK High Commissioner in Canada, 30 April 1955, para. 2(a), cited in FO 371/117380/UN 1192/306.
97. Letter from FO to New York (UK Delegation to the UN), 12 July 1956, cited in FO 371/123703/UN 1192/551.
98. Telegram No 690, from Geneva to FO, 27 November 1958, cited in FO 371/132680/IAD 111/134.
99. Telegram No 920, from FO to Geneva (UK Delegation), 19 November 1958, cited in FO 371/132679/IAD 111/90.

3 The attainment of a broad consensus (1960-1968)

The beginning of the sixties was the starting point for new directions in the UN. It coincided with the genesis of a new UN institutional framework for the conduct of the business of disarmament. The outcome was significant differentiations of approach to the part the UN should play in the negotiating process and to the appreciation of the principle of universal state participation in the process of arms control and disarmament decisions.

A long time had passed since the Soviet Union walked out of the UN disarmament bodies wherein its constant appeal for a parity of representation between the two blocs, East and West, had not been satisfied. Meanwhile there was mounting pressure for the resumption of negotiations.

The distinctive feature of this period is that all efforts which were undertaken for the resumption of negotiations took place in the light of two new development in the UN. Firstly, the establishment of the Ten Nation Disarmament Committee (TNDC), outside the UN's legal jurisdiction and secondly, the appearance of a third major political force in the UN: a group of states who refused to enter the East-West fray. Not limited to the third world, they were restless with antagonistic post-war ideologies and big power struggles for political hegemony.

It was at a Conference of the Foreign Ministers of France, United Kingdom, United States and the USSR which was convened in Geneva to discuss questions relating to Germany, including a peace treaty and the question of Berlin, that an agreement was reached in August 1959 for a new forum for disarmament negotiations. It was formed under the same institutional pattern that the technical conferences in the preceding year had been fashioned, that is outside the UN but with links to it. The superpowers used the technical Conferences, which had been established in the two previous years, as a vehicle for remodelling the political talks on that of the these Conferences and when they succeeded in doing so they jumped at the chance and returned to negotiations in a new forum. The agreement of 1959 called for a parity of representation between the East and West blocs, as five states from each bloc were to participate in the negotiations. This parity of representation, as an institutionalized expression of the bipolar military strength opened the way for new developments the final stage of which is that today the most significant arms limitations negotiations have taken place outside the UN.

The composition of the new forum was Eurocentric apart from United States's and Canada's participation. Its members were Soviet Union, Czechoslovakia, Poland, Romania, Bulgaria on the one side, and United States, United Kingdom, Canada, France, Italy on the other. Thus, the arrangement for the establishment of the TNDC did not go further than to institutionalize in a unique body the confrontation already existing between the two sides.

The TNDC met for a short period just from 15 March to 27 June 1960. It attempted to negotiate, quite unrealistically, matters of general disarmament at a time when relations between the East and West were still at a low ebb. Its direct search for disarmament did not go further than empty verbal exchanges of views between its members.[1] The TNDC adjourned for the scheduled summit meeting between France, the United Kingdom, the United States and the Soviet Union. The U-2 spy plane incident which occurred on May led to the cancellation of the summit even as the participants were arriving in Paris on May 17. The TNDC did however reconvene on June 7, only to have the Soviet bloc states walk out in June. In public at least, this was due to the Western powers 'having.... taken a position in this Committee which is calculated to achieve anything but success in the matter of disarmament'.[2] However, it is more likely that the withdrawal was partly due to the strained relations between the two superpowers during that period. The body because of its composition was very vulnerable to, or dependent upon, the existing political climate. However, even this cannot fully explain the abrupt disavowal of the forum.

The basic reason for its failure went deeper. It is related to a more general practical appreciation, according to which the most notable result of the way the TNDC was composed was that it could not negotiate nuclear arms control measures as an alternative to nuclear disarmament. What the TNDC really did was to bring the superpowers face to face in a period of strained relations where it was impossible to unlock the door of disarmament unless the international climate could be improved. Thus, a more modest approach to disarmament was required, the main feature of which would be for arms control measures to function as a confidence-building approach. However, the TNDC could not provide outlets for its participants so that it could put them comfortably in the way of questing for arms control measures. The absence of pure multilateralism and the restricted composition of the TNDC could not offer a commodious atmosphere or a wide range of arms control measures from which a discretionary choice for negotiations could be made. By definition, the problem here becomes multilateral and a wider multilateral forum would be the only appropriate basis for such negotiations. In practice, the TNDC found it impossible to consider arms control measures and especially the prevention of the wider dissemination of nuclear weapons despite the fact that it was requested by the General Assembly to do so. As a consequence, had the Committee been given the option to negotiate nuclear arms control over general disarmament, it might have been unable to proceed successfully. It could be argued that even then, because of its composition, it would in all likelihood have been useless.

Furthermore, although the TNDC's original task was to negotiate General and Complete Disarmament (GCD), it seems to be questionable whether it had the organizational ability to work so. 'General' means that every state in the world is committed to disarm and 'complete disarmament' means that all levels of weapons and forces are scaled down to a minimum defined at that point at which states retain just sufficient military capability to maintain order and to assist the UN internationally. What turns out to be a realistic approach is the appreciation that the GCD, if it was ever to be feasible and desirable, requires because of its complexity, the negotiation of the different stages of implementation of the treaties to take place in a unique body. This body should have been capable of reflecting in terms of composition the international community as it inevitably affects the interests of all the states. So far as the TNDC was concerned, due to its restricted membership it lacked the organizational unity and the homogeneous structure which could enable it to deal with GCD. Its composition did not fit it well to achieve this goal. As it was put, the proposals for comprehensive disarmament which were submitted during the short life of the TNDC led states 'to propose the establishment of a negotiating body, related to the UN, to replace the unsuccessful Ten-Power Committee'.[3]

The TNDC never got substantive approbation and endorsement from the UN despite the granting by the 'big four' of a package of assurances that 'the setting up of the Disarmament Committee in no way diminishes or encroaches upon the UN's responsibility' in this field; and that 'ultimate responsibility for general disarmament rests with the UN'.[4] The UN, in the person of the Secretary-General Hammarskjold, reacted promptly to the situation which emerged but in vain the Secretary-General took specific actions to prevent the disarmament negotiations from being removed from the UN.[5] The negative reaction of the UN should be attributed to the damaging impact the institutionalization of negotiations in a body outside the UN representing bilateral interests and understandings would have on the UN; and to the lack of representativeness of the world of the UN in the new body. In reality, the TNDC reflected just the East and West duopoly ignoring the rest of the world and especially the third major political force of the UN: the Non-Aligned world.

The emergence of a new political force in the UN

By the end of 1950s, the Afro-Asian group of states foremost in the historical process of the formation of the Non-Aligned movement, had increased rapidly and had become the largest regional group in the organization. In fact, more than fifteen new states emerging from their colonial status became independent and were admitted as members of the UN in this period. The inflow of these new states in the UN made the United States no longer capable of delivering automatic majorities. It could, however, register majority's decisions if it would ensure the votes of a number of Non-Aligned states. Under Article 18 paragraph 2 of the Charter of the UN, resolutions concerning important (non-procedural) questions require an increased majority of two thirds of the members present and voting. This inevitably meant that the Non-Aligned group could now prevent any resolution from obtaining the two-thirds majority in the General Assembly. This could happen only if its members were able to display a high degree of unity. However, this group of states was far from being cohesive and organized. This prevented them from undertaking a regulating role in international affairs in general and in the UN in particular through collective actions. In order to act in such a manner they began to organize conferences at the highest political level. The purpose of these conferences was to generate among the participants certain common interests and internal loyalties which could enable them to establish a common front in the face of the crucial problems arising on the international scene; to represent an alliance of the like-minded. Sponsoring draft resolutions and in approaching the UN generally, they based their position primarily on the political and economic guidelines of their conferences. The group had already reached a significant number of members, constituting nearly half the entire UN membership and its meetings could no longer be the occasional and sometimes apathetic assemblages that they had been in earlier years.

The Eighteen Nation Disarmament Committee (ENDC)

The TNDC, despite its short duration, had created an important development which the UN set about considering how not to discard completely. The establishment of the TNDC had created the precedent of a negotiating body on the management of which the superpowers kept a balanced grip. The UN seemed now to support the establishment on a more permanent basis of a body like the TNDC, provided that it could be expanded. Expansion was deemed to be essential so that representation of the three political groups of which the UN was now composed was ensured.

The reconsideration by the UN of its attitude *vis-à-vis* the continuation of the negotiations in an institution outside the UN was due to its assessment that the fundamental assumptions on which the superpowers relied to establish the TNDC undoubtedly remained valid. These assumptions may be deemed as having been determined by the channels through which subsequent negotiations on disarmament in both multilateral and bilateral schemes were directed.

The superpowers had been convinced that it would not have been politically possible in the future to establish within the UN a negotiating body where East and West could sit on an equal footing. The reason was that the newly independent states emerging from their colonial status were and would remain more sensitive to the notion of one nation-one vote, as part of the principle of equality among the states. It is interesting to note that the Soviet Union put its claim for parity of representation with the West within the organs of the UN at the very time that the *impasse* upon the admission of new members in the world organization was broken. Ironically, the superpowers chose this time, when the admission's flow of the new states became the annual business of the UN thus shifting political conditions within it in terms of voting power, to take the negotiations of disarmament outside the UN. Both sides it seems were prompted by similar considerations: to establish a new institutional scheme for disarmament negotiations in which they could keep degrees of a control over the pace and pattern of negotiations.

Taking these assumptions into account the UN at this time addressed itself to the immediate task of finding a way forward for the resumption of the disarmament negotiations. It appealed to the two superpowers urging them 'to reach agreement on the composition of a negotiating body which both they and the rest of the world can regard as satisfactory'.[6] In regard to the superpowers it became evident that the UN resorted to them for a balanced form of positive leadership. In consequence, the General Assembly of the United Nations, during the second phase of its fifteenth session, in March 1961, decided to postpone consideration of the disarmament question pending United States-Soviet Union consultations.[7] This reflected the extent to which the global organization itself and its member-states looked to the superpowers to play the decisive role in the resumption of the negotiations as well as to the matter of the determination of the composition of the negotiating body. For the UN it was more essential to contribute to the resumption of the negotiations. The central idea of the UN's tendency to approve a new framework for negotiations was that it would, at least, bring an element of flexibility into the situation which could be taken advantage of at later stage.

To satisfy the request of the UN for bringing the composition of the planned negotiating body into harmony with the changing membership of the world organization, the superpowers invited the Non-Aligned group, which the loose alliance of states uncommitted to the Cold War call themselves, to join in the work of the new body. The primary concern of this group of states was to ensure their participation in all the international organs, including those which were mandated to carry out disarmament negotiations, irrespective of the ties these organs maintained with the UN.[8] Consequently, they avoided momentarily being bogged down in the controversial issue of what precise role the UN had to play in the disarmament process.

Despite the expressed desire for inclusion in the new negotiating scheme, the Non-Aligned states were not well disposed to the Soviet proposal for equal tripartite presentation in the new body. As Jacobson and Stein wrote, 'as early as September 1960 the Soviet Union had suggested that the TNDC should be enlarged by adding five Non-Aligned states'.[9] The Soviet Union favoured an equal tripartite representation to the new negotiating body in order to implement more widely the troika political formula. To give broader legitimation to this formula, the Soviet Union had suggested a new forum of fifteen members.[10] The Western states raised objections insisting on proposing alternatives the main feature of which was the rejection of the idea of equal tripartite representation.

The Soviet troika proposal came at a time when the diplomatic attack on Secretary General Hammarskjold had been stepped up. Hammarskjold used to claim more than merely administrative powers. Moscow was infuriated by the way he performed his duties. He was regarded as partial, favouring Western policies in the UN. The central idea on which the troika concept was focused was the change of the structure of the UN Secretariat so that a new collective executive would take the place of the office of the Secretary General. This would consist of three administrators, each one representative of one of the three groups of states - the Eastern, the Western and the Non-Aligned - on a basis of equality. Each of them, and consequently each of the groups of states, would possess a right to exercise a veto over any action of the collective executive. The Non-Aligned states took the troika proposal for the tripartite control of the UN as an attempt to weaken the global organization to which they were unhesitatingly loyal. As one Non-Aligned state put it 'anyone who acts deliberately and with calculation to the injury of the UN, to weaken it or endanger its existence as an effective and energetic international institution, is the enemy of all of us'.[11] From a practical point of view, acceptance of the troika concept would mean that the UN Secretariat would have become unworkable as an organ of the UN just as the Security Council had been, by virtue of the right of the three administrators to use the veto power. Although the troika pattern seemed to offer the Non-Aligned states more participation in the Secretariat and therefore in the decision-making of the UN, in reality, it would bring about the neutralization of them as a potential political force in the UN. It would mean the subjection of their future role to a veto. The Non-Aligned states were in a state of anticipation that their role in the various institutions and the decision-making of the UN would be gradually increased in consequence of their constant growing numerical force. They had already begun to play a key-role in changing the UN step by step, including in the long term the Secretary-Generalship. This was the consequence of the political reality of a new geographical distribution of its members which resulted from the granting of independence to new states. As one commentator, Crabb, put it 'the more active a part a nation is playing in UN affairs, the more unpalatable the troika apparently becomes'.[12]

Thus, the Non-Aligned states saw the Soviet proposal for tripartite representation in the ENDC as a means of giving wider acceptance of the troika formula and, therefore, rejected it. This forced the Soviet Union to withdraw its proposal. This, in turn, enabled the superpowers to arrive at a compromise. Agreement between the superpowers on the membership of a new negotiating body was finally reached. The members put forward did not however coincide with the notion of equal tripartite partition sought by the Soviet Union. In the words of one observer 'the US accepted this membership insisting on the unbalanced numbers of neutrals to avoid the appearance of adopting the Soviet troika proposal'.[13] Even the inclusion of eight new states, namely Brazil, Burma, Ethiopia, India, Mexico, Nigeria, Sweden and the United Arab Republic, in the composition of the body came as the result of hard bargaining between the superpowers. During this bargaining, the United States constantly refused to accept the inclusion of radical states like Indonesia and Ghana, which it regarded as having an anti-western attitude.

The composition of the new body of eighteen states met the technical and political realities of the day. It reflected, as it had to do, a small representation of the world's technological and political forces for the time being. It succeeded, firstly, in representing on a more realistic basis than the UN itself the world power structure underlying so much of international relations at that time and, secondly, in integrating new comers, namely the Non-Aligned states, into these relationships. ENDC's limited membership including the most technologically advanced states was considered to take into account the technological factor as determinant in the nuclear race and, therefore, the basic criterion for determining its synthesis, and for the limitation of any trends towards further enlargement. Nonetheless, the new political realities in the UN were considered of vital importance and, although the body was not formally established as part of the UN structure, it constituted a microcosm of the UN even in terms of geographical distribution.

The establishment of the ENDC came about with the active encouragement of the General Assembly of the UN which with Resolution 1722 (XVI) of 20 December 1961 unanimously endorsed its birth. The wrangling over the question of what role the UN should play seemed to have ceased. It is noteworthy that the UN at this time did not react negatively, as it did in the case of the TNDC, to the establishment of the ENDC outside its legal framework. On the contrary, the General Assembly accepted the new negotiating body set up by the agreement of the superpowers commenting that it was 'an appropriate body'. There were fundamental reasons which accounted for the General Assembly to give its blessing to the establishment of the ENDC: firstly, the three political groups of which the UN consisted - the Eastern, the Western and the Non-Aligned - were admittedly in favour of such an institution format. Secondly, the representative insertion of the three main political groups of the UN was coupled with the provision for a representative of the Secretary-General to attend all the meetings of the negotiating body. This presentation ensured the political presence of the UN at this forum and brought about a close tie between it and the UN. This was inevitably a significant departure from the structures of the TNDC through which the superpowers made an attempt to isolate entirely the negotiations from the environment of the UN. In the context of the tenuous *liaison* which was established between the UN and the ENDC, the former welcomed the idea of providing the latter with financial services. Although the ENDC remained outside the UN, it operated in Geneva and utilized the facilities of the UN as well as the services of the Secretariat.

The quid pro quo for the acceptance by the UN of such a format for negotiations was the expectation that the ENDC would mirror the attitude shared by the UN membership, expressed in the form of the resolutions of the General Assembly.

The decentralization of the negotiating process

Decentralization of the negotiating process of disarmament was by the particular delegation of the conduct of negotiations by the General Assembly, the main and central authority of the UN, to an autonomous body, namely the ENDC.

The autonomous status of the ENDC offered the negotiating process protection from the political influences produced by the UN's grappling with the multi-faceted problems of day to day international relations and attempts to reform the system. The marked decrease in the so called inter-issue bargaining (i.e., the bargaining of aspects of disarmament concurrent to aspects of other processes which are 'on move' in the UN) helped the ENDC enjoy a comparative advantage to previous negotiating bodies which had worked from within the internal structures of the UN under the determinant role of the General Assembly. The commitment to such an autonomous body to stay (to the extent possible) out of politics not relating to the disarmament process had two outcomes. It was conducive to an effective focus on the issues, but its side-effect was to overemphasize the peculiarities of its services.

The resulting decentralization meant in practical terms substantial redefinitions of the role of the UN in general and of the General Assembly in particular. Eventually decentralization had the effect of undermining the direct political influence of the UN, and especially the General Assembly, whose supervisory role in the matter of disarmament was considerably diminished and substantially limited to that of merely making recommendations to the ENDC. In contrast, decentralization increased the role of the superpowers. The purpose of decentralization was the the claim to re-organize the UN's disarmament machinery according to the role states could play, especially the major powers, *vis-à-vis* the process of disarmament negotiations. It happened when the General Assembly left the superpowers to build up the new negotiating body according to their perceptions.

The co-chair institution and the superpowers' leadership

It was the primary responsibilities of the superpowers, political, military, strategic, and technological, as recognized by the world community of the UN, which conferred on them the leadership position in the ENDC. Indubitably, these responsibilities were the *raison d' être* for the setting up of the entirely new UN institutional framework for negotiations.

First of all, the co-chair institution derived, as did the ENDC itself, from the special role incumbent upon the superpowers in the UN disarmament business and the world at large. From a military point of view, as a commentator, namely Gotlieb, pointed out, 'the co-chairmen were chosen precisely because they were the two main powers concerned and in a sense those with the most at stake'.[14] However, the holding of the co-chair by the two not only reflected the political but also the strategic reality of the military environment which negotiations on nuclear disarmament had to confront. This meant that through such an institution the strategic dialogue especially of those 'with the most at stake' could be appropriately preserved, provided there was a willingness on the part of the superpowers to resort to it. Moves on nuclear disarmament and arms control were primarily based on decisions involving attempts at equalizing, as far as possible, the risks involved in taking them. In this respect, the institution of co-chair maintained a consistent relevance to the McLoy-Zorin Joint Agreement of agreed principles which was unreservedly endorsed by the General Assembly and which provided the basis for the oncoming negotiations.[15] Actually, these principles took into account the essential matter of strategic perception on the road to disarmament or arms control. They explicitly provided that measures of disarmament should be balanced so that at no stage of their implementation could any state or group of states gain military advantage, thus ensuring equal security for all. Furthermore it is beyond any doubt that the technical requirements of nuclear disarmament or arms control render the negotiating process quite different from any other. The negotiating process requires by definition mutual technological understanding; as well as means of searching for common ground and co-ordinating consultations which are largely based on advanced technological knowledge. It is these technical requirements which gave advantage to the institutionalization of the co-chair office.

The co-chair institution ensured a form of co-operative cohabitation of the superpowers at the head of the ENDC. Since it created the need for the United States and the Soviet Union to actively co-operate on the business agenda and decision-making of the ENDC, it significantly contributed to the reduction of the rivalry between them by providing balanced relationships and decision responsibilities. Through the co-chair the superpowers gained political control of the ENDC. Their joint decisions and functions covered its daily operations, including setting the agenda as well as the negotiation, preparation and presentation of draft agreements for decision. They were able to direct the ENDC mostly at their will. Furthermore, the practice to which the ENDC was accustomed whereby all its decisions had to be taken unanimously - the consensus principle - strengthened even more the power of the co-chairs and ensured for them overall control of the negotiating body.

One of their important duties was the preparation of reports to the General Assembly. These reports which were presented to the full Committee for formal approval should not be considered as a mere formality. It was largely on the basis of these reports that the General Assembly was kept informed about the progress being made in the ENDC. Discussions in the General Assembly and the particular content of its recommendations in the form of resolutions, as well as the actions of the Secretariat, were based largely on these reports. One eminent scholar commenting ironically on the powers that had been vested in the superpowers stated that 'even a visitor observing the formal proceedings of the negotiating body must request permission from the US and the USSR delegation, not through the UN Secretariat'.[16]

It is remarkable that the composition of ENDC's predecessor, the TNDC, consisting of five states from the East and West camps, had given the superpowers the opportunity to reach an agreement in which the chair of the TNDC rotated more democratically than in the ENDC among the ten delegation.[17] At the moment of the inception of ENDC, the addition of eight new states coming neither from the West nor the East coincided with the invention of the co-chair institution. The co-chair institution was a means of offsetting the admission of the eight Non-Aligned states into the negotiating body.

The pursuit of the arms control measures as the predominant policy

The problem for the UN in general and the ENDC in particular at this period was whether it would be possible for an indirect mechanism of the step by step construction of peace through nuclear arms control measures to take the place of the direct, overambitious search for all-encompassing plans for general disarmament. The arms control policy had been visualized, as was seen in the previous chapter, as a possible course in the past negotiations but the sudden cessation of the talks had interrupted the process of rendering it the predominant policy. However, it emerged as such in the early years of the sixties.

There appeared to be a decided willingness to start out from a new premise. This was that it was not possible to do away with the fundamental differences states had in relation to the process of disarmament, unless they were able to get rid of the uncompromising context of international relations which had been hanging over them, the UN and the negotiations hitherto. Even modest progress in the field of disarmament would be conducive to altering the existing climate. It was clearly admitted that there was a gap to be bridged on the political side prior to the working out of measures of disarmament. This general appreciation that surrounded the UN constituted a notable development in political thinking with regard to the negotiating process of disarmament.

Therefore, to make a modest start with the search for progress towards disarmament through its arms control phase would have a multiple effect. First and foremost, it would significantly contribute to a much improved atmosphere of political co-operation with international relations being normalized, stabilized and freed from the obstructions the Cold War created. Such an improvement would act as an imperative need for lessening the possibility of war in actual and negotiating basis and would inspire confidence among states. The realization of these sound expectations which would remove significant obstacles standing in the way to disarmament would give to nuclear disarmament a much greater chance to flourish than ever before. Furthermore, arms control measures were connected organically with the achievement of the ultimate goal of disarmament. In other words, these measures could render easier the attainment of disarmament agreements by removing also some of the existing threats to international peace and security.

The importance, urgency and immediate necessity of putting into motion this process had been the *leitmotif* of the work in the UN and the ENDC. The three major political groups, which made up the entirety of the UN and were represented in the ENDC, proceeded eagerly to approve the new process. It followed thereafter, that they became increasingly tied together by the common purposes such an approach could serve. The new process began to take concrete shape very early, indeed from the first working sessions of the ENDC. The Soviet Union, on behalf of the Eastern group, brought the matter to the forefront of consideration:

> while the Soviet Government regards the preparation of an agreement on GCD as the Committee's main task it would nevertheless consider it useful if a number of measures which would facilitate the relaxation of international tension, the strengthening of confidence among states were taken forthwith, without awaiting the completion of the negotiations on GCD.[18]

The Western group responded favourably to the challenges of the new approach. Following an Anglo-American initiative it approved the proposition for devoting ENDC's sessions to the search for limited measures in parallel with the direct pursuit of agreement on GCD. The United States agreed that certain measures can, by their very nature, be taken up and dealt with independently of the effort to reach agreement on GCD. The Secretary of State of the United States, Rusk, made clear this position by saying that 'wherever possible, we should seek specific commitments that could be put into effect without delay'.[19] Equally, the United Kingdom made an appeal to the ENDC 'to concentrate upon agreeing now on any possible confidence-giving measures without relaxing efforts for the conclusion of a treaty on GCD'.[20]

Furthermore, the ardent support, from the outset of the negotiations, of the Non-Aligned states for the ENDC to come to grips with the planned new directions derived basically from their determination to fulfil the spirit and recommendations of their summit conferences. As Mates, who has written extensively on Non-Aligned policies, describes, in Belgrade and Cairo the need was stressed for actions 'which do not appertain to the actual matter of disarmament but rather serve to help create the necessary climate for taking up measures which are directly related to disarmament'.[21] The group had also been predetermined to act as a sort of bridge between the two camps, the East and West, while at the same time maintaining an attitude of impartiality. As Crabb observed, the Non-Aligned states conceived their role as a 'golden bridge' between the superpowers on disarmament issues.[22] The 'golden bridge' platform was partly due to Indian Premier Nehru's political philosophy which to a degree guided the actions and determined the attitude of the Non-Aligned states. Nehru's view was that the Non-Aligned states should remain merely a political force which must not overestimate its own importance.[23] However, their moderate attitude should be seen much more in the context of the diplomatic strategy they pursued in the international arena. They deemed their role as mediators to be a necessity, contributing significantly to a change in international relations whereby the East-West conflict eased and the polarization is slackened. It is particularly in this state of world relations that the Non-Aligned states perceived that they could play a major role in the international arena. The arms race and particularly its nuclear aspect ran counter to the achievement of relaxation of tensions; indeed it encouraged confrontation. The political climate which accompanied the arms race appeared to be the very antithesis of the enduring efforts for international co-operation and accommodation. That explains why since the beginning of the sixties the Non-Aligned states committed themselves to use their outmost endeavours to arrest the trends towards aggravations in international relations.[24]

The Non-Aligned group came into line with the determinations of the East and the West groups in expressing the desire to see the ENDC get down to the practical issues involved and to begin the realistic and serious approach the superpowers had suggested. The Non-Aligned states unreversedly endorsed the new approach whilst simultaneously looking to the superpowers and their allies, especially the United Kingdom, to reach a consensus not only on what any agreements would mean in themselves but also for the stimulus they would give to so much of the work in the wider sphere of disarmament.[25] Any possible agreement that would make the superpowers tolerate a modicum of co-operation was essential to break the deadlock at long last. On behalf of the Non-Aligned states, Mexico defined accurately the position of the Non-Aligned states in the negotiations. Because of the fact that the Non-Aligned states 'have no immediate interest in the particular formula or formulas by which it is attempted to solve the problem, they are in a good position to play a part of moderation, to seek conciliatory formulas, to serve as a link between the great powers'.[26]

The similarity of attitude among the Non-Aligned states was apparent from the earliest working sessions, when they made clear that they were ready 'to refuse everything that aggravates polemics, emphasizes antagonism or delays settlement'.[27] Their predetermination to stand as conciliators between the superpowers and their eagerness to show that they did not constitute a bloc which pursued its own goals seems the reason why the Non-Aligned states did not attempt to take issue with the superpowers, either in the proposed approach or on the agenda of the specific measures which were proposed for negotiation.[28] On the contrary, 'being conscious that the General Assembly has sent them to ENDC with the mission to introduce an element of constructive impartiality'[29] they were vigorously attached to the pursuit of the new approach. Not only in their behaviour at the ENDC but also in the manifestation of their policy in the UN the Non-Aligned group appeared to support the suggested course of action. It should be borne in mind that significant resolutions of the General Assembly which repeatedly called for the first time upon the ENDC to give 'urgent attention' to the search for arms control measures came about as the result of the Non-Aligned states sponsorship or overwhelming support.[30]

Since the uncommitted states' mission was to bring the superpowers together, not foment the quarrels between them, they were prepared to associate themselves with any initiative proposed by the superpowers assuring an approach to disarmament through the search for arms control measures. Their attitude was equated with the granting of a broad and unequivocal backing, a *carte blanche* to the superpowers for actions which would be based and determined in principle and advance between them. Not only were the Non-Aligned states predisposed to refrain from making the agenda for negotiations, they were even prepared to accept negotiated arms control measures that presupposed their agreement to measures, such as, the prohibition of the vertical proliferation of nuclear weapons. It was India which explained that if the Non-Aligned states had a say on the selection of the agenda the question of the prevention of the proliferation of nuclear weapons would no doubt have figured at the top on that agenda.[31]

The moderate attitude they displayed added a great deal of flexibility to the efforts of the superpowers to make a discretionary selection of measures of arms control the consideration of which could offer immediate prospects for successful negotiation. If the Non-Aligned states had taken a share in the quest for arms control measures together with the superpowers they would inevitably have driven themselves to side with one or the other of the two blocs. The consequence would have been to destroy the picture of mediators they wished to display. Additionally, they abstained from the haggling over the agenda and the selection of arms control measures because such action would be difficult to reconcile with their persistent proclamation that they did not constitute a bloc. Furthermore, the recognition on their part of the technical intricacies involved in the negotiating process of disarmament, even in its arms control phase, made them accept that they lacked sufficient familiarity with such processes. Thus, the superpowers, the commanding power of the ENDC, emerged as the most competent authority to chart the course the negotiations had to take.

Thus, the ENDC started to lay out the foundation for the growth of a common approach to which, quite significantly, the three political groups consented. It took a unanimous decision that concurrently with the elaboration of agreement on GCD, and not to the detriment of this elaboration, the ENDC should consider and implement measures of arms control. According to such decision, these measures 'should be aimed at lessening of international tension; the consolidation of confidence among states; and facilitating general and complete disarmament'.[32]

GCD began to be visualized as the ultimate goal despite the fact that the General Assembly of the UN, by establishing the ENDC had mandated it to be occupied with immediate negotiations on GCD.[33] The conviction throughout the UN and the ENDC was strongly of the opinion that GCD and arms control measures were not mutually exclusive but supplementary processes. One of the specific guidances, the Joint Statement of Agreed Principles (the McLoy-Zorin principles) for disarmament, provided that efforts to achieve agreements on and implementation of measures of disarmament including arms control measures could be taken without prejudicing progress on agreement on the total programme of GCD.[34] Under such circumstances, the ENDC's work began to gradually drift away from the issue of GCD. It should be noted that the drift towards arms control measures was being reinforced throughout the whole period by a tactical play, a sort of dilemma, which was being put in action by the superpowers to the members of the ENDC and especially to the Non-Aligned states. The ENDC's members were offered two alternatives: either disarmament under the formula of GCD in a single treaty or a more modest approach, that of the quest for arms control measures. There was no midpoint between the two alternatives as the superpowers were persistently refusing to accept for discussion or negotiation measures of real disarmament isolated from the intricate context of GCD; they insisted on an all-or-nothing approach of GCD. Real disarmament measures had to be discussed, on the insistence of the superpowers, on the basis of a treaty on GCD and not to be selected and negotiated separately. The consequential fact was that the members of the ENDC were faced with a position whereby they were obliged to make a choice between the one or the other option.

The view that the search for arms control measures was a more viable and realistic option in comparison to GCD turned the scale in favour of arms control and presaged, to a certain extent, the course the negotiations would take. This appreciation was also reinforced in the practice during the first sessions of the ENDC. Since the superpowers tabled their individual plans for GCD, they increasingly tended to be wrapped up in their own radically different individual thoughts. The GCD was very likely to remain an issue for the two protagonists as its discussion was dominated by the superpowers. As such it could destroy the rich potential of the ENDC and could put the other participants on the margins of the negotiating process. Additionally, GCD seemed to be virtually unnegotiable at that time, not only because of its very comprehensive content or the existing climate but in terms of the fact that it required the presence of France and China in the negotiating team. France was still declining to take its seat in the ENDC[35] and China, which became the fifth nuclear power in 1964 was not yet a member either of the UN or the ENDC. For all these reasons, the UN, very wisely, took the decision not to let the brief sessions of the ENDC turn their attention to general disarmament plans, which did not provide any realistic basis for the multilateral activity surrounding the ENDC and UN. As a consequence, GCD retreated into the background as it was submitted as not amenable to coming within manageable limits.

The foundations of the moderate approach the ENDC decided to pursue through the quest for arms control measures was being built piece by piece. Negotiations in the ENDC were taken up in a rather haphazard manner depending either on the convenience of the superpowers, to whom all the states in the ENDC had granted considerable initiatory and regulatory powers, or their perspective of what was ripe for consideration. States in the ENDC were vigorously inclined to make their own earnest endeavour to build up the foundations of the new 'modest approach' to disarmament. It is important to say that whereas the meetings of the ENDC and the UN's disarmament business were overshadowed by the very serious incidents of the Berlin and Cuba crises, what emerged during and after these crises was not only justification in a dramatic manner for the approach taken but also led to the underlying of the need to hasten the course upon which the UN/ENDC had embarked. This need turned out, in the aftermath of the Cuba crisis, to be more urgent as the superpowers wanted demonstrative acts of reconciliation, which could at least restore each side's faith in the other's credibility. Lall, in his writings about the UN, indicates that 'the feeling within the ENDC was very strong that there should be concentration on single issues of arms control measures and especially the test ban issue'[36] had to be solved before there could be meaningful talk on GCD.

Negotiations on particular issues required long and demanding hours for study, formal and informal consultations, clarification of positions, meditation and, most of all, a great deal of bargaining to minimize the differences and, ultimately, to agree upon detailed provisions. As basic differences arose and had to be solved, the ENDC found it difficult to be engaged in more than one detailed nuclear arms control negotiation at a time. This observation is mainly concerned with the negotiation of the Non-Proliferation Treaty (NPT). As will be seen shortly, attempts which were made during the negotiation of the NPT for a simultaneous deal over other measures were finally abandoned. The abandonment resulted from the objective appreciation that such attempts would have delayed the conclusion of the NPT. The drafting of the NPT was by no means an easy matter on account of its very particular importance and the need to satisfy the often conflicting desiderata of the states. The negotiation of the Outer Space Treaty took place simultaneously with the negotiation of the NPT but in a subsidiary body of the General Assembly of the United Nations, the Committee on Peaceful Uses of Outer Space.[37]

The Partial Test Ban Treaty (PTBT)

The first treaty decided upon by the ENDC was that of establishing a direct communication link between the superpowers. The involvement of the ENDC in its negotiation and conclusion was decisive. The subject matter of the treaty had been initially discussed both by the TNDC and ENDC under the programme for GCD. Shortly after, as a strong movement was gaining ground in the ENDC in favour of the quest for arms control measures, the issue was isolated from the general context of GCD into which it had been initially incorporated. Its consideration as a special measure which would produce direct communication links between the superpowers with a view to averting the risks of accidental war was taken up by the ENDC. However, because of its bilateral nature the issue was referred to the superpowers and the details of the treaty were worked out by them in informal meetings. The conclusion of the treaty, therefore, should be credited to the ENDC and to the co-chair institution as in the case of its negotiation full advantage was taken of both institutions.[38]

The ENDC and primarily the United States and the Soviet Union very soon became engaged in the process of identifying other more practical measures which would offer immediate conclusion and implementation. These would stand as priority measures for negotiation in order to show that the ENDC was able to conclude successful arms control measures. It was agreed that the most serious consideration had to be given to those measures 'for whose adoption all the necessary conditions and practical opportunities are available and which the states are resolved to carry out without delay'.[39] Thus, the negotiation of the non-proliferation issue was recommended but was not taken up at that time. It was looked at as a composite issue not capable of being the subject of immediate action on the part of the ENDC. The non-proliferation issue if it had been taken up would have supposedly led to high controversy when negotiation reached a practical level. The main problem was centred on the compatibility of nuclear sharing within an alliance, which the United States and the United Kingdom had proposed, with the principle of non-dissemination. The problem of giving West Germany access to nuclear weapons through the military alliance of NATO seemed to be at the centre of the controversy.[40] It would presumably have brought the superpowers into such dispute as to render the negotiation of the NPT a very difficult objective. The question of prohibition of the military use of outer space was also suggested but, as already noted, it was decided that this should be dealt with not by the ENDC but by the Committee on Peaceful Uses of Outer Space which had already been established under the aegis of the General Assembly.

Generally speaking, all the measures which would have enabled the ENDC to go ahead with its predominant task were scrutinized. Finally, the ENDC decided to grapple with the issue of the nuclear test ban. The test ban issue gained ground because of the fact that it had reached a peak of necessity for serious negotiation. It was the closest to the substance of real disarmament among all the nuclear arms control measures. Its negotiation got the approval of all the three political groups as a matter of immense significance. The ENDC's plump for it as a matter of immediate negotiation coincided with the time when the harmful effects of radioactive fall-out were receiving extensive public attention. Additionally, whereas the taking up of the non-proliferation issue was postponed for the immediate future falling into the background as a secondary negotiating option, the negotiation on a test ban was being targeted to serve as a means of deterring non-nuclear weapon states (NNWS) from becoming members of the nuclear club. Continued testing had increased the danger of the spread of nuclear weapons to NNWS.

The opportunity to concentrate exclusively on the test ban negotiations was given when the ENDC proceeded with unanimous support to set up a sub-committee consisting of the United States, the Soviet Union and the United Kingdom, the three nuclear power states in the ENDC. The delegation of authority to the sub-committee was the outcome of the appreciation shared by the ENDC and all its groups that the question of a test ban revolved, apart from the question of political readiness, around technical considerations with which the most advanced technological states were the most qualified to deal. The sub-committee continued consideration of the test ban until the end of the year. The spirit of urgency with which the sub-committee took up the question at issue enabled the positions of the three nuclear weapon states (NWS) to be clarified and the crucial points of differences to be understood very soon. Due primarily to the Anglo-American initiative being accompanied by the submission of alternative solutions to the question of the test ban, the negotiating parties came to evaluate what would constitute the terminal point up to which they could proceed in order to arrive at an agreement. It was revealed that there was a great measure of agreement on a PTBT, as had been proposed by the United States and the United Kingdom, on the discontinuance of nuclear testing in the atmosphere, under water and in outer space. Control of the compliance with the banning of the tests in those three environments could be exercised by national means of inspection. What was the crucial point of difference on which the three NWS could not or did not wish to agree was the question of control over underground nuclear tests.

The question arises as to what extent was the implementation of control over the underground testing fraught with any serious technical difficulties? The United States maintained that seismological signals could not be easily distinguished from underground explosions and they are often indistinguishable from those associated with numerous earthquakes. However, even if we suppose that the 'technical' objections of the US were sustainable, it is still possible to argue that the problem here lay on the political side and should be attributed to the lack of readiness of the superpowers to accept a comprehensive test ban treaty (CTBT). This point is reinforced by the fact that there was an alternative to the natural means of identification of underground explosions, the acceptance of which was purely a political matter. It was the reliance upon a system of verification based on on-site inspection to which the Soviet Union, in turn, politically objected.

By the end of 1962 negotiations to work out an agreement on a test ban had reached a terminal point whereby the common agreement that existed determined the scope of a possible treaty as one which would put the brakes on the development of nuclear weapons by other NNWS. Since the treaty would ban nuclear tests in the atmosphere, underwater and in outer space at a time when the superpowers had been mastering the techniques of underground testing, it would turn out to be a measure directed at stopping proliferation.[41] It would not, however, infringe the interests of the superpowers, whereas it would affect those of the NNWS. As the treaty was projected to be open for accession by all states, it appeared to be more of a multilateral than of a purely trilateral character and as such it should have been widely acceptable.

The view that an agreement of such nature would require, most of all, universal acceptance and application dictated the transfer of the negotiations from the sub-committee to the plenary meetings of the ENDC. The multilateral approach seemed to be more essential at this time. Wide acceptance and application could be effected if the NNWS and especially the Non-Aligned states could have contributed or, to put it better, could have felt that they had contributed to the shaping of the treaty. This would guarantee their accession to the treaty. This could be achieved through their apparent but not substantive participation in the negotiations. It was in this direction that the subsequent negotiations within the plenary meetings of the ENDC were devoted rather than to genuine efforts to further the scope of the agreement to render it more comprehensive.

During the negotiations, the Non-Aligned states' mediatory role was tested. It is characteristic of the period of the negotiations of the PTBT that every formal initiative by the Non-Aligned states was expressed in the so called 'memorandum of eight' which represented their unanimous voice.[42] The eight Non-Aligned members of the ENDC acted as a homogeneous body in the negotiations. There was a credible follow-up to the self-commitments they had undertaken to stand as a political power of conciliation and moderation. They were in a position of passive mediators facing with increasing realism the technical complexities of the issue in question. Despite the fact that they were determined to accede to what the NWS had been agreed upon, they attempted to make a responsible political rather that technical contribution by attempting to bring the two closer with regard to the controversial issue of the control of underground tests.

Whilst the Non-Aligned states felt at that time that they were enjoying a considerable share in the shaping of the treaty making process primarily through their mediatory role, the superpowers announced that private consultations would be held in Moscow between them and the United Kingdom with a view to signing a treaty on a testing ban. In Moscow, after brief consultations, the three powers demonstrated their readiness to sign a treaty the aspects of which had been sufficiently explored during the negotiations in ENDC.[43] An agreement was concluded in August 1963 which by no means went beyond the terminal points reached in the ENDC. The announcement of the conclusion of the treaty put a stop to the negotiating activities in the ENDC which began to flounder in the same deep sea of arguments, counter arguments, manoeuvres, innumerable meetings and endless debate about whether or not it was possible to proceed further and conclude a more comprehensive agreement.

The UN itself and particularly the General Assembly appeared to come round to the view that if the negotiating parties were to say anything more in the ENDC this might make any agreement more difficult to arrive at. It should be admitted that the General Assembly never ceased throughout the period of the negotiation of the PTBT that took place in the ENDC, to exhort it to work for a CTBT. It asked for the maximum possible being aware that the pursuit of the best could lead the ENDC to pass something which could be considered, at least, good or acceptable. As a matter of fact, the General Assembly was forced to face with increased scepticism the idea of requesting the ENDC to strive solely for a CTBT. The dilemma was that if the UN was to renounce the search for a modest agreement like the PTBT, because it would fall short of the best solution, then the UN might arguably be said it have lost sight of the broader perspective it had put on to the negotiations on arms control measures and made as they say, the best the enemy of the good. Unreserved insistence on the negotiations of a treaty of broader scope might bring states and negotiations back on the rails of the old positions at a time when the UN through its moderate approach to disarmament was going to great pains to break the ice of the Cold War. The foundations of the new approach it had initiated might be jeopardized or destroyed by the political storm any prolongations of negotiations aimed at putting the test ban treaty in a more comprehensive context could cause. A PTBT, according to the UN's opinion, should not be rejected outright for the simple reason that it did not go far enough, but should be welcomed. A PTBT would afford a respite pending the preparations for the continuation of the quest for other arms control measures. Thus, the General Assembly of the UN called on the ENDC to thrash out the actual possibilities offered and if, against all hope, the negotiating parties could not reach an agreement on a CTBT, they then should immediately enter into an agreement on a PTBT.[44]

The PTBT generated a feeling of compulsion to the negotiating parties to move forward. It made them perceive that there was a community of interests which had been left in the shade by the differences which separated them and that this community of interests could be converted into other valuable arms control measures like those prohibiting the horizontal dissemination of nuclear weapons. The conclusion mainly of the PTBT went a long away towards creating encouraging signs of easing tension and a distinct improvement in the Cold War position.

The negotiation of the NPT: A two step process

Non-proliferation became the next dominant issue in the UN since it appeared to be amongst the most urgent issues which could also provide a rapid solution. In the following years it was kept in the forefront of the UN and ENDC deliberations and negotiations respectively, because it emerged incontestably as the next logical and most necessary step.[45] The urgency of its consideration was dictated by the need which the UN and the ENDC had already felt, especially after the Chinese nuclear test of 1964, for the adoption of effective measures against a further spread of nuclear weapons. This need was based upon the acknowledgement of the serious consequences for world peace which would result from the acquisition of such weapons by other states. The risk run was that in a relatively short time, the number of nuclear powers might considerably increased.

The subsequent monopolization of the ENDC's sessions with the negotiation of the NPT seemed to mirror the attitude shared by the members of the UN. Successive resolutions of the General Assembly, after they expressed the conviction of the General Assembly that the emergence of additional nuclear weapon powers would provoke an uncontrollable arms race, reiterated that 'the prevention of further proliferation of nuclear weapons is a matter of the highest priority demanding unceasing attention of both nuclear weapon and non-nuclear weapon powers'.[46] In line with such a view, the Secretary-General of the UN seemed to share the optimism that the shift towards nuclear arms control measures and more specifically towards the negotiation of an NPT would render disarmament more attainable. He regarded 'the successful conclusion of a treaty for the non-proliferation of nuclear weapons as an indispensable first step towards further progress in disarmament. In fact, it is difficult to conceive of any agreement in the foreseeable future or any other measure of disarmament, if it is not possible to reach agreement on a treaty to prevent the spread of the nuclear weapons.[47]

The negotiation of the NPT can be regarded as a two step process. The first initial stage involved prolonged negotiations between the superpowers including intra-alliance consultations. By methods similar to that for conflict resolution they made efforts to overcome a major hurdle to an agreement, the problem of nuclear control within their military alliances. The second stage involved similar methods but this time between the two superpowers supported by their allies on the one hand and the NNWS which were mostly identified with the Non-Aligned states on the other hand. The process as a whole was of great importance not just because it led to the conclusion one of the most significant arms control measures in the history of the negotiations which were conducted almost exclusively within the UN disarmament institutions (General Assembly and ENDC) but for an additional profound reason. It coincided with the first appearance of a demand on the part of the Non-Aligned group for substantive participation in the negotiating process. Actually the transitional period from the one stage of the process to the other stood out as a noticeable change in the direction of the negotiations towards a broader, more universal approach.

The negotiation of the NPT resulted in cutting across the traditional political environment for negotiations in the UN. The prevalent feature until that time had been the unchecked dominant role of the superpowers. From this standpoint, it was a strike at the existing framework of negotiation and had significant implications for the role of the UN. Particularly the second stage of the negotiations of the NPT functioned as one of the fundamental progenitors of the subsequent demand of the Non-Aligned group for equitable participation in the disarmament negotiations. It is fitting to point out that non-proliferation was the issue that presupposed more than any other measure of disarmament or arms control the active participation of all the NNWS. As such, it could be argued, it had the potential of bringing them into the mainstream of the political process of the negotiations even in its arms control phase.

Negotiation of an agreement on non-proliferation began to take concrete and practical shape in 1965. It was at this juncture that the superpowers became deeply engaged in negotiations between themselves. These bilateral negotiations were accompanied, or followed, by frequent consultations with their allies with a view to determining how various collective nuclear defence arrangements within their military alliances could be reconciled. The reconciliation was mainly concerned with the elimination of the suspicions that if the non-proliferation regime were not void of loopholes, then states, particularly the Federal Republic of Germany, might gain possession of nuclear weapons indirectly under the camouflage of internal defence alliance arrangements.

Negotiations resulted in superpowers submitting, from the vantage point of their status as co-chairs, the first draft treaties designed to prevent the spread of nuclear weapons. The American draft treaty provided in its operative text:[48]

ARTICLE 1

1. Each of the nuclear states party to this treaty undertake not to transfer any nuclear weapons into the national control of any non-nuclear state, either directly, or indirectly through a military alliance, and each undertakes not to take any other action which would cause an increase in the total number of states and other organisations having independent power to use nuclear weapons.

2. Each of the nuclear states party to this treaty undertakes not to assist any non-nuclear state in the manufacture of nuclear weapons.

ARTICLE 2

1. Each of the nuclear states party to this treaty undertakes not to manufacture nuclear weapons, each undertakes not to seek or to receive the transfer of such weapons into its national control, either directly, or indirectly through a military alliance; and each undertakes not to take any other action which would cause an increase in the total number of states and other organisations having independent power to use nuclear weapons.

2. Each of the non-nuclear states party to this treaty undertake not to seek or to receive assistance in the manufacture of nuclear weapons or itself to grant assistance.

The American draft treaty did not meet the requirements of the Soviet Union for a text on non-proliferation without such loopholes that would prevent indirect access, particularly of West Germany, to the weapons through the projected NATO multilateral nuclear force (MNF).[49] The draft treaty which the Soviet Union tabled shortly after the tabling of the American draft was a working document that reflected its discontent. The operative part of the Soviet treaty intended to eliminate the loopholes of the American plan and it reads as follows:

1. Parties to the treaty possessing nuclear weapons undertake not to transfer such weapons in any form-directly or indirectly, through third states or group of states to the ownership or control of states or groups of states not possessing nuclear weapons and not to accord to such states or group of states the right to participate in the ownership, control or use of nuclear weapons.

The said parties to the treaty shall not transfer nuclear weapons or control over them or over their emplacement and use, to units of the armed forces or military personnel of states not possessing nuclear weapons, even if such units or personnel are under the command of a military alliance.

2. Parties to the treaty possessing nuclear weapons undertake not to provide assistance directly or indirectly, through third states or group of states not at the present possessing nuclear weapons in the manufacture, in preparations for the manufacture or in the testing of such weapons and not to transmit to them any kind of manufacturing, research or other information or documentation which can be employed for purposes of the manufacture or use of nuclear weapons.[50]

Article 2 of the draft treaty provided, with a similar wording, for the states not possessing nuclear weapons to undertake corresponding obligations.

The request for a balance of mutual obligations and responsibilities: A strike on the governing decision-making process?

Discussion in the ENDC continued to be a dialogue between the superpowers. For the superpowers reliably to preclude any possibility for an indirect spread of nuclear weapons through military alliance remained the outstanding issue. First and foremost, attempts had to be concentrated on the text of a treaty which 'should avoid any loopholes which might permit nuclear weapon powers to proliferate directly or indirectly nuclear weapons in any form'.[51] To do so in such a manner as to cover all possible means of transfer of nuclear weapons, negotiations should be conducted primarily between the two camps, the East and West, which the superpowers represented. To correspond with such a position, new altered versions of the previous drafts were submitted which eventually facilitated a better approximation between the two sides. It can be said that up until late 1966, the way the superpowers had determined the scope of an NPT justified their position regarding the course the negotiations had taken. The distinctive feature of this course was that the consultation had been principally between them and their allies.

It is fitting to point out, at this juncture, that as long as the negotiations in the ENDC tended to be between the superpowers the concept of a non-proliferation regime began to be visualized as a matter of agreement between the United States and its allies on the one hand and the Soviet Union and its allies on the other. Such visualization was absolutely reflected in the texts of the draft treaties cited above. They did not take account of the particular concerns and interests of the NNWS which were to forego their option to acquire nuclear weapons. The draft treaties which had been submitted gave a clear indication of what the superpowers expected of the Non-Aligned states.[52]

This kind of visualization could have meant the assignment of a secondary status to the Non-Aligned states in the subsequent negotiating process or even the substantial limitation of their role to that of making a commitment to a non-proliferation regime exclusively negotiated by the East and West. When Stoessinger wrote that the superpowers 'attempted to sell a non-proliferation treaty'[53] to the NNWS, he indicated the clear position that the East and West had taken that they would frame such a regime according to their own interests. Accordingly, this East-West position became little more than manifestations of the superpowers' wish to retain by all means the decision-making process under their absolute control; the non-proliferation regime should be one that would unilaterally impose obligations and responsibilities on the NNWS.[54]

The way the negotiations had been framed made the Non-Aligned states, whose substantial participation had been loosely articulated, take actions to protect their legitimate right to have a decisive say in regard to the formulation of the non-proliferation regime. The surfacing of the issue of the involvement of the Non-Aligned world in the negotiating process came about when the Non-Aligned states decided to rally around a political platform-request for a 'proper balance of mutual obligations and responsibilities'.[55] Their systematic rallying around such a platform-request was a concrete form of mobilization they chose in their effort to accommodate themselves in the decision process involved in the negotiations. This continuous request for such a balance was tantamount to the Non-Aligned states offering a different negotiating position from that which the East and West maintained on the scope and the content of a treaty to halt the spread of nuclear weapons. The new approach on the part of the Non-Aligned group was at variance with the attitude they had followed since the ENDC began working on disarmament and subsequently, before and immediately after the conclusion of the PTBT. Then, as it has been stressed, this group had the predisposition to accord with everything the superpowers had agreed upon or what they wanted to regulate in the future negotiations.

At the time of the negotiation of the NPT they began to shape a new international response *vis-à-vis* the negotiating process. It reflected the manifestation of their wish to intervene decisively in it. The request for a treaty which would ensure a balance of mutual obligations and responsibilities presupposed that both the views of the NWS and the NNWS would receive more or less equitable consideration and adoption. It meant a shift in the decision-making process on which the superpowers had a stranglehold in order to put it into a more democratic shape. As was pointed out by the Non-Aligned states, debates and negotiations 'must take place between nuclear and non-nuclear, between Aligned and Non-Aligned countries: it is undeniable that in regard to the treaty (of non-proliferation) the Non-Aligned and non-nuclear countries have equitable claims to put forward which must be taken into account in the negotiations'.[56]

It is of particular value to note that this platform for a balance of obligations was put forward in the negotiations at the time the Non-Aligned states started complaining that the ENDC had been 'apparently paralyzed or hypnotized by the preoccupations of some of the larger powers'.[57] For the

Non-Aligned group there was no denial that a treaty of such nature as that on non-proliferation carried in its very concept a certain discriminatory appearance since it confirmed and perpetuated the disparity between 'nuclear haves' and 'have-nots'.[58] What they meant by balance in this context was something more than the making of provisions whereby merely NNWS would have the responsibility and the obligations not to acquire nuclear weapons with corresponding responsibility and obligation on the part of the NWS not to proliferate nuclear weapons to them.[59] This is precisely what the first draft treaties of the superpowers provided. The platform of acceptable obligations and responsibilities between the NWS and the NNWS tended to be conceptualized in a way that was different from that already envisaged in the negotiations by the superpowers.

From the Non-Aligned point of view, their platform amounted to a variety of demands that the Non-Aligned states sought as means of safeguarding those of their interests which seemed to be at stake. These demands constituted the significant part of the 'deal' for the NNWS-Non-Aligned states giving up the right to obtain such weapons.[60] To use the words of Goldblat, representative of the delegation of Poland in the ENDC, what was being asked was like 'a kind of exchange of one commodity for another over a bargaining counter'.[61] They should be embodied as basic elements in a treaty on non-proliferation in compliance with the principle of balance and the mutuality of obligations. If the Non-Aligned states were to relinquish their access to nuclear weapons, they had to be given assurances for their security and essential guarantees that their commitment to the non-proliferation regime would not hurt their interests in economic development. To be deprived of the peaceful applications of atomic energy was equated with their deprivation of 'access to the economic benefits and technological spin-offs of the nuclear age at a time the developing countries were facing severe economic and resource problems'.[62] Actually, the platform for balanced obligations embraced with varying degree of emphasis the whole package of demands of the Non-Aligned states. This varying degree of emphasis, as Epstein indicated, was due to the fact that 'the Non-Aligned, non-nuclear weapon countries were not a solid bloc with a single point of view, but rather were divided among themselves and constituted a whole spectrum of opinion'.[63] Thus, the platform upon which the Non-Aligned states were standing had been comprehensively expanded by them so that it covered all the variations in opinion that existed among them. Being so, it opened up the way for the Non-Aligned states to have a common bargaining position; a broad unity which enabled them to maintain a more or less reliable common position during the negotiations. It can be argued, however, that the wide spectrum of opinion within the group diluted the strength of their bargaining position.

Furthermore, the Non-Aligned states appeared to have seen as an element of balanced obligations and responsibilities the prospect of the superpowers undertaking explicit commitments on specific measures of nuclear disarmament. In this context, they jointly attempted to link the negotiations of the non-proliferation issue with nuclear disarmament. In this way they refused to see the non-proliferation measure, as either the East or the West saw it, as a measure in the right direction which even if it were left to stand by itself after being concluded 'would create more favourable conditions for the attainment of further agreements on the urgent measures of disarmament'.[64] They jointly argued that the measure of the horizontal prohibition of nuclear weapons 'should be coupled with or followed by tangible steps to halt the nuclear arms race and to limit, reduce and eliminate the stocks of nuclear weapons and the means of their delivery'.[65]

The compromise formula for an NPT 'to be coupled with or followed by' additional measures of nuclear disarmament covered the differences of opinion which appeared regarding the nature, scope and form of the link to be attempted between NPT and nuclear disarmament. It reconfirmed that the Non-Aligned states were not in absolute agreement but they had broadly similar views. The most extreme positions regarding such a link were heard much more in the General Assembly than in the ENDC. It should be pointed out that those who occupied the seats in the deliberations occurring in the General Assembly in New York, being on the sidelines of the negotiating process taking place in Geneva, kept the discussion more free and somewhat academic. Without having to put their minds to mastering the difficulties emerging in the negotiating process it was not necessary for them to manifest the negotiating responsibility they ought to show if they were to participate in the ENDC. Voices were repeatedly raised in the discussion in the General Assembly like the following one:

it is imperative that real progress should be made in the conversations of the great nuclear powers on the practical means for their own disarmament since the renunciation by the small states of any attempt to develop their own nuclear weapons will be of no avail unless it is accompanied by the nuclear disarmament of all states.[66]

The differences of opinion as to the precise link between an NPT and nuclear disarmament were between the most militant and the moderate parts of the Non-Aligned group. The former attempted for the first time in the

ENDC to use the necessity for a NPT as a political vehicle to put pressure on the superpowers to go ahead with nuclear disarmament.[67] Brazil, India, both members of the ENDC, as well as Pakistan were identified as being among the most militant. With such a position they required the placing of the horizontal non-proliferation issue within a much wider context which would include a simultaneous deal involving substantial steps of nuclear disarmament. Views were expressed before both the General Assembly and the ENDC that 'the commitment of non-nuclear weapon states to sign away the right to manufacture or otherwise acquire those weapons must be coupled with a specific and binding commitment on the part of the nuclear powers to take concrete steps to halt the nuclear arms race'.[68] On the other hand, for the moderates, such as Mexico and Sweden, the negotiation of the NPT should not be encumbered or associated with the solution of other complex problems of nuclear disarmament. They were assuring the ENDC and the UN that 'the repeated reference to the insistence on balanced obligations does not certainly stem from any desire to cause unnecessary difficulties in the already complicated negotiations on the non-proliferation issue'.[69] The moderates' position basically derived from their willingness to see the ENDC keeping faith with the moderate approach it had credibly followed since its inception. Additionally, if the treaty was to be negotiated on the stipulation that it 'should include specific measures to be implemented by the nuclear powers in the immediate future, this would be tantamount to opposing the very existence of an NPT'.[70] They relied upon those profound reasons to take the view that an NPT should be seen as an essential single step forward which would be followed without delay by other and more effective measures leading to disarmament. They rejected the idea of seeing the NPT as an instrument that would embody an agreement on disarmament. They were categorically against any attempts to manipulate the negotiation of an NPT as an appropriate vehicle to exert pressure on the NWS, so that they would be obliged to go ahead with the disarmament process. For the moderates, measures of real nuclear disarmament should not be used as a compensation, a quid pro quo in return for something.

The subsequent course of actions of the Non-Aligned states made it clear that if the negotiations continued to take place in utter disregard of their views it could prevent any agreement whatsoever. The Non-Aligned states were of the opinion that if they were to play the role of a non-reacting catalytic agent they had displayed from the beginning of the sixties up to that time, they would have been condemned to a position of drift. They would have been destined to make a passive accession to a treaty agreed, to a large extent, in informal meetings between the superpowers. That is why they became now somewhat different and more assertive. The nature of the non-proliferation issue was such that they would have to be committed to an international instrument with far-reaching political, military, strategic and even economic implications for them.

The first burst of pressure aimed at pressing the superpowers to open the negotiations to the NNWS-Non-Aligned states came when all the eight members of the Non-Aligned group in the ENDC submitted a memorandum in mid-1966. This amounted to the presentation of their basic approach to the question of the NPT with extensive implications for the decision-making process which takes place along with it. Their belief that the negotiation of an NPT was a matter of urgency was reconfirmed. However, its conclusion was possible only if the talks were enlarged in favour of the substantial participation of the Non-Aligned group. For the first time since the birth of the ENDC, the Non-Aligned states took a position against both the superpowers and subjected them to criticism over the way the negotiations had been directed so far. As was pointed out, the non-proliferation issue had so far been discussed between the major powers and attention had been focused on the differences concerning nuclear armaments within alliances which was certainly an obstacle for consideration but not the main issue. What should be the central issue in the negotiations, according to the memorandum, was compliance with the request for the achievement of a balance of mutual obligations and responsibilities. Such a compliance was a key criterion to test the acceptability of any new draft treaties on non-proliferation. From this viewpoint, the Non-Aligned states launched a severe criticism against the draft treaties submitted so far by the superpowers as not ensuring their interests. Their stance was tantamount to an ultimatum that if the views of the Non-Aligned states were left out of account such a situation would lead not only to an increase of nuclear armaments but also to a spread of nuclear weapons over the world.[71] It might lead to a treaty which since it would constitute more or less a bilateral contractual arrangement would be useless because it would not be acceptable 'to all concerned'.

This was the advent of an entirely new process whereby the Non-Aligned states started making constant efforts to utilize to the utmost, within the limits of the UN moderate approach toward disarmament, the favourable possibilities which resulted from the necessity of their required adherence to the non-proliferation regime. The effectiveness of an NPT depended on the power of its universal attraction. The circumstances were more auspicious than ever before. By negotiating skillfully and politically the non-proliferation issue and manipulating the necessity of their requested adherence to such a regime as a bargaining chip, the Non-Aligned states could gain political bargaining power. This, in turn, would enable them to ask the superpowers to make concessions which would substantially lead to the upgrading of the role of the Non-Aligned states; whilst simultaneously bringing them very near to the centre of the political process of the decision-making. The disillusionment of the Non-Aligned group with the amorphous and limited participation they had had so far and the fact that they had been largely ignored in the negotiating process was unremittingly expressed both in the UN and the ENDC. The new course of action seemed now to be justifiable for the Non-Aligned states as they felt distressed

> because in the past, the superpowers had tended to treat the non-nuclear states as if they counted for little and as they had no interest in this vital question of war and peace. The superpowers were always apt to agree behind the scenes and to present us with a *fait accompli*, on the confident assumption, helpless as we are, we would have to accept their conclusions.[72]

They went on to give a warning that 'if the proposed NPT is to have the support of the have-nots, then it must meet their legitimate concerns'.[73]

A first trial search for democratization of the negotiating process

The attempt of the Non-Aligned states to get to the heart of the negotiating process generated a substantial increase in their sense of collective responsibility. The way the Non-Aligned states at that moment interpreted such joint responsibility meant the undertaking of further drastic actions aimed at giving full impetus to their demands for strengthening their position in the process of negotiations. A further significant step they took provides further evidence that in negotiating an NPT they were also negotiating for a better position in the overall international decision-making process concerning disarmament. They became directly responsible for the sponsorship of a set of resolutions[74] by which the General Assembly decided to convene a Conference of NNWS to meet not later than 1968 to consider the following and other related questions, which had so far not been dealt with by the ENDC: (a) how can the security of NNWS best be assured?, (b) how may NNWS co-operate among themselves in preventing the proliferation of nuclear weapons?, and (c) how can nuclear devices be used for exclusively peaceful purposes?

This was an initiative which had no precedent in the history of the UN. The central political organ of the UN, the General Assembly, decided to convene a Conference under its aegis with participants solely from the non-nuclear weapon group. The other groups of the UN were excluded. By such means the General Assembly institutionalized within the UN a cleavage between NWS and NNWS. The cleavage which was formalized and perpetuated during the negotiation of the NPT had far reaching consequences as it put in serious danger the coherence of the UN over an issue of such importance as that of non-proliferation. The sponsorship and the unanimous support of the UN's community for the General Assembly's resolutions came about as the result of a constant complaint from the Non-Aligned world that they had not been given sufficient opportunity to become familiar with the problems and to receive explanatory illustrations, before they had to decide whether to commit themselves to the planned non-proliferation regime.[75] The lack of such familiarity was attributed to the fact that the largest number of members of the group remained outside the ENDC, while those inside had not so far been invited to participate substantially in the negotiating process.

However, there were alternative means by which the Non-Aligned states not present in the ENDC could have appropriately followed the negotiations on the proposed treaty and expressed their views. Apart from the General Assembly and its First Committee, the Disarmament Commission might have been reactivated at their request; while along with the negotiations and consultations which were to be continued in the ENDC a wider multi-sided forum than that of the ENDC could have been arranged through the General Assembly.

The preference the NNWS-Non-Aligned states showed for the convening of their own Conference under the auspices of the General Assembly came to serve simultaneously a complexity of interrelated important purposes. A long time after the Cairo Conference, which was held in 1964, where they had made general appeals for the UN to take up the non-proliferation issue, they felt the need to pass to more concrete formulations of policy *vis-à-vis* the negotiations of the NPT and the superpowers. Under these new formulations they could determine on a more solid, commonly acceptable way their attitude for the sake of insurance of their interests and decisive participation in the negotiating process. Substantive participation presupposed, most of all, the conversion of the somewhat loose character of political co-operation they then had into a more solid tie-up. It was repeatedly said from rostrum of the General Assembly that the Conference of the NNWS 'was intended to serve primarily as a forum of consultation among non-nuclear-weapon states with a view to collectively ensuring their legitimate interests of national security and economic well being'.[76] Furthermore, the Conference would inspire co-operation among them, tapping new energies and shaping more concrete directions so that the Non-Aligned states would be armed with stronger collective bargaining power to exert pressure on the superpowers for improving or altering the political context of the negotiations and the decision-making process. As Pakistan, original sponsor of the General Assembly's resolutions calling for the convening of such a Conference pointedly said 'the aim of the Conference would be to evolve a common standpoint of non-nuclear weapon countries which would enable them to enter into a fruitful dialogue with the nuclear weapon states'.[77]

The way in which they began to channel their willingness to affect the negotiating process deserves special consideration. A new political pattern was emerging as the result of a new international response which the Non-Aligned states were adopting in the negotiations. It was related to the appearance for the first time of the notion of the democratization of the negotiating process and its decision-making. For a better understanding of the emergence of the new response on the part of the Non-Aligned states it is of particular importance to consider another profound reason which made them resort to such a Conference. With the view to gaining more influence upon the negotiations they attempted to activate the the question of the number of the Non-Aligned states which would participate in the Conference of the NNWS. The opinion of the group as a whole carried great political weight since its accession to the non-proliferation regime was more than essential. The group intended to depart from the Conference, in order to resume negotiations, with the establishment of a more or less concerted negotiating position. There is conflicting evidence as to the group's real intentions. Mates, for example, seems to argue that the objective of the convening of the proposed Conference was merely to expand the political activities of the Non-Aligned states in relation to the negotiations.[78]

The change of the behaviour of the Non-Aligned states in the negotiations of the non-proliferation issue was the initial step on the road towards the Non-Aligned states searching for the means of putting in motion the process of democratic change in the UN disarmament machinery. The fact that the Non-Aligned group was on the way to a new long-lasting process aimed at seeing disarmament negotiations taking place with the widest possible participation of their members was confirmed by the increasingly frequent references like that which Pakistan made:

> The Conference is not going to establish a trade union of non-nuclear countries. The idea of the Conference is to establish new channels of consultation whereby non-proliferation of nuclear weapons and nuclear disarmament will become, not the preserve of few, but the concern of

all. We remain unshaken in our conviction that the questions involved in a non-proliferation affect the destiny of each and every nation. We therefore want to ensure that each and every nation has its full say in the matter. [79]

During the negotiation of the NPT there were constant appeals from this group to the world organization that 'not only should its universal character be thrown into relief but all the aspects of the universality enhanced to the maximum'.[80] One of the most significant aspects of universality, as it was made clear, would be the participation of the rapidly expanded membership of the UN in the decision-making process of the disarmament business. The fact that most of the newly admitted states had enlisted in the Non-Aligned group had far-reaching implications for the existing UN disarmament structure; especially the ENDC which seemed not to be given political credit by the Non-Aligned states in the long term. What had been perceptible was an indirect questioning of the modus operandi of the institutionalized UN decentralized structure and particularly the ENDC. The dissatisfaction of the Non-Aligned group with the extant institutional scheme resulted from the fact that their majority in the UN had been left out of the negotiations in the exclusive club of the ENDC. Their dissatisfaction with the present structure for negotiations became immediately discernible when they resorted to the Conference of the NNWS and attempted to associate its members with the negotiations in the ENDC. Their appeal to such a Conference which, as they explained, 'must surely be regarded as complementary to the ENDC'[81] was tantamount to a recognition by them that the present disarmament structure of the UN and particularly the ENDC was to say the least inappropriate.

Following the powerful intervention of the Non-Aligned states in the negotiating process, the superpowers had to exert all their influence to conclude a NPT prior to the convening of the Conference of the NNWS so that the Conference would have to deal with a *fait accompli*. The ENDC and especially the superpowers had now to face a very crucial question: how such an agreement on non-proliferation could be made acceptable to the NNWS-Non-Aligned states? If they had to pursue the object of widely increasing the treaty's acceptability, then they would not be able to ignore basic objections favoured by the Non-Aligned states. Correspondingly, if they did so, then the Conference of the NNWS would occur, as the ultimate judge, to examine what would otherwise have been overlooked. It became obvious that even the preparations which were under way for the convening of this Conference were exerting a considerable degree of influence on the negotiations. In the UN, the superpowers were taking extreme care to succeed in having the Conference postponed until after the NPT was concluded.

At this particular stage, the Non-Aligned states were brought to the forefront of the negotiations as their role in the politics of negotiations was substantially augmented. The superpowers consequently came under strong pressure. Under such conditions they felt the need to adopt a wider perception of democratization in order to avoid the complication of the negotiation of the NPT beyond remedy. Any new draft text of the treaty under negotiation submitted by the superpowers to the ENDC would be a distinct improvement on the previous text. The superpowers, at this crucial point, appeared to make concessions and offer improvements in the balance of obligations and thus widen the scope of the NPT. The last act of the democratic behaviour they displayed involved, as will be seen shortly, the submission of the final draft treaty for further consideration and approval to the General Assembly.

United Nations General Assembly: An outright intervention.

Although the Non-Aligned states had come very close to exercising a considerable influence in the international decision-making process regarding the context of the NPT, the superpowers were still in control of the process. The close co-operation of the superpowers, loyally followed by their allies, significantly increased a favourable balance of political and psychological factors that bore upon the last phase of efforts to conclude the NPT. Furthermore, the fact that the NNWS-Non-Aligned states were divided over the question of the scope of a non-proliferation regime, as it had been framed so far in the ENDC, rendered these factors more influential.

Capitalizing on these factors, the East and West groups jointly sponsored a resolution in the General Assembly which met with acceptance from the overwhelming majority of UN members. The decision of the General Assembly in the form of Resolution 2346 of November 1967 should be regarded as of paramount and decisive importance. It constituted an outright intervention in the negotiating process and ensured for the superpowers further control over the final and more important stage of the negotiations. Because of its important character, the most important parts of the General Assembly's decision merit explicit reference. They read as follows:

The General Assembly
Noting the progress that the ENDC has made towards preparing a draft international treaty to prevent the proliferation of nuclear weapons,

Reaffirming that it is imperative to make further efforts to conclude such a treaty at the earliest possible date,

Expressing the hope that the remaining differences between all the states can be quickly solved,

3. Requests the ENDC to submit to the General Assembly, on or before 15 March 1968, a full report of the negotiations regarding a draft treaty on the non-proliferation of nuclear weapons.

4. Recommends that upon the receipt of that report appropriate consultations should be initiated, in accordance with the rules of procedure of the General Assembly, on the setting of an early date after 15 March 1968 for the resumption of the twenty-second session of the General Assembly, to consider agenda item 28(a) entitled: non-proliferation of nuclear weapons: report of the ENDC.[82]

From an operational and institutional point of view, what came out of the General Assembly's action was the strengthening of the functional ties between it and the ENDC. The character of the General Assembly's initiative showed a desire for some regulatory power on the part of the UN *vis-à-vis* the negotiations. Such a role on the part of the General Assembly exceeded the margins of the role it had played since the beginning of the sixties in relation to the ENDC. The General Assembly was no longer content merely with recommending items for inclusion on the agenda for the ENDC. As a result of this intervention, the UN and the ENDC improved their relationship. After a further period of negotiations this relationship became even closer as the General Assembly called on the ENDC to submit the draft treaty on NPT to it for further consideration.

Both the Non-Aligned group and the superpowers seemed to benefit from the General Assembly's action but for different reasons. As far as the Non-Aligned states were concerned, they were predisposed to welcome any initiative which could upgrade the regulatory and intervening power of the UN with regard to the disarmament business. The initiative of the General Assembly seemed to serve the purpose of expanding of the role of the UN in general and the General Assembly in particular. For the superpowers, the undertaking of certain regulatory initiatives on the part of the General Assembly would have short term positive effects related to the conclusion of an NPT. In particular, the compliance of the ENDC with the request of the General Assembly for a submission of a draft treaty to it would be beneficial to the superpowers. Thanks to the General Assembly's intervention, the world community of the UN would set the democratic seal of its approval on the text of a treaty the scope of which fell more or less, as it will be explained shortly, within the scope of the superpowers' expectations, and which would be free from undesirable commitments for them especially those concerning vertical proliferation.

In reality, what constituted the essence of the intervention of the General Assembly was the judgement it passed on the controversial issue of the scope of a NPT. Its judgement was tantamount to an appeal to all members of the ENDC and especially to the Non-Aligned states to concentrate for the moment on the possibility of agreement on the common ground and not to strive for their own versions of perfection. The common ground was solely concerned with the prohibition of the horizontal proliferation of nuclear weapons. It was held to be the essential part of an NPT. By stressing that considerable progress had been made so far in the negotiations and expressing the view 'that the remaining differences between all the states can be quickly resolved', the General Assembly implicitly redefined the scope of the NPT. Thus, it determined such common ground as existed. This common ground could be found in the key-provisions of the separate but identical draft treaties the superpowers had submitted to the ENDC, before the General Assembly's decisive intervention and which had been thoroughly considered in the ENDC.[83] They constituted, according to the General Assembly's view, the essentials of the treaty. This is why the General Assembly claimed that the conclusion of a treaty on non-proliferation brooked no delay. The operative part of the identical texts of the draft treaties that the superpowers had submitted and of which the General Assembly thought highly had been formulated as follows:

ARTICLE 1

Each nuclear weapon state party to this treaty undertakes not to transfer to any recipient whatsoever nuclear weapons or other nuclear explosive devices or control over such weapons or explosive devices directly or indirectly, and not in any way to assist, encourage or otherwise acquire nuclear weapons or other nuclear explosives, devices or control over such weapons or explosive devices.

ARTICLE 2

Each non-nuclear weapon state party to this treaty undertakes not to receive the transfer from any transferor whatsoever of nuclear weapons or other nuclear explosive devices or control over such weapons or explosive devices directly or indirectly: not to manufacture or otherwise acquire nuclear weapons or other nuclear explosive devices; and not to seek or receive any assistance in the manufacture of nuclear weapons or other nuclear explosive devices.

Those two articles which constituted the very essence of any prohibition of the horizontal proliferation of nuclear weapons were adopted without alterations as Articles I and II of the final NPT. More negotiations, however, had to be conducted in order that the text of the NPT might provide more clarity on a number of important questions of specific interest to the NNWS-Non-Aligned states, thus satisfying the request for a balance of obligations and responsibilities. There was speculation, of which the General Assembly had been aware at the time it issued its resolution, that the negotiating parties would come to negotiate, within a short time, provisions which would be drafted with due regard to certain basic considerations and proposals of the Non-Aligned states. Such proposals had met with the favourable response in the ENDC. They were concerned with the drafting of positive provisions for an effective system of international safeguards and for a more complete article on the peaceful uses of nuclear energy. Both were provided in the draft treaties which met with the favourable response of the General Assembly but the necessity of setting them forth in greater detail in the treaty was recognized. There was also the need for provisions concerning the sharing of potential benefits from peaceful applications of nuclear reactors and the undertaking on the part of the nuclear weapon states to pursue negotiations in good faith (a good-faith clause) on measures regarding cessation of the nuclear arms race and disarmament. Both subjects were treated in the preamble of the draft treaties in the form of declarations of intention. However, the Non-Aligned states suggested that they should be formulated as an express obligation and as a more positive commitment in the main body of the treaty. There was also a remaining area of concern which was still being considered in the ENDC, with which the draft treaties, which seemed to have the endorsement of the General Assembly, did not deal. These were the 'security assurances'. If the NNWS renounced the manufacture or acquisition of nuclear weapons, they had to be given guarantees for their security. Thus, they had asked for security assurances in a positive as well as a negative form. Positive assurances would be promises on the part of the NWS that they would come to defend the NNWS in the event of a nuclear attack against any of them. Negative assurances would be promises whereby the NWS undertook that they would never use or threaten to use nuclear weapons against the NNWS.

A significant part of the General Assembly's powerful intervention in the negotiating process lies with the fact that this organ of the UN cleared up the great difficulty created by virtue of the continued insistence of the most militant part of the line up of the Non-Aligned states which were attempting to tie up in a single package of the NPT a number of other complicated questions of nuclear disarmament. The General Assembly fixed a very short time limit for final negotiations in the ENDC. By such means, it discouraged the prospects of concluding a NPT dependent on the simultaneous implementation of, or the explicit commitment on the part of the superpowers to, specific measures of nuclear disarmament. Such demands exceeded, according to the General Assembly, the commonly acceptable scope of the treaty. By giving the ENDC a specific mandate to be carried out by a certain time limit, the General Assembly judged the character of the NPT as a single arms control measure. The ENDC found itself in a position where it had to make a decision between what was ultimately desirable and what was practically possible within the margins of such a time limit. Even the most militant states among the Non-Aligned states in the ENDC seemed now to be tied down; they could do nothing but endorse the ENDC's singleness of purpose: the prohibition of the horizontal proliferation of nuclear weapons. A threat which was being systematically used that 'to press for such measures (i.e., measures of nuclear disarmament) at this stage in the negotiations would throw the whole non-proliferation issue back to the bilateral stage of the negotiations'[84] seemed to influence the choice the Non-Aligned states made. To considerable relief for them the ENDC was beginning to emerge from the bilateral context of negotiations, that prevailed in the ENDC up to the mid-sixties. Additionally and especially after the conclusion of the Outer Space Treaty in 1967, the chance to shake up the moderate policy of pursuing arms control measures, primarily as a political-settlement approach in the interest of commonly building up conditions of detente, had a decisive impact on Non-Aligned group decision-making.

The ground for such intervention by the General Assembly which rendered practically impossible the connection of the NPT with disarmament measures had been diligently prepared by the superpowers a long time ago. They had drafted and submitted to the General Assembly, on behalf of the ENDC, interim reports on the work of the negotiating body.[85] Thus, the General Assembly was kept informed during the negotiations occurring in the ENDC that it was intensively continuing its efforts to achieve agreement on the NPT. Therefore, consideration of disarmament measures either in the ENDC or in the UN could not be taken up in the present work of these bodies. They could perhaps be taken up in future work. Otherwise, consideration of such measures might turn out to be detrimental to the very purpose of the conclusion of the NPT. By such means, the way was paved for putting a damper on any attempts in the UN or the ENDC to bring real measures of disarmament to issue. In essence, any discussion about nuclear disarmament in the General Assembly or the ENDC was fragmentary and very tentative and took place only during the consideration of the non-proliferation issue and the chance of associating it with disarmament measures. It was clear that substantive discussion on the specific issue of GCD had ceased a long time before.

Since the General Assembly defined the timetable for submission of a draft treaty to it, the superpowers were able to retain control over the negotiating process. Because of their discretionary power to present draft treaties on a take it-or-leave it basis when they deemed it essential, they submitted to the ENDC new identical draft treaties in a very advanced stage of readiness, shortly before the due time of submission of the final draft treaty to the General Assembly.[86] By doing so, not only did they control the inclusions sought by the Non-Aligned states but also delivered to them the weight of the political responsibility to decide whether they would acquiesce in the completion of the negotiations as the General Assembly required. This weight of responsibility was increased by the intervention of the UN Secretary-General, who made a plea that the years of patient negotiations on a treaty on non-proliferation 'must now be brought to fruition'.[87] Finally, the text of the treaty was approved after it was improved by more detailed provisions as to a system of international safeguards and the development of peaceful uses of nuclear energy; also with provisions concerning the pursuit of negotiations in good faith for the cessation of the arms race, the promotion of disarmament and the availability of any potential benefits from any peaceful applications to the NNWS. The question of granting security assurances to the NNWS was to be met by the undertaking of the commitment on the part of the NWS to submit, as they eventually did, a resolution in the Security Council to make parallel declarations which amounted to promises of positive assurances. After all this a joint text of the treaty left the ENDC and came to the General Assembly which, after minor revisions in the text, commended by an overwhelming majority its adoption by the world community.[88]

The 'forgotten Conference'[89] of the NNWS-Non-Aligned states was held later on that year. However, as it had to deal with a subject which already constituted a *fait accompli*, since the NPT had been approved and signed by the world community, its role was necessarily redefined: it dedicated its working session to finding means for the NPT to obtain the widest possible adherence.

Conclusions

Very early in the sixties, a changing UN framework for negotiations came into existence. A so-called decentralized UN disarmament structure was established. The main feature of it was the establishment of a negotiating body, for the first time in the history of the UN, outside the world organization's legal purview but with links to it. The UN was called to play a rather more limited role in comparison with the past, that of making recommendations to the ENDC, while its direct influence on the negotiations was diminished. The fact that the UN was restricted to making only recommendations without attempting to enforce concrete policies of its own facilitated the disarmament negotiations on the ground that it left states with freedom of action in their search for common approaches to disarmament.

As the UN conceded its primary role to the superpowers to construct the negotiating body, namely the ENDC, there was an East-West grip on its management and operation. The continuation of ENDC's life came about as a consequence of a broader consensus reached by the UN's community.

During this period, the UN including the decentralized ENDC proved to have a realistic vision of the nature and the scope of the solutions which had to be sought in the negotiating process. What the UN and the ENDC achieved during this period was to take a decision that disarmament was not directly negotiable but could be successful in the long run if a reliable degree of common understanding could be created and moves by all sides in matters of common interest could be inspired. To do so, they had to avoid to dealing solely with the complicated comprehensive plans for disarmament and concentrating more on the quest for arms control measures as a political-settlement approach; disarmament should await until after a political settlement.

An essential criterion for any judgement concerning the UN's contribution should depend on the importance of the problems solved looked at within the broader context of international relations. In the light of this assumption upon which a criterion of substance should rely, it should be accepted that an assessment of the work done by the UN and the ENDC during this period should depend on a judgement on the political contribution of the solutions arrived at, not on their efficiency as disarmament measures. As a consequence, it may be concluded that the UN provided the most convenient means of putting into effect the foundations of the period of *detente*; while the UN's quest for arms control measures should be regarded as the most positive action in the field of political *detente*. At the beginning of the sixties, the UN embarked on disarmament negotiations under Cold War conditions; by the end of the decade it had managed to break the Cold War barriers. The world entered into a serious dialogue and a constructive rapprochement was achieved between states and particularly those with which nuclear disarmament was concerned, thanks to the UN's constructive search for arms control measures. Peace and negotiations were put in a better perspective and accomplishments like the PTBT, the Outer Space Treaty and the NPT disposed states to undertake further commitments.

Beyond this point, further analysis of the role of the UN in this period can illustrate how the likelihood of the maximization of its potential to act effectively can be achieved. The effective negotiations of the years dealt with in this chapter were based upon a wide consensus which consisted of the co-operative attitude of all the three political groups of the UN. The central and dominant idea or thesis is that the UN dealing with the disarmament business should reflect the will of the world community in terms of structure, agenda and scope of the negotiations.

However, it should be pointed out that there are certain limitations which come into play and determine the conditions upon which the consensus should come to rely. These conditions derive from an inter-correlation analysis between the nature of the UN; the issue which it intends to remedy; and the existing realities of the world. In this case, a correlation analysis between the scope of the organization and the nuclear disarmament issue verifies and focuses the centrality of the issue around the great powers which are the nuclear weapon states and, therefore, have the power to contribute to the solution of the problem. This logic leads to the conclusion that the UN's disarmament seeking practices should provide an entity wherein structures and functions including the scope of the negotiations, are built up along lines drawn or necessarily approved by the great powers. Furthermore, the successful response of the UN becomes more likely to be increased when the other powers accede to such great-power leadership of the UN, or to put it differently, when the major powers are ready to determine jointly with the other states the negotiating arrangement.

The study of the period covered in this chapter should be regarded as a leading case-study, since it has produced and reinforced the assumptions and axioms to which reference has been made. A consensus means a broad agreement on the institutional format and agenda of negotiations which either will be made primarily by the major powers or will receive a very positive welcome by them. Both are decisive factors towards allowing the major powers to have a decisive, not exclusive say in the negotiations.

In the sixties, such a broad consensus was achieved and marked the life of the UN with success. At the beginning of the decade, the UN passed from being an organization of American dominance to an organization wherein there was a very positive balanced East-West participation in the making of the new framework for disarmament. The new framework was characterized by the innovation of the decentralization of the negotiating process from the ambit of the UN. Thus there arose a paradoxical but well-suited situation whereby, despite the shift in the UN's membership taking place throughout the whole period in favour of neither the Eastern nor the Western group, there was an increase of the role for the superpowers to the point where they could have a significant degree of influence over the disarmament business. This was the result of an unprecedented phenomenon of the broad consensus of the three political groups which constituted the entirety of the UN to the institutionalization of a new framework for disarmament negotiations. The superpowers ensured, under such institution building, a leadership to which, it should be remembered, the Non-Aligned group did not object. On the contrary, the Non-Aligned group not only supported such institutional setting but also its continuation.

If the real consensus of the three political groups on the UN's institutional building was the one prerequisite for the UN's successful response to the nuclear disarmament problem, the other was the consensus on the agenda for negotiations. The unanimity among the political groups led unreservedly to the quest of peace through arms control measures which were selected by the superpowers in advance.

The Non-Aligned states had just began their rise as political force and would increase the importance of their role in the subsequent phases of the UN's disarmament activities. However, at this time they were more interested in securing and making apparent their political presence in the international organs which dealt with the disarmament question than to challenge the way they had been built up. This was manifested as a willingness to accede to what the superpowers were ready to agree. Their concern for the ban on test explosions and for curtailing the proliferation of the nuclear weapons was expressed in the successive Conferences held in Belgrade and Cairo. Their declarations at those Conferences and their concrete actions taken and policies followed all were characterized by their political determination to act as mediators or conciliators between the two blocs. Moreover, as has been noted, when the process of negotiations for the NPT came very close to its completion, the Non-Aligned group modified its modest position in order to make its involvement in the decision- making relating to disarmament and arms control negotiations more substantial. The group passed from the original position it held at the beginning to mid-sixties, when its profound concern was to participate in the international negotiations, to the evolution of a new position. This was concerned with the growing desire to maximize the group's arithmetical force by its substantial participation in the disarmament business. This desire should, in turn, be associated with the remarkable shift in UN membership which was taking place at the time and through which the UN was becoming truly universal. The tracing of the course of change in the Non-Aligned group's attitude provides a picture of the evolution on their part of a new variable behaviour. At the end of the day, the Non-Aligned states were found to have learned to seek disarmament or arms control measures through universal approaches. The ENDC had already felt their attempt to affiliate the NPT with disarmament steps as a strong expression of their willingness to have a say in the agenda making process. The universal approaches *vis-à-vis* the negotiations to which they had been introduced during the NPT were accompanied by their desire to enhance the presence of their arithmetic force in the substance of the decision-making of the negotiations. This would have been more fitted for a worldwide institutional framework than that which the UN currently provided which meant that the very suitable and realistic decentralized institutional UN framework for the conduct of negotiations would attract reformist attention and could be destabilized.

Notes

1. Document TNDC/3, 16 March 1960.
2. Letter from Mr. Krushchev to Mr. Macmillan, 27 June 1960, cited in Parliamentary Papers, CMND, Paper 1152, April 1962.
3. UN Document A/C.1/24/PV.1966, 21 November 1969, p. 6.
4. UNGA Resolution 1378 (XIV) of 20 November 1959.
5. Brian Urquhart (1960), *Hammarskjold*, Bodley Head: London, pp 323-324.
6. UNGA Resolution 1660 (XVI), 28 November 1961.
7. United Nations (1970), *The United Nations and Disarmament, 1945-1970*, United Nations: New York, p. 86.
8. First Conference of Heads of State or Government of the Non-Aligned Countries: Declaration, Belgrade, September 1961, cited in Odette Jankowitsch and Karl Sauvant (eds) (1978), *Third World Without Superpowers, The Collected Documents of Non-Aligned Countries*, Oceana Publications: New York, p. 6.
9. Harold Jacobson and Eric Stein (1966), *Diplomats, Scientists and Politicians: The United States and the Nuclear Test Ban Negotiations*, University of Michigan Press: Ann Harbor, pp. 356-357.
10. Sydney Bailey (1964), *The Secretariat of the United Nations*, Pall Mall Press: London, p. 50.
11. Yugoslav Government (1961), *The Conference of Heads of State or Government of Non-Aligned Countries*, Yugoslav Government:

Belgrade, pp. 85-98: Speech delivered by Haile Selassie I. For further discussion upon the troika proposal from a Non-Aligned point of view see in the same publication the speeches delivered by Tito, President of Yugoslavia, pp. 153-170, esp. p. 167, and by Bandaranaike, Prime Minister of Ceylon, pp. 175-182, esp. p. 179.

12. Cecil Crabb (1965), *The Elephants and the Grass: A Study of Non-Alignment,* Praeger: New York, p. 130.

13. Ruth Russell (1968), *The United Nations and United States Security Policy*, The Brookings Institution: Washington, p. 73. For the draft resolution submitted by the Soviet Union concerning the troika concept see UN Document A/C.1/L. 249, 13 October 1960.

14. Allan Gotlieb (1965), *Disarmament and International Law,* Canadian Institute of International Affairs: Toronto, p. 66; for the co-chair institution see Document ENDC/1 of 14 March 1962,

15. Noel Baker and Others (1978), *Disarm or Die : A Disarmament Reader for the Leaders and the Peoples of the World*, Taylor & Francis: London, pp. 30-31, 40-42; see also Hedley Bull (1961), *The Control of the Arms Race*, Chatto & Windus: London, pp. 37-39.

16. Michael Sullivan (1975), 'Conference at the Crossroads: Future Prospects for the Conference of the Committee on Disarmament', *International Organization*, vol. 29, no 2, Spring, p. 399.

17. Document TNDC/PV. 2, Agreement on Procedural Matters, 15 March 1960, para. 5.

18. Document ENDC/PV. 2, 16 March 1962, p. 12.

19. Document ENDC/PV. 2, 16 March 1962 p. 21. Document ENDC/C.I/PV. 6, 22 May 1962, Mr. Dean, United States.

20. Document ENDC/C.I/PV. 9, 26 May 1962, p. 43, Sir Michael Wright, United Kingdom.

21. Leo Mates (1972), *Non-Alignment: Theory and Current Policy,* The Institute of International Politics and Oceana Publications: Belgrade, p. 263.

22. Crabb, op.cit., p. 102; see also Avi Beker (1985), *Disarmament Without Order: The Politics of Disarmament at the United Nations*, Greenwood Press: Westport (Conn.) & London, p. 62.

23. The Yugoslav Government, op.cit., p.113; for the Nehru's view see pp. 107-118.

24. Robert Mortimer (1980), *Third World Coalition in International Politics*, Praeger: New York, p. 12.

25. For the arms control policy of the Non-Aligned states see: UN Document, A/C.I/17/PV.1724, 14 November 1962, p.152, Mr. Vakil,

Iran; see also Document ENDC/C.I/PV. 2, 5 April 1963, p. 40, Mr. Lall, India and Document ENDC/C.I/PV. 6, 22 May 1962, p. 35, Mrs. Myrdal, Sweden.

26. Document ENDC/PV.7, 23 May 1962, p.7, Mexico.

27. Samir Ahmed (1963), 'The Role of the Neutrals in the Geneva Negotiations', *Disarmament and Arms Control*, vol.1, p. 22.

28. G. H. Jansen (1966), *Afro-Asia and Non-Alignment*, Faber & Faber: London, p. 299.

29. UN Document, A/C.I/17/PV.1253, 22 October 1962, p. 42.

30. For example UNGA Resolution 1762 A (XVII), 6 November 1962.

31. Document ENDC/C.I/PV.7, 23 May 1962, p. 29.

32. Document ENDC/I/Add.I, 23 March 1962.

33. The GCD received a concrete shape immediately after the ENDC came into existence. It happened when the superpowers submitted in year 1962 separate draft proposals. Both proposals envisage three stages. The original draft of the Soviet Union proposed a four year programme with fifteen months for each of the first two stages, while a later Soviet draft extended the period for implementing the whole programme to five years and extended the first stage to two years. The United States proposal provided for two stages of three years, each to be followed by a third stage the duration of which would be fixed at the time the treaty would be signed. For a good discussion of the GCD plans see Leonard Beaton (1972), *The Reform of Power: A Proposal for an International Security System*, Viking Press: New York, pp. 73-117.

34. Baker and Others, op.cit., pp. 40-41.

35. Jean Bureau (1983), 'Decision Making for Arms Limitation in France' in Hans Braunch and Duncan Clarke (eds) *Decision Making for Arms Limitation: Assessment and Prospects*, Cambridge University Press: Cambridge (Mass), pp. 81-85. President Charles de Gaule explaining why France refused to take its seat in the ENDC argued: 'If there should one day be a meeting of states that truly want to organize disarmament and such meetings should, in our mind, be composed of the four atomic weapon states, France would participate in it whole heartedly. Until such time, she does not see the need for taking part in proceedings, whose inevitable outcome is disillusion'. See also *New York Times*, 20 February 1962.

36. Arthur Lall (1964), *Negotiating Disarmament, The Eighteen Nation Disarmament Conference: The First Two Year, 1962-64*, Cornell Research Papers in International Studies, no 2, Center for International Studies, Cornell University: New York, p. 70.

37. Treaty on Principles Governing the Activities of States in the Exploration and Use of Outer Space, Including the Moon and Other Celestial Bodies. Signed at London, Moscow and Washington on 27 January 1967. Entered into force on 10 October 1967.

38. Document ENDC/70 of 12 December 1962. The Memorandum of Understanding Between the United States and the USSR Regarding the Establishment of a Direct Communications Link was signed at Geneva on 20 June 1963. Entered into force on 20 June 1963.

39. Document ENDC/C.1/PV. 6, 20 May 1962, Mr. Zorin, USSR.

40. E. L. Burns (1965), 'Can the Spread of Nuclear Weapons be Stopped?' *International Organization*, vol. xix, no 4, Autumn, pp. 857-860, esp. p. 859.

41. Document ENDC/SC.I/PV. 48, 11 December 1962, p. 30.

42. For the role of the Non-Aligned group in relation to test ban negotiations see Samir Ahmed, (1964), *The Neutrals and the Test Ban Negotiations*, Carnegie Endowment: New York, 1964.

43. Homer Jack (1964), 'Seventeen Continue', *Bulletin of Atomic Scientists,* June, pp. 43-45.

44. UNGA Resolution. 1762 A (XVII), 6 November 1962, para. 6.

45. On the negotiation of the NPT, see Elizabeth Young (1969), *The Control of Proliferation: The 1969 Treaty in Hindsight and Forecast*, Institute for Strategic Studies: London; see also Georges Quester (1973), *The Politics of Nuclear Proliferation*, University of Illinois Press: Urbana; George Fischer (1971), *The Non-Proliferation of Nuclear Weapons*, Europa: London.

46. UNGA Resolution 2149 (XXI), 4 November 1966, adopted by 110 votes to 1 with 1 abstention; see also UNGA Resolution 2153 A (XXI), 17 December 1966, adopted by 97 votes to 2 with 3 abstentions.

47. UN Document A/C.1/22/PV. 1552, 15 December 1967, p. 14.

48. Official Records of the Disarmament Commission, Supplement for January-December 1965, UN Document DC/227.

49. John Simpson (1982), 'Global Non-Proliferation Policies: Retrospect and Prospect', *Review of International Studies*, vol. 8, p. 73.

50. General Assembly Official Records, Twentieth session, Annexes, Agenda item 106, UN Document A/5976.

51. Document ENDC/PV. 297, 18 May 1967, p. 5; see also UN Document A/21/PV. 1448, 9 November 1966, p. 123.

52. Michael Mandelbaum (1979), *The Nuclear Question: The United States and Nuclear Weapons, 1946-1976*, Cambridge University Press: Cambridge, p. 139.

53. John Stoessinger (1977), *The United Nations and the Superpowers: China, Russia & America*, Random House: New York, p.173.

54. Myrdal, op.cit., pp.166-168, esp. p. 168.

55. For the text of the UNGA Resolution 2028 see United Nations, op.cit., pp. 277-280.

56. Document ENDC/PV. 294, 16 March 1967, p. 5, Mr. Khallaf, UAR.

57. UN Document A/C.1/22/PV.1555, 18 December 1967, p. 5, Mr. Salim, Tanzania.

58. Document ENDC/PV. 323, 14 August 1967, p. 14 Mr. Zelekke, Ethiopia.

59. For the Eastern and Western point of view see the following Documents: ENDC/PV. 326, 29 August 1967, p. 6; ENDC/PV. 327, 31 August 1967, p. 4, and ENDC/PV. 373, 5 March 1968, p. 13, Mr. Winkler, Czechoslovakia; ENDC/PV. 358, 23 January 1968, p. 9, Mr. Mulley, United Kingdom; ENDC/PV. 326, 29 August 1967, p. 6, Mr. Goldblat, Poland. A similar view can be found in the literature; see for example John Edmonds (1984), 'Nuclear Spread and Test Bans' in Josephine O' Connor Howe (ed.), *Armed Peace: The Search for World Security*, Macmillan for the Council for Arms Control: London, p. 73.

60. For the Non-Aligned viewpoint with regard to the platform for a balance of obligations and responsibilities see the following Documents: ENDC/PV. 298, 23 May 1967, p. 9; ENDC/PV. 300, 27 May 1967, pp. 5 and 11; ENDC/PV. 295, 21 March 1967, p. 20; ENDC/PV. 331, 17 September 1967, p. 9; ENDC/PV. 348, 16 November 1967, p. 7; ENDC/PV. 364, 13 February 1968, p. 15.

61. Document ENDC/PV. 326, 29 August 1967, p. 5.

62. Ralph Townley (1968), *The United Nations, A View from Within*, Charles Scribner's Sons: New York, pp. 113-114.

63. William Epstein (1976), *The Last Chance: Nuclear Proliferation and Arms Control*, Collier-Macmillan: London, p. 122.

64. UN Document A/C.1/22/PV.1551, 14 December 1967, p. 27.

65. Ibid.

66. Ibid., p. 17.

67. John Barton and LawrenceWeiler (eds) (1976), *International Arms Control*, Stanford University Press: Stanford, pp. 296-297.

68. UN Document A/C.1/22/PV.1551, 14 December 1967, p. 27, Mr. Correa Do Lago, Brazil; see also the views of Pakistan in UN Document A/C.I/21/PV.1434, 28 October 1966.

69. Document ENDC/PV. 300, 30 May 1967, p. 12; see also Document ENDC/PV. 304, 13 June 1967, p. 6, and Document ENDC/PV. 331, 19

September 1967, pp. 17-19, Mr. Castaneda, Mexico.

70. Document ENDC/PV. 331, 19 September 1967, p. 9, Mr. Castaneda, Mexico.
71. UN Document A/C.I/22/PV. 1551, 14 December 1967, p. 13, Mr. Dhar, India.
72. UN Document A/C.1/22/PV.1553, 15 December 1967, p. 2, Mr. Akwer, Ghana.
73. Ibid., p. 2.
74. UNGA Resolution 2153 B (XXI), 17 November1966 adopted by a vote of 48 to 1 with 59 abstentions; UNGA Resolution 2346 B (XXII), 19 December 1966, adopted by a vote of 110 to none with 8 abstentions.
75. E. L. Burns, op.cit., p. 804.
76. UN Document A/C.1/22/PV.1552, 15 December 1967, Mr. Malary, Ethiopia.
77. United Nations, op.cit., p. 307.
78. Mates, op.cit., p. 347; see also Jasip Djerdja (1968), 'The Non-Nuclear Countries and Their Course of Action', *Review of International Affairs,* vol. xix, no 130, March, pp. 1-3. See also Ciro Zoppo (1969), 'Nuclear Technology, Weapons and the Third World', *Annals of the American Academy of Political and Social Sciences,* November, pp.113-125, esp. pp.120-2.
79. UN Document A/C.121/PV.1469, 17 November 1966, p. 4, Mr. Ali, Pakistan.
80. Leo Mates (1965), 'Universality of the United Nations', *Review of International Affairs,* vol. 16, no 316, April, p. 15.
81. UN Document, A/C.1/22/ PV. 1552, 15 December 1967, p. 12.
82. UNGA Resolution 2346 A (XXII), 19 December 1967 was adopted by 112 to 1 with 4 abstentions.
83. Official Records of the Disarmament Commission, Supplement for 1967 and 1968, UN Document DC/230 and Add.1, Documents ENDC/192 and ENDC/193.
84. Document ENDC/295, 21 March 1967, p. 4, Lord Chalfont, United Kingdom.
85. UN Document A/C.1/21/PV. 1551, 14 December 1967, p. 17.
86. Document ENDC/PV. 320, 8 August 1967, p. 4.
87. Document ENDC/PV. 357, 18 January 1968, pp. 4-5, Mr. Protitch, Special Representative of the UN Secretary-General.
88. UNGA Resolution 2373 (XXII) 12 June 1968, was adopted by 95 votes to 4 with 21 abstentions.
89. Epstein, op.cit., pp.128-134.

4 A retreat from the consensus (1969-1977)

A strategic dilemma for the UN

During and after the negotiation of the Sea Bed Treaty, in 1970 and 1971,[1] a parallel to the Outer Space Treaty of 1967 and the Antarctic Treaty of 1959,[2] the case at issue at the UN was whether the tendency to discuss and negotiate arms control measures should be carried on endlessly in a haphazard way or be set more clearly within the overall framework of progress towards disarmament. A continuation of the UN's focus of attention on arms control measures in the seventies would have resulted in a diversion of the world organization from the real business of disarmament on a more permanent basis. It was a tactical choice among equally disagreeable alternatives which faced the UN. The UN's dilemma seemed to be shared by the Non-Aligned states which, as their arithmetical force in the UN was rapidly growing, were keen on strengthening the role of the UN in the disarmament process; and they therefore claimed dissatisfaction with the pursuit of piecemeal arms control measures.

A more active engagement of the UN in the disarmament process could only be seen in connection with the Conference of the Committee on Disarmament (CCD, 1969-1977), the new label attached to the former ENDC, and its willingness to comply with the directions of the General Assembly of the UN. The extent to which the CCD would correspond to the mandates coming from the Assembly depended almost entirely on the two superpowers because of their privileged position within the CCD. The consensus principle and the presence of their military allies in terms of numerical power neutralized the political presence of the Non-Aligned states.

During the sixties the superpowers' selective agenda in the ENDC favoured measures which strengthened the non-proliferation regime (PTBT and NPT) and which thus accorded with the General Assembly's directions expressed through its resolutions. It can be concluded that the agenda of the ENDC and the mandates of the General Assembly of the UN were mutually reinforcing. In the seventies the General Assembly attempted to play its role as an agenda setter in a different way from the one it had played in the sixties. With the massive support of the Non-Aligned states, which had established during the negotiation of the NPT a lively sense of collective responsibility on disarmament mainly due to the commitment of most of them not to acquire nuclear weapons, the UN made an overall reappraisal of its strategy. It called more consistently for specific measures of nuclear disarmament, a comprehensive test ban treaty (CTBT) as a specific arms control measure to lead substantially to nuclear disarmament, and the adoption of a comprehensive programme of disarmament. The influence of the Non-Aligned states in the General Assembly created a distinctly new approach: the so called request for a 'comprehensive programme of disarmament'.[3] The initiative was the first in the history of the negotiations at the UN where a group of states not belonging to the East or West camp attempted to revive the concern of the world organization for disarmament by submitting proposals which not only called for the adoption of a programme of disarmament but constituted substantial modification of the previous unrealistic plans for GCD which the superpowers had submitted in 1962.[4]

The new approach attempted to associate the arms control measures with 'the ultimate goal' of GCD. According to this new approach, GCD was regarded as an end state which could be reached only gradually with an organized sequence of measures.[5] As a matter of fact, such a comprehensive programme of disarmament did not run counter to the objectives of the GCD. Furthermore, it attempted rather to rehabilitate and 'sidestep the central difficulty of GCD' by means of looking for a succession of systematic moves towards GCD.[6] As such, it was thought it would introduce some orderliness and rationality into the negotiating process. Myrdal, one of the leaders of the Non-Aligned group in the negotiations in the CCD, giving the history of the negotiations at the UN made an accurate assessment of the scepticism that surrounded the UN and afterwards gave the real meaning of the new approach:

> The history of disarmament should have been a series of positive, purposeful, effective steps towards the goal which is acclaimed by everybody. We are still waiting for a first decisive or even a serious step to be taken.
>
> In attempting here to formulate a rational and ethical strategy for disarmament, I conclude from experience that we have regrettably to give up the holistic approach of GCD by means of an orderly series of steps for implementation and a present timetable.
>
> A new comprehensive grasp of the disarmament problems is necessary. While abandoning the attempt to get a general agreement in one stroke, we must seek a solution that combines specific measures into an integrated whole. These may take the form of international legislation of multilateral or bilateral agreements or of unilateral moves on the road to the acknowledged goal. [7]

The comprehensive programme of disarmament seemed to follow the middle course between two existing schools of thought concerning the way to achieve disarmament thus filling the gap between them. Advocates of the one school favoured the idea of seeing general disarmament come about by way of an all-encompassing agreement; while the other school of thought, being far more flexible and realistic, was attached to the idea of gradualism as a step by step approach, where each step taken is a significant move towards disarmament that creates confidence, brings experience and generally makes easier the taking of further steps in the future.[8]

The new approach was espoused with enthusiasm by its supporters, the Non-Aligned states and the Secretary-General of the UN, because, as it was amplified by the resolutions of the General Assembly and the annexed working papers of the Non-Aligned states, it sought to reassert the primary responsibility of the UN in the field of disarmament with subordinate roles for the bilateral institution of Strategic Arms Limitation Talks. (The SALT talks began in 1969 between the United States and the Soviet Union and led, if fitfully, to the Stategic Arms Reduction Talks and Reduction of Intermediate Range Nuclear Forces). To be effective, the broadening of the UN's role in all arms control negotiations was asked for and was accompanied by constant appeals from the UN to the superpowers to keep the UN informed on the progress of their bilateral negotiations. Generally, if the new approach was to be adopted for negotiations by the CCD it would have to accommodate the participation of all states in disarmament in an effort to resist the centripetal tendencies of UN members and especially of the two superpowers. The comprehensive programme of disarmament was far more realistic than the GCD plans of the United States and the Soviet Union; not overambitious but still ambitious. Moreover, the General Assembly's mandate to the CCD was concerned with the undertaking of serious negotiations alternating between realistic measures of nuclear disarmament, the working out of a specific comprehensive programme for disarmament and the negotiation of a CTBT.

The effect in the seventies of the redefinition of the General Assembly's role as an agenda setter for the CCD led to a major deterioration in the relationship between these two institutions as it became increasingly clear that the real agenda-setting role remained in the CCD and, more particularly, in the hands of the two superpowers. The superpowers turned a deaf ear to the claims for the CCD to concentrate on broader issues of disarmament based on being 'duty bound to take into account the will of the majority of the General Assembly as reflected in relevant resolutions'.[9]

This scenario remained substantially unchanged until 1978. Furthermore, the superpowers maintained their pattern of refusing to keep the UN and the CCD abreast of the bilateral negotiations they were undertaking elsewhere in spite of repeated calls by the General Assembly and the Secretary General of the UN to do so. The superpowers claimed that the bilateral talks were not within the purview of the UN and they did not therefore create an obligation to give information to the UN about them.[10] This refusal to give information amounted to a lack of common demands, identifications, and expectations - i.e., the perspectives of the effective elites of the world could not produce what is more traditionally described as political will for productive co-operation within the UN *vis-à-vis* the CCD.

The negative response of the CCD to the General Assembly's calls made the Non-Aligned states realize that the decision-making in the UN was substantially circumvented by that body. Whereas in the UN, Assembly progress in the seventies had become dependent on the Non-Aligned states, their role in the decentralized multilateral body in Geneva was substantially limited. The Non-Aligned states were becoming restless since they felt confined by the existing UN disarmament structure as if they were wearing suits and boots tailored for someone else. However, having established themselves as an irreplaceable factor in the work of the world organization, these states identified themselves with the prospective fortunes of that organization which seemed to be, in their perspective, at stake.

Challenges to the old orthodoxy: The Non-Aligned group's changing view of the role of the UN in the global process of disarmament

The Non-Aligned states in the decade of the seventies were concentrating their efforts towards maximizing the UN's effectiveness on the international scene. International relations, according to the convictions of the Non-Aligned group which were expressed in its successive conferences, were entering a new phase characterized by increasing political and economic interdependence. New centres of power were emerging and they considered that it was time that the bipolar power structure gave way to a growing multipolarity in international relations the main feature of which was an expanding interdependence. The UN should become the centre of reflection of such interdependence, an instrument for the accomplishment of economic and political change. It is by virtue of these fundamental reasons that the organization should shoulder more responsibility for economic and certainly political changes in the broad context of international relations. They believed that a universalist-oriented international organization, like the UN, was a necessary component of any successful attack on the major problems of the world. As Beker observed, 'the United Nations, which was initially established as a security instrument was transformed into a forum in which new states began to press their claims for changes in the international system'.[11] Mojsov, head of the permanent mission of Yugoslavia to the UN, put it rather more prescriptively when he argued that 'the UN should become a forum for the establishment of a new system of international relations which should be responsive to the contemporary requirements of the entire international community'.[12] He added that the UN should be shaped in a different way which could guarantee equitable co-operation in international relations.

It is significant that whenever the Non-Aligned states addressed their conferences on the subject of democratization of international relations, they immediately proceeded to call for the fostering of such democratization through increasing recourse to the institutions of the UN. Such interconnection was abundantly manifested and declared constantly in their conferences throughout the decade. Accordingly, they declared in Belgrade in 1969 that 'the United Nations should be a more representative and effective instrument for the regulation of international relations in the lasting and long term interests of all countries'.[13] They also repeated at the summit meeting which was held in Lusaka in 1970 that the UN provided the most suitable forum to facilitate the democratization of international relations.[14] The significance of this categoric statement lies with the fact that the political declaration of the Lusaka conference of the Non-Aligned states was entirely concerned with the democratization of international relations. This being so, the democratization of international relations emerged as a major political platform that opened up new prospects for concerted actions on the part of the Non-Aligned states throughout the seventies. Once again, at their summit meeting in Algiers in 1973 they expressed the firm conviction that states and particularly the Non-Aligned states that constituted the majority of the UN membership should continue to work 'with a view to bringing about a change in international relations towards democracy and equality of all states and to ensure that decisions which could affect big and small countries are not taken without their full participation on an equal basis'.[15] Immediately after, they proceeded to confirm what they had agreed upon in their meeting at the UN headquarters and Georgetown in 1972 that 'the United Nations should be universally supported as the principal democratic instrument of equitable and peaceful co-operation among states'.[16] At the last of their conferences during the specific period examined in this chapter, that was held in Colombo in 1976, they reiterated their viewpoint that the UN constituted the principal instrument in the pursuit of the objective of the democratization of international relations and of creating conditions serving the cause of peace, justice, equality and international co-operation.[17]

While, as was mentioned previously, in the sixties the Non-Aligned states had acted upon the sweeping political determination to strengthen their presence in the international scene and not exclusively within the UN, in the decade of seventies they approached the UN with their preoccupation that the upgrading of the world organization would develop their status in the international scene. Already constituting the majority of the UN, politically controlling the General Assembly, they were proceeding with confidence to promote the world organisation's role. They no longer wished for the status of mediators or observers which they had been willing to accept up until now. Their policies followed their fundamental axiom of demand; in the UN it was they, not the superpowers, who were in the mainstream of global decision-making, and, hence, they had to be placed similarly in all other world structures of authority. For them, the global decision-making could not find any better centralized structure of authority - in which effective participants in world power process can interact - than that of the UN system. As the UN in its constitutional scheme maintains the nation-state as the basic unit of its political structure, a significant increase in the competence and role of the UN and its democratization - with increases in the range of participants - would have the positive effect of upgrading their world status, both individually and as a group. The more powerful the UN's authority, the greater becomes the role of the Non-Aligned states.

It was their primary concern with the democratization of international relations, which they perceived should be pursued through the United Nations system, that made the Non-Aligned states assign the primary role and responsibility to the world organization in the field of disarmament. It should be said that any transfer of power from the UN to any other political institution, expressing bilateral or non-multilateral understandings, would have been deemed by the Non-Aligned states as diminishing the prestige of the UN organization in an age when it was used systematically to bring about political and economic changes in the international field and more specifically the advent of calls for a new international economic order.

This argument becomes even more convincing if one takes into consideration the tendency of the Non-Aligned states, manifested in the activities and resolutions of the UN, to regard disarmament as being generally aimed at overcoming economic disparities and supporting the process of eliminating underdevelopment. This was the manifestation of a new approach whereby the UN, on the insistence of the Non-Aligned group, had begun reappraising and questioning the consideration of disarmament as an independent political issue. There was a tendency of viewing it not only in its security dimension but as a process which could lead to the diversion of the resources used for military purposes to peaceful ones and therefore to the improvement of the economic position of the developing states.

The new approach manifested itself very soon in the organs of the UN. Already in 1962, the Secretary-General of the UN U Thant, in the introduction of a study he submitted to the General Assembly on the economic and social consequences of disarmament, emphasized that the sense of urgency with respect to disarmament not only sprang from 'the existence of a threat to mankind that has grown into one of mass destruction'; but also 'from the consequences that the resources that make this threat possible are being diverted from the tasks of lightening the burdens and enriching the lives of individuals and of society'.[18] Since then the process had developed step-by-step and from the mid-sixties began to command increasing attention in both the General Assembly and the Economic and Social Council (ECOSOC).[19] However, it should be pointed out that during this period this approach did not gain any substantial linkage with the disarmament debates and negotiations.

The near completion of the decolonization process in the beginning of the seventies led the Non-Aligned states faced with staggering economic problems to occupy the UN with the issues of international economic relations and especially with the problem of the advancement of their economic position. The hyperactive diplomacy of the Non-Aligned world to make the UN pay intermittent attention to their economic problems shifted the main centre of attention to the difficult problems of economic development. As Townley noted, the debate on economic development 'permeated practically every discussion in the organization, whatever the subject, be it human rights or disarmament'.[20] Any subject which could promote development came increasingly into the focus of interest and attempts were made to associate it with the efforts for economic progress of the developing states, the Third World. Among them was disarmament. In this context, actions were taken by the organs of the UN in favour of the organization taking seriously into consideration such a widened approach to disarmament. Very early in 1970, the General Assembly formalized the link between disarmament and development calling for a close link between the second development decade and the disarmament decade. By doing so it realized that

> the success of international development activities will depend in large measure on improvement in the general international situation, particularly on progress towards general and complete disarmament under effective international control. Progress towards general and complete disarmament should release substantial additional resources which could be utilized for the purpose of economic and social development, in particular that of developing countries. There should, therefore, be a close link between the second UN development decade and the disarmament decade.[21]

Thus, the Non-Aligned states endorsed the supreme authority of the UN regarding disarmament because of their predominant perception which ran through the UN during the whole period, that disarmament generally including nuclear disarmament, must be negotiated as an integral part of wider global issues and most importantly should not be pursued in isolation from considerations of economic viability. The Non-Aligned states argued that 'it is incontestable that there is an integral connection between politics and economics and it is erroneous to approach economic affairs in isolation from politics'.[22]

The Non-Aligned states saw the opening, institutionalization and the further strengthening of the talks which took place outside the UN after 1969 as evidence of increased bilateralism and regarded it as anathema to the democratic pattern of international relations they were attempting to impose through the UN system. The group also saw SALT as an institution that emerged to perpetuate the status quo and therefore as eroding the prestige, status and competence of the UN. Their position became gradually a strong conviction that the bilateral scheme of SALT in the way it was developing, would prove to be concerned more with nuclear arms control and the balance of power than with disarmament. The Non-Aligned states did not hesitate to complain during the whole period that there was an apparent tendency on the part of the superpowers to bypass the world organization in dealing with international issues of crucial importance.[23] As such 'it have had a negative effect not only on the world organization but also on international relations as a whole'.[24] 'The destiny of the world', they argued, 'should not rest with a small syndicate of states'.[25] For them it was more than essential to hold out against all tendencies which could undermine the attachment to the UN or weaken its involvement in the world issues like disarmament. The prevalent analysis among the Non-Aligned states, therefore, was that the superpowers were prepared to use the multilateral machinery that surrounds the UN when it suited their convenience and had been willing to ignore it when their interests so dictated. They believed that this approach should come to an end; the basic international issues and among them disarmament should be settled in the UN in such a way as to contribute both to the role and prestige of the world organization. It was their view that the UN should be restored as the central focal point in the international scene.

The restructuring process

The beginning of the seventies signified the undertaking of large scale efforts at reforms of the CCD by the Non-Aligned states. Having initiated the restructuring process, they seemed to see two choices. On the one hand, they could allow the arms negotiations to be dependent on the initiatives and agreements reached primarily between the two superpowers, with only a marginal role for their group; on the other hand, they could take over the initiative in the UN and in the CCD; and use both arenas to reorient both institutions towards strengthening the role of the organization as well as the role of the uncommitted nations. They decided for the latter. 'To strengthen the role and the efficacy of the UN', to 'work towards future democratization of the UN' [26] to secure the 'widest participation of member-states on a footing of equality in the decision making process'[27] were objectives formulated at gatherings of the Non-Aligned states in Lusaka in 1970, in Georgetown in 1972, and Colombo in 1976, aiming at confronting the 'big power tendency to monopolize' or manage the world organization in the direction of their own interests.[28] Directed to give effect to the democratization of the UN where all the states independent of size have equal footing, the Non-Aligned position used these goals translated into demands to confront the recognition of the 'main responsibilities' of the superpowers. In reality, the restructuring process which the uncommitted states engaged in was a challenge to the privileged position the superpowers enjoyed in the decentralized framework of disarmament negotiations.

In conformity with such trends of restructuring, the Non-Aligned states insisted that the negotiations should be brought back under the UN and the General Assembly's control of the global policy-making process. One claim of the Non-Aligned states in their campaign for restructuring was that reforms would allow the participation of France and the People's Republic of China in the activities of the negotiating body. France declined to take its seat in the ENDC-CCD, and the People's Republic of China, which was not yet a member of the ENDC or its successor CCD, entered into the UN in 1971. Their absence was for the Non-Aligned states due to the existing so called undemocratic structures for disarmament negotiations.[29] Mexico, supporting the initiation of the restructuring exercise stated on behalf of the Non-Aligned group that :

> bearing in mind that the entry of the People's Republic of China into the United Nations has introduced a new element of prime importance for disarmament negotiations, we feel that the time has come to start thinking about the changes which will have to be made in this committee if we want to create favourable conditions for its continued existence as a negotiating body.[30]

It is important to note that the autonomous status of the CCD facilitated the participation of any member or non-member of the UN in the arms control proceedings. This was a matter entirely dependent on the superpowers, the candidate state itself and the pressure for such action on the CCD from the world community. Instead of acting in this direction, the Non-Aligned states preferred to use this demand of participation as a blunt instrument to beat the CCD in their public campaign for its restructuring.

In a period when disarmament problems had begun to take on the appearance of an habitual exercise in the CCD, the reformers claimed that they did not have anything to lose from challenging its structure. On the contrary, for them reform of the CCD could lead to the uniting of all the diverse factions (i.e., United States, Soviet Union, United Kingdom, China, France, Non-Aligned states) in the disarmament process. The reformers capitalized upon the potentialities of the polycentrism of those diverse factions to put up a powerful fight against the 'bilateral tendencies' which, according to their perspectives, had eroded the role of the UN and prevented the CCD from coming more clearly under the world organization's wing.

However, the entry of all the five states, which had the veto power in the Security Council, into the negotiations contained a risk. This risk was related to the probability of bringing the Security Council into play which, in turn, could bring about the substantial exclusion of the Non-Aligned majority in the UN from the negotiations. That is why, by claiming, the entry of France and the People's Republic of China into the negotiations, the reformers hastened to insist that such a probability would not 'contradict the healthy trend towards the democratization of international relations'[31] in that the concomitant strengthening of the role of the General Assembly would occur.[32] More importantly for the uncommitted nations, the General Assembly was the body wherein majority votes are unchecked by a great power veto and an organized majority is able to use its voting strength to press its demands on the organization. It seems that France's stance in the UN encouraged the restructuring efforts for their own tactical considerations. France used to state repeatedly in the UN:

> Does not the ineffectiveness of the CCD stem from the fact that this organization, is less than ever equipped to deal with the circumstances, and that neither its composition nor its procedures enable it to keep pace with the developments that have occurred in recent years? The Charter expressly entrusts our organization with the specific task of dealing with disarmament negotiations. One may well wonder whether the UN has not been too hasty in giving up one of its most basic responsibilities, by delegating the study of current problems to an organ not directly dependent on it, an organ that operates according to procedures that do not respect the principle of equality that must prevail among member states.[33]

The superpowers and their allies were unwilling to act collectively with the Non-Aligned states to revitalize the existing UN disarmament machinery and, therefore, to place the CCD under the aegis of the General Assembly. Pressure on the superpowers led them to a tacit agreement to co-operate, to preserve the existing machinery under their control, thus defending the great-power structures of the UN. As a consequence, the political confrontation between the Non-Aligned states and the superpowers became the central issue in the restructuring exercise. Remodelling of the UN disarmament machinery brought the Non-Aligned states inevitably into political confrontation with the states which were regarded as responsible for the existence of this machinery.

The restructuring exercise which was undertaken by the Non-Aligned states had a damaging effect on the negotiations. It generated political conflict on a North-South basis which prevented the CCD from being seriously involved in the negotiating process. It was not only the political climate which surrounded the UN/CCD which should be regarded as a frustrating factor for serious negotiations; it was also the fact that as long as the superpowers refused to acquiesce in the remodelling of the CCD, the restructuring efforts had reached an impasse and therefore took up an undue proportion of the work of the body. Members in the CCD were negotiating not nuclear disarmament but the politics of the reforms of its structure and organization. Taking the lead in a steady campaign to make the CCD responsible to the General Assembly and towards establishing a more centralized and integrated UN framework for disarmament, the Non-Aligned states initiated and perpetuated polemics against the superpowers. However, the CCD was not a political organ or a committee of the UN to be governed by the rule of the majority which could at any time impose its conditions; instead, it relied on the consensus principle and as the United States and the Soviet Union, backed by their allies, consistently refused to endorse the restructuring of the CCD the internal conflicts were perpetuated and became the day to day events in the multilateral negotiating body. As the transitional period was drawing to its close in 1977, a year before the convening of the first special session of the General Assembly devoted to disarmament, these conflicts were intensified. They, in fact, made the CCD a very divergent political unit. Indeed, one academic, Sullivan, commenting on the work of the CCD admitted that during the seventies the viability of the world's multilateral forum in Geneva was 'in jeopardy' and noted that the quest by the Non-Aligned states was for a 'procedural revolution'.[34] A significant part of the work of the CCD after 1972, the year the lasting restructuring efforts were put into effect, was diverted to the discussion of organisational and procedural matters. Demands for changes in the CCD's structure thus affected the substance of negotiations. The delegation of German Democratic Republic put it quite emphatically:

we regret that a large place is being given to organisational matters, which not only take time but also distract attention from the consideration of important questions. The discussion of these matters must be concluded as soon as possible. We are in favour of the Committee's concentrating on the main issues of the programme of work.[35]

Similarly, another delegation argued that the CCD 'leaving aside the high priority problems of disarmament... lost its sense of perspective and neglected the most urgent problems involved in a true effort at disarmament'.[36] On the other hand, the reformers sought to determine the political context under which negotiations were conducted in the CCD. The following example of the viewpoint of the reformers lends powerful support to the main argument of this chapter: 'the negotiation in the Committee will have to meet the requirements of democratization and equal participation of all states in the solutions of international problems and to reflect greater shifts and transformations which have taken place in international relations.[37]

It might be questioned whether the particular group of states which wanted to carry out institutional reforms of the UN environment was exactly the same as the group which was calling for democratization of the political context of negotiations. Indeed, as one scholar observed, 'the group of the Non-Aligned states led by Sweden, Mexico and Yugoslavia had intensified its efforts to shake up the foundations of the international arms control machinery'.[38] However, there was quite a split among members of the group over the issue of the application of the principle of democratization to the disarmament framework for negotiations.[39] Part of the explanation for this lies with the fact that the platform of democratization was not a concrete one to be applied only to the disarmament process. It was to apply initially to all the other activities in which the UN was engaged and especially to those relating to international economic relations. When, finally, it was decided to extend the proposed norms of the democratization platform to the disarmament activities of the organization, certain states opted out of the orchestrated actions the uncommitted group was taking probably because they could not identify with and, therefore, support its application in the field. It should be added that while the Non-Aligned group had established ad hoc bodies in the UN's headquarters to co-ordinate and implement the group's objectives, as they were determined at their Conferences, it lacked such a co-ordinating unit in Geneva where the meetings of the CCD were held.[40] Besides, the split was also due to the fact that certain states in the group, including militarily significant states, like India, strongly dissented from restructuring the existing UN framework for negotiations. India refused to endorse the package of restructuring proposals claiming that 'the CCD has no written charter, statute or constitution. It has worked on the basis of the principle of consensus. And its basic structure has proved to be sound for its work as a multilateral negotiating body'.[41] On the other hand, the rest of the uncommitted states seemed bent on making the constitution of the CCD mirror that of the UN. Yugoslavia was explicit in demanding that 'the negotiating machinery should be based on the role of the UN as determined by the Charter. It is necessary to review the activity of the CCD and its closer link with the UN'.[42]

The outcome was that the group, initiating restructuring, was, incapable of achieving a common strong bargaining position from which to bargain. In fact, up to 1975, the restructuring proposals of the most militant of the Non-Aligned states, namely, Mexico, Yugoslavia and Sweden, did not secure the enthusiastic support of the whole Non-Aligned group. Fragmentary efforts were characterized by the lack of strong loyalties among the members of the group and reinforced the negative attitude of the superpowers towards the demands for reforms. However, when the process of restructuring finally got under way, the position of the coalition was strengthened, but it was not until after the mid-seventies that deviations were eliminated from the more or less common attitude the Non-Aligned group had adopted. It was prospects of the General Assembly convening its first special session exclusively devoted to disarmament matters that actually united the Non-Aligned group.

Within the UN itself the restructuring undertaking met with a weak response. The General Assembly, through its recommendations, tried to address the CCD and its members by expressing its willingness to keep the basic framework of the negotiations, particularly nuclear disarmament, within the organisation's purview. In the systematic efforts to give a universal character to the negotiating process, the General Assembly was seen to conceptualize such universality. Virtually all the resolutions of the General Assembly claimed that disarmament is no longer the exclusive responsibility of a few states; that it is a matter of grave concern to all states; and that the UN must, therefore, make manifest its central role and its superior status in the field.[43] Behind such predispositions lay the demand of the Non-Aligned majority of the UN for democratization which, as it was developed conceptually and pursued in practice, meant equal participation of all the states in decision-making concerning world affairs. Such an enhanced role for the uncommitted nations included the nuclear aspect of disarmament.

It is of particular importance that the UN, particularly the General Assembly and the Secretary-General, failed to take action to solve the dispute that erupted. Their conflicting claims, thus, contributed to the prolongation of a more or less festering situation where the UN provided an institutional setting for disarmament which came under serious question due to the differences of approach of the three political groups over the role it should play in the negotiating process. The only step taken after recognizing that 'the role of the UN was far from adequate' was the establishment by the General Assembly of an Ad Hoc Committee with the task to review the role of the UN in the field of disarmament and to make recommendations. However, due to the atmosphere which prevailed, the Committee never touched upon the underlying causes which incapacitated the UN in dealing - within a commonly accepted institutional framework - with the question of disarmament. Instead, procedural matters occupied its sessions and its findings. The General Assembly was capable merely of endorsing the Committee's findings and requesting that the question of the role of the UN should remain 'under continued review'.[44] It was only when in 1978 the Assembly decided to take action through the first special session on Disarmament that the three groups finally gave their consent to such political intervention by the UN.

The claim for democratization took the form of restructuring efforts by the uncommitted states which they mainly manifested within the multilateral body of the CCD where the predominant position of the superpowers had been well founded. This participation seems to be reasonable because the CCD was preserving its status of being independent from the General Assembly of the UN, and the restructuring exercise had to be conducted, and its results to come from, decisions within that body itself. Additionally, the failure of the UN itself to take concrete action in favour of the restructuring enterprise forced the Non-Aligned states to focus a significant part of their efforts at restructuring within the CCD.

It is possible to identify two particular phases of the restructuring process engaged in by the uncommitted nations as applied to decision-making on disarmament, arms limitation, and weapons regulation. The first phase lasted until 1975 and the second from 1976 to 1978. What differentiates the one from the other is the degree of coherence with which the Non-Aligned states were endowed. During the second phase the Non-Aligned states due to the prospects of convening the General Assembly via a special session on disarmament were compelled to act in a purposive unison.

Phase one of the restructuring process

The first steps by the uncommitted states were taken with the purpose of reversing the declining trend of UN involvement in the disarmament negotiating process. Although it brought about no rapid changes it may be regarded as a 'revolutionary stage'. It served as the background to the further escalation of the restructuring activity witnessed at the second and crucial stage.

The attack on the superpowers' leadership

The starting point for reforms of the CCD consisted in demands for changing the co-chair system. States like Mexico, Yugoslavia, Romania[45] and Sweden called on the superpowers to resign from this post. They called repeatedly for the discontinuation of the co-chair institution on the basis of a traditional claim in international law, namely, to 'reflect the basic principle of the sovereign equality of states'.[46]

This common drive towards seeking the abolition of the co-chair was an attack on the superpowers within the CCD; mounted by throwing down the gauntlet to the CCD in rejecting the previous trend in decision allocating 'primary responsibilities' in the field of disarmament to the superpowers. Furthermore, if this trend was to cease, the consequential abolition of the co-chair could lead to the democratization of the CCD and, more important for the purposes of the uncommitted nations, to the facilitation of its compliance with the General Assembly of the UN. Additionally, the resultant structure would have been similar to that of the UN, thus contributing significantly to its easier incorporation into the UN system.

The attack on the co-chair emerged as the first step in a long-run plan towards intensifying the efforts for a firmer link between the UN and the CCD. The dispute indicates how much political credibility the co-chairs and existing structure of the CCD had lost in the eyes of the Non-Aligned states. They attacked the superpowers that supported the co-chair office because it was a political device that served the latter's particular political interest. They attempted to restrict the superpowers' role solely to dealing with procedural matters. Representatives of the group, such as Iran, argued that:

> The co-chairmen should be co-chairmen and nothing more. When they act as the representatives of their countries the co-chairmen have every right to defend the views of their countries, but it would not be advisable to become convinced that the relationship between the co-chairmen and the negotiating body was the same as that which Louis XIV regarded as existing between himself and the French state.[47]

However, despite the fact that the majority of the Non-Aligned states in the UN appeared to agree with the restructuring initiatives there were strong disagreements, much more visible in the CCD, about their soundness. India responded negatively saying that 'the cause of disarmament will receive a setback if the work of the CCD were disrupted. It would be difficult, if not impossible, to hold meaningful disarmament discussions, if a proven forum was to be destroyed or changes to be made in it on the basis of preconceived expectations'.[48] In agreement with this view was the belief of two other Non-Aligned states according to which the required changes 'are issues on which the discussions should be rather cautious and realistic. We are aiming at perfection in our committee and this can only come about through careful reasoning'.[49] At this time, the uncommitted states were unable, or reluctant, to comprehend the failure of the CCD to keep a close watch on practical compliance with the General Assembly, thereby permitting the majority of their group to blame this failure on the superpowers. A lack of coherence characterized the restructuring efforts of the Non-Aligned states, offering both the Eastern and Western blocs, and especially to the superpowers, another reason to put up a stubborn defence of the institution in question.[50] In defence of the institution of co-chair and of the existing structure of the CCD, the British delegation, expressing the perspectives of the West, stated pointedly: 'In a climate of belief in the sovereign equality of states, it may not be congenial to have to acknowledge that some countries are bigger and more powerful than others. But it is a political reality. And the present arrangements of our Committee (i.e., CCD) reflect political realities.[51] This observation went to the heart of the matter. It focused on the political foundations upon which both blocs relied to insist on the continuation of the life of the CCD under its existing structure: the disarmament machinery of the UN should correspond effectively to the prevailing power situation in the world.

Expansionism as means of limiting superpowers' roles

The attack on the superpowers was accompanied by persistent efforts for expansion of the CCD. It became obvious that the Non-Aligned states were fighting the 'bilateralism' presented in the CCD by seeking its enlargement. Such enlargement, if it was to be accompanied by the abandonment of the co-chair office, would have gradually lessened the claimed stranglehold the superpowers had on the CCD and, simultaneously, strengthened the role of the Non-Aligned states. As one state speaking on behalf of the Non-Aligned group put it: 'the time has come to consider the question of the UN's presence in the Committee's deliberations'.[52]

Enlargement was a frequent demand made by the Non-Aligned states throughout this period. They claimed that it would provide a closer representation of the UN and more democratization of the CCD. It would have the effect of restricting the superpowers' dominant political role and, thereby, it would achieve the purpose of the Non-Aligned states to gain political control of the CCD, provided that it was accompanied by the requested abandonment of the co-chair institution. However, with the exception of France, China, the German Democratic Republic and the Federal Republic of Germany, there was no organisational (i.e., functional) justification for enlargement. For the practice, which had been established during the negotiation of the NPT and consistently followed ever since, to submit to the General Assembly a significant part of the negotiation at an advanced stage from the CCD resulted in associating the work carried out in the CCD with the rest of the General Assembly.

The demands for expansion of the CCD were supported by all the Non-Aligned states. But most of the same states which raised strong objections to the proposals for the abolition of the co-chair institution were reluctant to support changes in the composition of the CCD apart from those concerned with inviting China and France to join in and participate in its decision. And again, the disagreement among the members of the Non-Aligned group[53] over the question of the expansion of the membership of the body allowed the superpowers to propose a compromise formula which worked as an ingenious device by which they could retain and perpetuate the control of the CCD for a long time.[54] Despite the strong opposition they expressed towards the enlargement of the CCD, because there would be functional risks if it was not to remain limited in size, the superpowers finally acquiesced in a further enlargement of the CCD. Consequently eight new states were allowed to participate in the work of the body after 1969, six more after 1974, including the two Germanies.[55]

The quid pro quo for the acceptance by the superpowers of such an enlargement was the preservation for themselves of the co-chair institution. By such means, the superpowers divorced the issue of expansion from the issue of the co-chair and, consequently, they delayed the process the Non-Aligned states initiated for the earliest possible adaptation of the CCD to the structures and organizations of the UN. As Verona noted, despite the process of democratization that was taking place the institution of two co-chairs was still all powerful in the mid-seventies.[56]

Because its composition ceased to be based on the criteria of realistic political and military balance which correspond to the peculiar dimensions of the process of decision-making on disarmament, and because it tended to be based on the simple criterion of geographical distribution, the expansion of the CCD was detrimental to its functioning as the negotiating body on disarmament decisions. It lost the optimum of balance between participant composition and requisite decisional competence which it had managed to build up during the earlier years.

The World Disarmament Conference (WDC)

As long as the first restructuring efforts turned out to be unsuccessful and were largely refuted by the superpowers, the Non-Aligned states were prompted to consider alternative means of accomplishing the institutional changes they sought. By 1973, it was generally accepted by states in the Eastern or Western camp that it was no longer a question of whether there should be restructuring but of when and how. The timing of a restructuring was dependent on the willingness of the most important states, including the superpowers, to accede to the elements of the demands. The restructuring of the CCD was not confined to the presentation of the proposals on behalf of the reformers within the CCD itself. The quest for remodelling the UN disarmament machinery led Non-Aligned states to set their hopes on the prospects of the UN convening a World Disarmament Conference. The discussion of this proposal and of the question of restructuring of the CCD largely overlapped.

Holding a WDC was originally an idea of the Non-Aligned group which advocated the convening of such a conference since the mid-sixties.[57] The debate in favour of convening a World Conference of this kind surfaced again at the beginning of 1970s. As a consequence, careful consideration was being given in the General Assembly over several years for the adequate preparation for, and the desirability of, universal participation in such a conference. A conference on a world scale was commonly seen as an instrument which could give a new political impetus to multilateral negotiations as well as putting dramatic focus on developments in the field of armaments and on the relative inadequacy of measures taken since the creation of the UN to achieve nuclear disarmament. Additionally, it could contribute towards the universal acceptance of, and adherence to, multilateral treaties already concluded, most especially the NPT.

A WDC built a constituency of support among members of the Non-Aligned group because it was perceived to be a vehicle for achieving the basic objectives of the restructuring campaign. Sullivan, having accepted that an institutional revolution was in progress attempting to establish an entirely new world disarmament negotiating structure, identified the prospects for the convening of such a conference as one of the first steps towards the institutionalization of this new structure.[58] In line with this observation, Myrdal, speaking on behalf of the Non-Aligned group, noting that the CCD 'is not yet brought into a logical relationship with the United Nations', proceeded immediately to stress that 'a World Disarmament Conference should obviously deal both with substantive disarmament proposals of a major kind - and with plans for establishing a more permanent structure for a continuous handling of disarmament issues'.[59]

In fact, the Non-Aligned states had deliberately left open two options. The first was that the WDC, because of the universality of its membership, to accomplish the restructuring they wanted by remodelling the existing UN machinery, including the CCD. The second was to replace the CCD by the WDC itself which would function as a negotiating body in the future.[60]

In general terms, a WDC could achieve any one of three main results. The first would be the establishment of a disarmament negotiating machinery under the political control of the UN. Yugoslavia, explicitly pointing out such an objective for the WDC, claimed 'returning to the United Nations of the role in the sphere (i.e., disarmament) that was entrusted to it under the Charter so that all aspects of disarmament are to be examined and negotiated within the framework of the UN, as the most universal and authoritative forum for the international community'.[61] The achievement of this objective would have led to the two remaining consequences desired which would follow from the subjugation of the multilateral disarmament negotiations to the UN, namely, securing universality and ensuring the abolition of the co-chair of the superpowers and thus, better observance of the principle of equal status among states.

The predisposition of Non-Aligned states to treat the WDC, if it was convened, as a suitable institutional framework for grappling in depth with the restructuring process, and the problem of substantial UN involvement in the negotiating process of disarmament, did not arouse enthusiasm in either the superpowers and their allies or, for that matter, a number of states belonging to the Non-Aligned group. The recourse of Non-Aligned states to the WDC as a means for carrying out reforms was, in effect, the consequence of their discontent with the existing framework for disarmament negotiations which was not delivering influence for them. The statements of many members of their group reflect that they reacted favourably towards the convening of a WDC precisely because of their disapproval of the existing general framework and functioning of the negotiations for their aims. This explains why they expected a WDC to shoulder the burden of responsibility for the accomplishment of restructuring and, even further, why they saw such a conference as a viable alternative to 'the obviously non-functioning CCD'.[62]

On the other hand, the superpowers disputed the assumption of the non-suitability of the existing framework for disarmament negotiations. They dissented strongly from the direction the reformers wished to give to a WDC on the ground that they were content with the existing disarmament machinery for decision-making. The United States took the opportunity to sound a warning that a new arena would not overcome the real problem: 'it is not the lack of a suitable forum, but the lack of political agreement which prevents us from taking more far reaching steps towards a more peaceful order with reduced levels of armaments. A World Disarmament Conference would be less likely to overcome this lack of agreement than to fall victim to it'.[63] Adding that the shortage of political agreement could be exarcebated and impair working institutions: 'a large, unwieldy, Conference would not provide the sort of atmosphere conducive to real progress: it could indeed be harmful to institutions that have already achieved a record of proved accomplishments (i.e., CCD and SALT) and are currently conducting ongoing negotiations'. Because of all this, the United States stated that they were 'highly skeptical about the value of a WDC'.[64] Its allies expressed similar views. The Netherlands, for example, expressed strong disagreement with the attempt to engage a WDC in the politics of restructuring and concluded that 'we believe that such a conference will not be able to take the place of a limited negotiating forum'.[65] In conformity with such views, the Soviet Union stated categorically that 'the discussion of all of those (disarmament) questions at the Conference should not, of course, be a substitute for disarmament talks which have proved their value, in particular those of the CCD'.[66] Thus, it may be concluded that the policy of the non-adherence of the Western and Eastern states to the restructuring agenda not only produced obstacles to the process of remodelling of the existing multilateral disarmament institutions, but also to the prospects of convening a WDC.[67]

Phase two of the restructuring process

After 1975 the restructuring process held out a very attractive vision for the Non-Aligned movement which was infused with the spirit of the New International Economic Order (NIEO), the most influential political and economic platform upon which the Non-Aligned states had ever acted. From the mid-seventies they were preoccupied with the perennial request for the creation of a NIEO which called for reforms on an international scale. It was accepted at the Colombo summit conference of the Non-Aligned states that 'in international negotiations the economic issue has become the major concern in international politics',[68] an they concluded that the 'arms race is inconsistent with the efforts aimed at achieving the New International

131

Economic Order in view of the urgent need to divert the resources utilized for the acceleration of the arms race towards socio-economic development, particularly of the developing countries'.[69] The incompatibility between the arms race and the pursuit of the NIEO, which was clearly emphasised in the General Assembly's resolutions,[70] became instrumental in persuading the Non-Aligned states even more than in the previous years that disarmament was too important a subject to be left in the hands of the superpowers and their allies which controlled the CCD and which refused to make it responsive to the UN. For the reason that 'measures of disarmament could be used to promote the economic development of the developing countries and would certainly contribute towards a bridging of the gap between developed and developing countries within the foreseeable future',[71] also meant that the call for a NIEO itself required a greater role for the UN in the achievement of its goals.[72] The special session of the General Assembly devoted to economic development, which was convened in 1974, made specific and urgent appeals 'to all organisations, institutions, subsidiary bodies and conferences of the UN system to be entrusted with the implementation of the NIEO'.[73]

The stakes now for the Non-Aligned states became higher than ever before insofar as they involved the establishment of a NIEO. In addition, the group was exhorted to endeavour more actively to enhance the impact of the majority they enjoyed in the UN by means of channelling the disarmament question within the framework and under the patronage of the UN. This would put on a sounder basis the group's access to the negotiating table where their problems could be taken into account and where, according to their viewpoint, they could really influence decisions affecting their economies and their future. Under these circumstances the UN and the CCD witnessed a sharpening of the restructuring activities and, therefore, of the North-South contention.

It is important to note that the sharpening of the North-South confrontation due to the restructuring exercise was not only apparent in relation to the disarmament activities of the organization, but also to other institutions of the UN system and especially those which were concerned with economic and social issues. The huge increase in the number of independent states together with the demands for a NIEO had changed dramatically the political power correlations within the UN system which had to adapt its structures and its functions to the requirements of the new political and socio-economic environment. The reshaping and strengthening of the UN system in favour of securing the participation of all state in the responsibilities of international life to replace the traditional sectionalism through the introduction of greater centralization under the authority of the General Assembly was set in action everywhere. As one UNESCO official noted 'the UN system has thus been given an opportunity, rich in exceptional responsibilities, to prove the irreplaceable nature of its services; it is a challenge which cannot be evaded'.[74]

In the light of these developments, perpetuation of the existing structure and organization of the UN's disarmament machinery including the CCD was, according to the Non-Aligned view, anachronistic. The prevailing mood in the UN's institutions was for restructuring and strengthening of the organisation's role in international affairs. It followed that, during the sweeping reforms which took place within the UN system there was a state of inactivity in the particular institutions and organs of the UN. It should also be observed that work of the CCD was probably one of the worst afflicted because of the high politicization of the disarmament issue.

Entangling the UN General Assembly

The most decisive step towards restructuring came from the General Assembly. Once the idea of convening a WDC under the aegis of the UN ran into irreconcilable difficulties due to the fundamental divergence of opinions on many aspects, the prospects for the convening of a special session on disarmament gained surprisingly rapid ground. The idea was given strong impetus when it was considered as a viable alternative to the WDC by the foreign ministers of the Non-Aligned states at their Lima meetings in 1975, declaring that 'if it becomes evident that it will not be possible to convene a world Disarmament Conference, a special session of the General Assembly of the UN devoted to disarmament issues should be convened'.[75] The initiative met with further support when one year later at Colombo the Non-Aligned states decided unanimously 'to request the holding of a special session of the General Assembly as early as possible but not later than 1978'.[76]

At this time in the UN, the idea of special sessions of the General Assembly had become fashionable as two such special sessions had been devoted to international economic relations and particularly to the declaration of the pursuit of a NIEO. Following these developments the General Assembly, propelled by the enthusiastic support of the Non-Aligned states, decided to convene a series of special sessions. The first special session was to be devoted exclusively to disarmament, to be held in 1978. The superpowers were sceptical of the wisdom of holding a special session, retreating after the mid-seventies on the ground that the political costs of continuing opposition would go against the popular will as expressed by the majority of the UN, the Non-Aligned states. Accordingly, the General Assembly established a preparatory committee composed of fifty-four members to co-ordinate the whole business of preparations for the convening of the special session.[77]

At this time the UN disarmament machinery including the CCD, entered the last stage of its transition. This was when the UN through its General Assembly demonstrated a desire to handle the burdensome range of disarmament issues and to improve its involvement in the disarmament process of negotiation and decision. The convening of a special session on disarmament provided the best opportunity for the Non-Aligned states to revive the UN's role in disarmament and one in which they decided to invest all their hopes.[78] The idea of convening a special session on disarmament seemed to be consistent with their greatest concern - the promotion of the UN's role and their drive for institutional reforms of the UN disarmament machinery whereby they would gain their measure of equality with the major powers. The General Assembly, which was to take action, provided them with the proper forum for such venture. They expected that through its session it would allocate to the UN the substantial direction of negotiations and decision-making, thereby ensuring the overall subjection of the multilateral negotiating body to its control. The Non-Aligned group claimed, the General Assembly bears the ultimate responsibility for disarmament 'as the principal political decision-making organ of the UN'.[79]

The agenda of the special session on disarmament, as it was adopted by the preparatory committee, appeared to reflect the Non-Aligned states' concern that the General Assembly should undertake an interventionist role in the disarmament process in order to bring about increased democratization through the greater centralization of all disarmament activities in the UN. The agenda was prepared so that it preserved for the General Assembly the prospects for a powerful regulating function: first, there should be a review and evaluation of the present situation, secondly, the adoption of a declaration on disarmament; thirdly, the adoption of a programme of action and, finally, a review of the role of the UN in disarmament.[80] The political orientations of the Non-Aligned group became evident from the papers their Co-ordinating Bureau in the UN circulated. They expressed the somewhat wishful demand that the special session on disarmament should 'reassert the responsibility of the United Nations' and 'should contribute toward strengthening the role of the UN and its overall involvement in the field of disarmament and disarmament negotiations'.[81]

Meanwhile there was increasing frustration in the work of the CCD.

Negotiations on a CTBT which was the top priority agenda item, were removed from the CCD agenda by the United States and the Soviet Union in 1976. These two states preferred to continue consultations in private and the following year the United Kingdom joined them in trilateral negotiations. In reality, the CTBT negotiations had ceased to be conducted in the CCD much earlier, since the superpowers took them away from the multilateral body and concluded the treaty on the limitation of underground tests, the 'Threshold Test Ban Treaty', in 1974. Under the terms of this treaty the two superpowers undertook not to carry out underground testing of explosives with a yield in excess of 150 kilotons. To conceptualize this, reference may be had to the 12.5 kiloton atomic bomb dropped on Hiroshima, 6 August 1945, killing more than 100,000 inhabitants and destroying completely 13 square kilometres of the city. The superpowers went on to sign the 'Peaceful Nuclear Explosions Treaty' regulating underground explosions for peaceful purposes below the 150 kiloton threshold in 1976.

The official records of the negotiations in the CCD reveal that virtually every delegation in each speech it delivered to the body raised the issue of negotiation of a CTBT according to the view its own group supported. When the criticism against the superpowers seemed to reach unacceptable proportions, the United States and the Soviet Union resorted to their favourite diversionary tactic: they introduced, as a result of a series of bilateral discussions within the CCD, a joint draft treaty for the undertaking by the CCD of intensive negotiations on a treaty on environmental modification warfare (ENMOD Treaty). The proposal was a new non-nuclear arms control measure but one which seemed to the uncommitted states of little significance. The extended duration of these negotiations in the CCD made stronger the conviction that the superpowers lacked the resolve to be involved in a serious discussion about disarmament;[82] it also probably justified the perspective that it was a strategy designed to relieve pressure on the superpowers and to switch attention to an ENMOD Treaty in order to avoid bringing the structure of the CCD into further disrepute.[83]

The prolongation of the negotiation of the ENMOD Treaty by the CCD brought an immediate reaction from the Non-Aligned group. Claiming to lessen the superpowers' discretionary power of systematically keeping the CCD occupied with the negotiation of arms control measures of little significance, the group proposed the institutionalization, within the CCD, of a standing sub-committee, the chairpersonship of which would rotate democratically among the member-states. The ostensible purpose of the sub-committee, as it was officially described, was to negotiate texts of draft conventions, treaties, agreements, and other documents and questions of the agenda of the CCD to which the CCD might refer.[84] However, the actual intention was for the standing sub-committee to be entrusted with the negotiation of secondary arms control measures, and, by this means, it would leave time for the full Committee (i.e., the CCD) to deal exclusively with real disarmament measures. Additionally, it could be used to lead to the limitation of the role of the co-chairs to manipulate the CCD at their will. As expected, the superpowers opposed the proposal, questioning its value. As a consequence, the proposal was finally rejected but the failure of their proposal impressed on the Non-Aligned group the importance of unity in action in order to achieve their objectives pending the convening of the special session on disarmament.

Despite the negotiation of the ENMOD Treaty in 1976, the political storm did not abate. On the contrary, the prospect of the convening of the special session of the Assembly and a commitment to restructuring the UN disarmament machinery was closely linked with the tactical consideration by the Non-Aligned states to maximize the movement's influence. The prospects of the Assembly's special session on disarmament made the Non-Aligned states realize that they could succeed in bringing about their desired ends if they displayed cohesiveness and unity in action. Even India, which up to 1977 had systematically questioned the political soundness of the institutional reforms for which the Non-Aligned group was demanding, came around to the need to reach agreement on the group's objectives for the special session on disarmament. Shortly afterwards and pending the opening of the special session, India and other Non-Aligned states dropped their reservations to the restructuring process. They now perceived the need to align themselves with the rest of the Non-Aligned group and to seek the institutional changes the group was demanding the General Assembly to carry out.

It can be said that the approaching special session on disarmament helped to endow the Non-Aligned group in advance with solidarity against the predisposition of the East and West to maintain the existing disarmament machinery of the UN;[85] and in favour of the revision of all the 'bilateral inheritances' which had been maintained since 1961 as well as the abandonment of the previous political framework under which negotiations had been conducted.

Conclusions

In the sixties, there was unanimity among the three major political groups within the UN on the disarmament institutional format as well as on the particular agenda for negotiations. As a consequence, the UN's quest for peace through nuclear arms control measures proved successful and established *detente* conditions conducive to the undertaking of further serious negotiations on nuclear disarmament.

In the seventies, serious developments that had not previously arisen took place. The UN, first of all, found itself in a crisis which was the result of the different perceptions of the three political groups as to its role in the disarmament negotiating process. There was a sudden swing of all the three political groups from the consensus which had been achieved in the sixties. The rise of the Non-Aligned states as the major political force in the General Assembly coincided with their intensive activity to make the UN's role predominant and central in the disarmament process in such a way that the global decision-making relating to disarmament would be entrusted to the universal community the UN expresses. On the other hand, the East and West camp institutionalized the disarmament and arms control dialogue through the institution of SALT and virtually assigned to the UN limited responsibilities of a 'purely multilateral nature'.

With their predisposition to wage a fight against all bilateral tendencies prevailing inside and outside the UN (particularly SALT) the Non-Aligned group initiated proceedings for restructuring the existing UN disarmament machinery against the wishes and the options of the superpowers.

In fact, the attempts at restructuring reflected the growth of a North-South axis in world politics in general in addition to that of East and West, which already existed and which had dominated the international scene since 1947. The new axis generated an overcommitment on the part of the Non-Aligned states to the utilization of the UN as an instrument for change in world politics. Such an overcommitment was combined with large scale proposals for restructuring the disarmament machinery on the part of the Non-Aligned group and developing countries with the very purpose of challenging the existing framework for negotiations in the interest of its democratization. They wanted a new framework which would become more responsive to the changes, they saw, in international relations. In this context, they tended increasingly to conceptualize the issue of disarmament including its nuclear field in fundamentally North-South terms.

The pressure on the superpowers led them to reach a tacit agreement to co-operate to withstand the strong political pressure of the Non-Aligned group with the view to preserving the existing machinery under their control. They, thus, defended the great-power institutional building of the UN as better reflecting the power realities which are involved in the disarmament process. Resistance to changing the existing framework for negotiations was persistently maintained. Under such circumstances, a serious political confrontation erupted between the Eastern and Western group on the one side and the Non-Aligned group on the other.

The restructuring efforts damaged any potentialities the CCD might have had for serious negotiations on nuclear disarmament. The only achievement during the period between 1972 and 1978 was the negotiation of the ENMOD Treaty. The CCD appeared to be something of a battleground between proponents of restructuring the UN framework for negotiations and those who refused to support such restructuring. Indicative of the exigencies the divisions between the political groups brought about was the fact that the UN itself failed to exercise its influence to arrest the continuing conflict between the three political groups. The inability of the UN to 'take notice' of such conflict was a catalytic factor leading to a decay of its role. The Non-Aligned majority of the UN challenged the superpowers' power to establish and perpetuate institutions for negotiations according to their perceptions and, most of all, it sought more widely to lay down new principles and different standards for the future building up of the disarmament machinery of the UN as well as for the conduct of negotiations in the debates and the resolutions within the UN. These principles and standards were based on the continuing quest for complete democratization of the UN's institutions and changes which would enable all states to be linked more closely to the negotiating process. Such changes and the collective involvement in the negotiations was only possible if it was also to coincide with the total abolition of the great-power structure. In other words, the UN's disarmament machinery was being driven away from those structures which would ensure the support and substantive participation of the most powerful states. The UN and its forthcoming special session had to give definitive answer to this problem and to prove itself capable of managing efficiently the crisis, after taking account the power realities existing in the world. The reactivation of the world organization in relation to the actual process of nuclear disarmament would in the final analysis depend on what the UN itself could do to improve the quality of international co-operation.

Notes

1. Treaty on the Prohibition of the Emplacement of Nuclear Weapons and Other Weapons of Mass Destruction on the Seabed and the Ocean Floor and in the Subsoil Thereof. Entered into force 18 May 1972. It is effective outside a 12-mile coastal zone and provides for the

denuclearization of the sea bed, the ocean floor, and the subsoil. For a useful analysis of the treaty see SIPRI (1970), *Yearbook of World Armaments and Disarmament 1969/70,* Almqvist & Wiksell: Stockholm, pp. 92-184.

2. Entered into force 23 June 1961. It provides for the demilitarization and nuclearization of Antarctica. It bars any nuclear testing or disposal of radioactive waste material in the Antarctic. For the structure of the treaty see SIPRI (1973), *Yearbook of World Armaments and Disarmament 1973,* Almqvist & Wiksell: Stockholm, pp. 477-493.

3. UNGA Resolution 2602 E (XXIV) 16 December 1969, para. 4; see also UNGA Resolution 2661 C (XXV), 7 December 1970 which passed with 106 votes to with 10 abstentions; see also UNGA Resolution 2825 B (XXVI), 16 December 1971 which passed with 92 votes to 0 with 1 abstention.

4. UN Document A/8191, 1 December 1970.

5. Nicholas Sims (1971), 'The Return of the GCD?', *Millennium: Journal of International Studies,* vol.1, no 1, Summer, pp. 54-66; see also Nicholas Sims (1976), 'General and Complete Disarmament, The Italian Initiative of 1969-1970 and the Synoptic Approach to the Disarmament Process', *Reconciliation Quarterly,* vol.1, March, pp. 41-45.

6. Philip Windsor (1971), 'GCD Again?', *Millennium: Journal of International Studies,* vol.1, no 1, Summer, pp. 66-70.

7. Alva Myrdal (1976), *The Game of Disarmament, How The United States and Russia Run the Arms Race,* Pantheon Books: New York, pp. 109, 110,114 and 115.

8. Kenneth Lee (1973), 'Disarmament, GCD, Small Steps and the Future', *World Issues,* vol.26, no 1, Spring, pp. 6-8.

9. Michael Sullivan (1975), 'Conference at Crossroads: Future Prospects for the Conference of the Committee on Disarmament', *International Organization,* vol. 29, Spring, pp. 392-3.

10. See for example UNGA Resolution 2932 B (XXVII), 29 November 1972, voted by 87 to 0 with 27 abstentions including the United States, Soviet Union, United Kingdom and France.

11. Avi Beker (1986), *Disarmament Without Order: The Politics of Disarmament at the United Nations,* Greenwood Press: Westport & London, p. 67.

12. Lazar Mojsov (1973), 'Non-Aligned Countries in the United Nations', *Review of International Affairs,* no 562, 5 September, p. 8.

13. Consultative Meeting of Special Governmental Representatives of Non-Aligned Countries, Belgrade, July 1969, cited in Odette Jankowitsch and

Karl Sauvant (eds) (1978), *The Third World Without Superpowers:The Collected Documents of the Non-Aligned Countries,* Oceana Publications: New York, p. 160.

14. Third Conference of Heads of Government of Non-Aligned Countries, Statement on the United Nations, cited in ibid., p. 104.

15. Fourth Conference of the Heads of State or Government of the Non-Aligned Countries, Political Declaration, September 1973, cited in ibid., p. 195.

16. Ibid., pp. 203, 461 and 507.

17. Fifth Conference of the Heads of State of Government of Non-Aligned Countries, Colombo, August 1976, cited in ibid., pp. 747, 749, 750, 785, 787 and 873.

18. United Nations (1962), *Economic and Social Consequences of Disarmament: Report of the Secretary-General,* New York, 1962, UN Document E/3593/Rev. 1.

19. See for example UNGA Resolution 1837 (XVII), 18 December 1962.

20. Ralph Townley (1968), *The United Nations, A View from Within,* Charles Scribner's Sons: New York, p. 59.

21. United Nations (1976), *The United Nations and Disarmament 1970-1975,* United Nations: New York, p. 201; see also UNGA Resolution 2626 (XXV) of 7 December 1970; see also Resolution 2685 (XXV) and 2831(XXVI) of 16 December 1971.

22. Fifth Conference of the Heads of Government of Non-Aligned Countries, Colombo, August 1976, Political Declaration, para. 168, cited in Jankowitsch and Sauvant, op.cit., p. 786.

23. Third Conference of the Heads of State or Government of Non-Aligned Countries, Statement on United Nations, cited in ibid., p. 104; see also Jasip Djerdja (1970), 'First Messages From Lusaka', *Review of International Affairs,* vol.xxi, no 491, September, p. 2.

24. Consultative Meeting of Ministers of Foreign Affairs of Non-Aligned Countries at the United Nations during the 26th session of the General Assembly, 16-18 September 1971, cited in Jankowitsch and Sauvant, op.cit., p. 505.

25. Conference of Ministers of Foreign Affairs of Non-Aligned Countries, The Georgetown Declaration, August 1972, cited in ibid., p. 443.

26. Lusaka Conference of the Non-Aligned States, Declaration on Peace, Independence, Co-operation and Democratisation of International Relations, cited in ibid., p. 82.

27. Ibid., p. 507.

28. Algiers Conference of the Non-Aligned Countries, Political Declaration,

para. 81, cited in ibid., p. 203.

29. See the following UN Documents: A/C.1/28/PV.1947, 5 November 1973, para. 59; A/C.167/I/Add. 3 and Cor. 1, 22 July 1975; see also Document CCD/PV. 683, 21 August 1975, p. 23.

30. UN Document A/C.I/28/PV.1942, 31 October 1973, p. 23.

31. Document CCD/PV. 580, 1972, p. 11.

32. UN Document A/C.I/28/PV.1941, 28 October 1973.

33. UN Document A/C.I/28/PV.1942, 31 October 1973, p. 220; see also UN Document A/C.I/28/PV. 1969, 23 November 1973.

34. Sullivan, op.cit., p. 393.

35. Document CCD/PV. 698, 30 March 1976, p. 13, Mr. Herder; see also the following Documents: CCD/PV.714, 22 July 1976, p. 32; CCD/PV. 708, 1 July 1976 p. 9; CCD/PV. 690, 24 February 1976, p. 12; CCD/PV. 692, 9 March 1976, p. 15

36. UN Document A/C.I/28/PV.1948, 6 November 1973, p. 265; see also UN Document A/C.I/28/PV. 1942, 31 October 1973, p. 212, para. 29.

37. Document CCD/PV.714, 22 July 1976, p. 27.

38. Sullivan, op.cit., p. 393.

39. See for example Document CCD/PV. 712, 15 July 1976, p. 20.

40. Peter Willetts (1978), *The Non-Aligned Movement, The Origins of a Third World Alliance,* Francis Pinter: London, pp. 38-40.

41. Document CCD/PV.736, 1977, p. 10.

42. Document CCD/PV.762, 1977, p. 11.

43. UNGA Resolution 2823 (XXVI) adopted at the 2022nd Plenary meeting,16 December 1971; UNGA Resolution 2930 (XXVII), adopted at the 2093rd Plenary meeting, 29 November 1972; UNGA Resolution 3183 (XXVIII), adopted at the 2225th Plenary meeting, 18 December, 1973; UNGA Resolution 3260 (XXIX) adopted at the 2309th Plenary meeting, 9 December 1974; UNGA Resolution 3469 (XXX) adopted at the 2437th Plenary meeting, 11 December 1975. All these Resolutions should be read in connection with the UNGA Resolutions which complain the SALT for a lack of substantial progress in the field of disarmament. For example, UNGA Resolution 2932 B (XXVII) 29 November 1972 or UNGA Resolution 3216 C (XXIX) 9 December 1974.

44. UN Document A/31/PV. 98, 14 December 1976; UN Document, General Assembly, Official Records, Supplement No 36, A/31/36, para. 18; see also UNGA Resolution (XXX), 12 December 1975.

45. Romania was not a member of the Non-Aligned group since it joined the ENDC/CCD as a member of the Eastern bloc. However, it is regarded as

belonging to the 'group of 77'. It joined almost all the Economic Conferences of the Non-Aligned states since 1964 as a full member; it allied itself to the group of the Non-Aligned states. Beker listed Romania among the states which belong to Non-Aligned front: see Beker, op.cit., pp. 74-76.

46. Document CCD/PV. 545, 1972, p. 35; see also the following Documents: CCD/PV. 685, 26 August 1975; CCD/PV. 687, 28 August 1975, p. 22; CCD/PV. 688, 17 February 1976, p. 10; CCD/PV. 689, 19 February 1976, pp. 10-13; CCD/PV. 697, 25 March 1976, pp. 18-20 and 27; CCD/PV. 708, 1 July 1976, p. 22; CCD/PV. 713, 20 July 1976, p. 13; CCD/PV. 714, 22 July 1976, pp. 7 and 13; CCD/PV. 724, 26 August 1976, pp. 11 and 22; CCD/PV. 727, 3 September 1976, pp. 8-9.

47. UN Document A/C.I/24/1691, 17 November 1969, paras 178-9, p. 17.

48. Document CCD/PV. 552, 1972, p. 8.

49. Document CCD/PV. 553, 1972, p. 14.

50. See for example the following Documents; CCD/PV. 727, 3 September 1976, pp. 27-28, USSR; CCD/PV.724, 26 August 1976, p. 18, Italy; CCD/PV. 688, p. 22, United States; CCD/PV.720, 12 August 1976, Hungary.

51. Document CCD/PV. 654, 1975, p. 22.

52. Document CCD/PV. 669, 1975, p. 9.

53. See for example Document CCD/PV. 688, 17 February 1976, p. 23.

54. Document CCD/PV. 767, 1977, p. 32, United States.

55 Argentina, Hungary, Japan, Mongolia, Morocco, Netherlands, Pakistan and Yugoslavia became member-states of the CCD in 1969; Federal Republic of Germany, German Democratic Republic, Iran, Peru and Zaire joined the CCD in 1975.

56. Sergio Verona (1976), 'The Geneva Disarmament Conference, Some Considerations', *Instant Research on Peace and Violence*, vol.6, no 1-2, pp. 62-71, esp. p. 69.

57. See the final Communique of the Belgrade and Cairo Summit Conferences of the Non-Aligned states, cited in Jankowitsch and Sauvant, op.cit, p. 6 and p. 54; the desire of the Non-Aligned states for the convening of a WDC was reflected in both the Disarmament Commission and General Assembly Resolutions, see UNGA Document 224, 11 June 1965 and UNGA Resolution 2030 (XX), 29 November 1965.

58. Sullivan, op.cit., pp. 404-408, esp. p. 405.

59. Document CCD/PV. 610, 1973, p. 7, Mrs. Myrdal.

60. Document CCD/PV. 572, 1972, p. 34, Yugoslavia.

61. UN Document A/10028 (GAOR: 30th Session, Supplement No 28), pp. 57-8.
62. See the following UN Documents: A/AC.167/I/Add.5, 27 August 1975, Peru and Guinea; A/AC.167/L.2/Add.6 and A/AC.167/I/Add.2, 6 June 1975, Indonesia; A/AC.167/ADD.I, 21 April 1975, Kuwait; see also the important view of Mexico in UN Document A/AC.167/I, 27 March 1975, and UN Document A/AC.167/I/Add.I, 5 June 1975, Norway.
63 Nicholas Sims (1979), *Approaches to Disarmament*, Quacker Peace & Service: London, p. 129.
64. Document CCD/PV. 560, 1972, p. 16; see also UN Document A/AC.167/I/Add.2, 20 June 1975.
65. Document CCD/PV. 552,1977, p. 13; see also the British view cited in UN Document A/AC.167/I/Add.I, 21 May 1975.
66. UN Document A/10028, op.cit., pp. 53-55; see also Document CCD/PV. 554, 1972, p.18; Document CCD/PV. 572, 1972, p. 34.
67. Nicholas Sims (1975), 'UN Deadlocks and Delaying Tactics: the First Three Years of the Soviet Proposal for a WDC, 1971-1974', *Millennium: Journal of International Studies,* vol.4, no 2, Autumn, pp. 113-117; see also Louis Sohn (1978), 'Disarmament at the Crossroads', *International Security*, vol.2, no 4, Spring, pp. 4-9.
68. See Jankowitsch and Sauvant, op.cit., pp. 792 and 800.
69. Ibid., p. 782; see also the following Documents: CCD/PV. 714, 22 July 1976, pp. 8-9, Sweden; CCD/PV. 724, 26 August 1976, p. 12, Mexico.
70. A/Resolution 3462 (XXX), 11 December 1975; see also UN Document A/AC.185/56, 19 May 1977, p. 2; and Document CCD/PV. 688, 17 February 1976, p. 34.
71. Fifth Conference of Heads of State or Government of Non-Aligned Countries, Economic Declaration, Chapter III, para. 10, cited in Jankowitsch and Sauvant, op.cit., p. 796.
72. Walter Kotsching (1968), 'The UN as an Instrument of Economic and Social Development', *International Organization,* vol.xxii, no 1, Winter, pp. 16-43.
73. Sixth Special Session of the UNGA, Programme of Action on the Establishment of a New International Economic Order, UNGA Resolution 3202 (S-VI), Section IX, para. 4, 1 May 1974. One should see this resolution in conjunction with UNGA Resolution 3281 (XXIV), 12 December 1974, Article 15; see also Karl Sauvant (ed.) (1979), *Changing Priorities on the International Agenda: The New International Economic Order*, Pergamon Press: Oxford, p. 209.
74. UNESCO Document 18 C/103, 1 October, 1974: Comments and

Suggestions of the Director-General: Ways and Means whereby UNESCO Could Contribute to the Establishment of a NIEO.

75. UN Document A/10217, 5 September 1975, Annex, pp. 28-30; see also Homer Jack (1977), 'The Special Session on Disarmament,' *Review of International Affairs,* vol. 28, 5-20 August, pp. 4-5.
76. Fifth Conference of Heads of State or Government of Non-Aligned Countries, Colombo, Political Declaration, cited in Jankowitsch and Sauvant, op.cit., p. 782; see also UN Document A/31/232, 28 September 1976, pp. 13-14.
77. UNGA Resolution 31/189 B, 21 December 1976.
78. UN Document A/C.I/31/PV. 25, 8 November 1976, pp. 67-72; see also UN Document A/AC.187/3, 30 March 1977.
79. UN Document A/AC.187/55, 18 May 1977, p. 9.
80. UN Document A/32/41.
81. UN Document A/AC.185/55, 18 May 1977, pp. 3-6; see also Parliamentary Papers, 1977-8, vol. LIV, Annex C, p. 49.
82. Laurence Juda (1978), 'Negotiating a Treaty on Environmental Modification Warfare: The Convention on Environmental Warfare and its Impact upon Arms Control Negotiations, *International Organization,* vol.32, no 4, Autumn, p. 987.
83. See the views of some of the Non-Aligned states in the following Documents: CCD/PV. 693, 11 March 1976, Nigeria; CCD/PV. 695 18 March 1976, Argentina; CCD/PV.701, 8 April 1976, Egypt.
84. Document CCD/PV. 530 of 23 March 1977, Working Paper on Procedures of the CCD, submitted by the Non-Aligned members of the CCD.
85. Pending the convening of the SSOD-I, the Conference of Foreign Ministers of the Co-Ordinating Bureau of Non-Aligned Countries, which was held in New Delhi (7-11 April 1977), issued a communique according to which 'the Non-Aligned states should act together' in achieving their predetermined goals: see UN Document A/AC.187, 11 March 1977, p. 2.

5 The UN after the first special session on disarmament (1978-)

The rise of an artificial consensus

The special session on Disarmament was the first specialised convocation to bring representatives of the world community together to discuss disarmament since the Disarmament Conference which was called by the League of Nations in the 1930s. The General Assembly of the United Nations convened three such special sessions to deal exclusively with disarmament: the first from 23 May to 30 June 1978, the second from 7 June to 10 July 1982, and the third from 31 May to 25 June 1988.

The most important function of a special session is to sensitize the public to the issues by raising consciousness through drawing public attention to the magnitude and dangers of a race of arms as well as to give new impetus to the disarmament process.

The first special session of the General Assembly (SSOD-I) changed entirely the previous structures of authority and courses of negotiations. It was the most important of the three sessions and the other two failed in that they could not keep up the momentum of doing what the first did. It alone of the three put the previous structures of authority in a new political context with significant implications for the UN itself and the process of disarmament. It constituted the broadest and most representative UN forum ever convened to deal with the question of disarmament in all its aspects. It brought together participants for the first time in the history of UN disarmament activities from various non-governmental organizations. The SSOD-I was supposed to be an extraordinary event the importance of which was heightened by the problem whether the special session would serve as a mechanism for decision-making about resolving a long-lasting crisis within the UN as to its role and actual involvement in the negotiating process of disarmament.

For the UN to succeed at the special session, it had to perform its essential role, neglected in some measure in forcing through controversial measures favoured by the uncommitted nations: to harmonize the perspectives and actions of the three political groups manifested in the seventies to diverse UN involvement in this process of disarmament - by decision-making based upon shared interests. For the SSOD-I conflict management was one of the most forward-looking targets. Its effectiveness would provide a significant basis for assessing appropriately the capabilities of the UN as a world organization itself. Thus, the success of any conflict management would have to comprise not only the conflict recognition but also the conflict handling process of decision-making. The time had come for the UN to identify the underlying causes of the growing marginalization of its role in the ongoing disarmament negotiations. Having done so, it would have to correct past mistakes and chart its future course of action by decision with greater prospects of success.

Little carries more far-reaching significance for the effectiveness of the UN's performance than the choices of the roles and the kind of organization required by the member-states. However, such choices have to be made with the measured constraint of sensitivity for the inherent constitutional scheme and work of the UN on disarmament: the UN is not an actor, but an arena. It cannot command or dictate disarmament and weapons regulation. Rather, the UN can be used at most to encourage and facilitate disarmament achievement by its member-states. In order to protect interests that are inclusive to all communities about the globe, the work of the UN involves three stages, each stage building upon the other. The first stage is international dialogue and intelligence for identifying and minimizing the differences on claims as to issues that can be immediately negotiated, the second is conceptualizing solutions by promoting and appraising, the third is recommending solutions by invoking basic community policy. The next component decision function involves prescription and application (or termination) of community law through making law or other decisional activity.

Depending on what the member-states expected from the UN, their different positions surfaced during the SSOD-I and fell within the framework of two major avenues to their demands. On the one hand, Eastern and Western states, led by the United States and the Soviet Union respectively, explicitly maintained that the UN had only 'a central' or 'an important' but never 'the primary' role to play in the sphere of disarmament negotiations.[1] In essence, this function was to be quite complementary to that of the bilateral institution of SALT-START. For them, the agenda of the UN remained limited, focusing on the purely multilateral aspects of certain important issues, such as, conventional and chemical weapons, nuclear test and the strengthening of the non-proliferation regime. They remained constant in their anti-reform campaign claiming, as they had done over the years, that no changes in the existing UN structures were required. This position was paralleled to the reasonable argument that if the authority of the General Assembly of the UN were to be increased, its more powerful and political intervention would undermine the 'technical service' of the negotiating forum which, given the nuances of negotiating arms reduction, maximize the possibilities of common understanding on issues of disarmament requiring decision. Consistent with this perspective was their position that the UN should not offer initiatives of its own, but, in the form of an impartial body, should be a coherent whole to cultivate and inspire international dialogue and action.[2] The General Assembly, which now by virtue of the SSOD-I emerged as the policy-making organ, would have to avoid giving decisions of specific guidance as to the means to be employed and the course of action to be followed, thus, prejudging the path of negotiations. Similar views were expressed by the United Kingdom and the Netherlands which not only did not propose a concrete policy-action for the UN but argued that a specific action-oriented UN would complicate the negotiations.[3] The Netherlands, for instance, in a working paper it submitted to the SSOD-I emphasized that 'the special session must avoid drawing up a time table of specific targets dates for achieving certain measures'.[4]

On the other hand, the Non-Aligned group regarded the role of the UN as 'the central' one.[5] Uppermost in their minds was the demand that disarmament should be brought back into the mainstream of the UN's preoccupations. The SSOD-I should form, according to them, the final point for bringing their long-lasting restructuring efforts to an end. Their chief thrust in the SSOD-I process was to argue for the strengthening of the role of the UN in relation to disarmament. This position did not emanate from any idealistic inspirations, rather it was the result of the fact that equated a stronger UN with the prospects of promoting their own interests which were associated in the realm of the UN in general, and the General Assembly in particular, with disarmament.

One of their main objectives in the SSOD-I was to make a contribution towards the return of the UN to a more central role in dealing with disarmament in all its aspects, the other was to ensure that the problem of disarmament was seen from the perspective of their economic situation.[6] It can be said that the Non-Aligned states saw these two objectives as mutually reinforcing. As was noted in the preceding chapter, the Non-Aligned states being the majority of the UN, biased in their approaches to world issues with the view to advance their own concerns, began to use the world organization to broach the problem of disarmament through the prism of their economic interests. As a consequence, disarmament was looked at as a process which would help to stem the massive and increasing diversion of scarce resources to programmes of military expenditure and make possible their direction to the urgent tasks of economic development of the Southern states. Thus, from the seventies the concept of security had been conceptualized in fundamentally North-South terms in the General Assembly. It was being enlarged not only to acquire the military but also the economic dimension of disarmament, as the result of the broader interpretation which the Non-Aligned states gave to the arms race:

> the arms race is not only a destabilizing factor and a source of latent dangers of a military confrontation, but also a factor that greatly undermines the world economy, one of the main causes of the profound crisis that is being experienced on all continents and particularly the continents with the developing countries. It is for this reason that the struggle for peace is one closely related in with the efforts to solve the most pressing problems of those countries and it is at the same time linked to the struggle for an international economic order.[7]

The holding of the SSOD-I coincided with the time the group of the Non-Aligned states was endeavouring to institute a NIEO. The principal mission for those who formed the strategic direction of the Non-Aligned policy in the UN during the SSOD-I was not only to further contribute to theory building concerning the link between disarmament and development, but also to *enforce* such a link within the UN. Dissatisfied with the lack of progress in their efforts for restructuring economic relations between the rich North and the poor countries of the South since launching their campaign for the establishment of a NIEO in 1973, the Non-Aligned states came to the SSOD-I with the determination to *commit* the UN membership to a conduct of binding negotiations on disarmament in a way which would be of much benefit to them. The disarmament-development link presented dogma for them and as such it had to be institutionalized in the negotiations. Submitting joint or separate but nevertheless identical working papers, the Non-Aligned states demanded during the proceedings of the SSOD-I that 'the disarmament process must be organically linked with measures adopted at the world level to establish a new international economic order'.[8] For the Non-Aligned states there was no question that 'the pursuit of disarmament is at the same time the pursuit of development by all nations'.[9] It is because of this relationship that they claimed that 'the special session should reflect an awareness of the organic link between disarmament and security and the necessity of disarmament for development'.[10]

They were explicit about the argument of the Eastern and Western states that disarmament and development are two quite distinct aims. The response of the Non-Aligned states to this claim was somewhat aggressive as well as unequivocal. The disarmament negotiations, they said, 'must be linked with economic development. However unpalatable it might be to a few, the truth remained that disarmament could contribute to real development in a great number of states'.[11] They argued that 'the problems of development and disarmament are closely related, and the two tasks must therefore succeed together or fail together'.[12]

The way the Non-Aligned states approached disarmament determined the nature of the UN's contribution they looked for. Thus, they perceived that a UN which would act as a catalyst or facilitator could not keep the link they demanded between disarmament-development in the forefront, but would let it be submerged in the morass of the diplomacy of subsequent negotiations. In other words, a UN without a concrete policy of action and a General Assembly remaining confined to making only recommendations could not ensure the institutionalization of the disarmament-development link, nor guarantee that the UN would go about its work on disarmament expeditiously. A highly interventionist UN and in particular an initiative-taking General Assembly which would lay down a programme of action which would interrelate disarmament and development would be best suited to materialize the plans of the Non-Aligned states. That is why they campaigned for a UN which would take immediately 'forceful action' and the adoption by the SSOD-I of a Final Document which, in the words of Sweden, 'must be precise and action oriented'.[13]

The fact that the Non-Aligned states were convinced that the way they looked at the UN was the only way which could put their own interests in perspective led them to take an uncompromising stand during the SSOD-I.[14] A consensus would be preferred, but only on the basis of their positions and no other. They were prepared even to press for a majority's decision in the

SSOD-I. Indeed, for them issues related to the establishment of a NIEO had to be voted upon if the developing countries were going to have them fly.[15]

The superpowers, appreciating that the Non-Aligned group was unlikely to concede ground, did not attempt to take issue with it. On the contrary, they kept a low profile during the last stage of the SSOD-I and reluctantly made concessions, ensuring the adoption of a Final Document which approximated the Non-Aligned positions. The superpowers knew that no real change could arise without their acquiescence, no matter what the General Assembly might resolve.

There were important reasons why the superpowers chose to make concessions. The priority of commitment to sincerity and truth was jeopardized because what was essential for the East and the West was to maintain a degree of popular appeal for their policies in the UN. They wanted to avoid the high political cost of being outvoted by the Non-Aligned majority at an extraordinary event like the SSOD-I which attracted enormous public attention around the globe. Furthermore, an explicit refusal on the part of the superpowers to agree with the Non-Aligned group in a Final Document would probably have had adverse effects on certain substantive disarmament and arms control policies they pursued through the UN. The world organization was and remains an agenda-setter for a variety of issues of vital importance to the superpowers ranging from those relating to disarmament and arms control to many which are not disarmament-related issues. In the realm of arms control measures, for instance, a negative attitude by the superpowers towards the UN and its disarmament activities during the SSOD-I would have made the Non-Aligned states doubt the commitment of the superpowers to reverse the horizontal proliferation of nuclear weapons;[16] and lead them to decide the bargain they made in signing the NPT was repudiated under the good faith clause of Article VI.

Additionally, such a negative attitude of the superpowers would be taken by the Non-Aligned states as a 'hostile' political act against them with certain consequences for the superpower's policies on certain non-disarmament related issues. The result would have placed the superpowers on the political defensive and, in consequence, weakened their position in the inter-issue bargaining process which very often takes place in the UN. Ambassador Maynes, who served as a negotiator for the United States in Geneva, wrote that 'it would be foolhardy to argue' that the United States is not concerned with the role of the UN as an agenda-setter for disarmament and non-disarmament issues. He further cited Ambassador Nitze's argument that 'neglecting UN disarmament issues runs the risk of placing the United States on the political defensive inside and outside the UN'.[17] A 'non-hostile' attitude of the superpowers during the SSOD-I was perceived to lead to the preservation of a minimum degree of political co-operation with the Non-Aligned states, making them at least hesitant to take unilateral decisions on other important issues by their majority.

As a consequence, a diplomatic compromise was finally reached on the text of the Final Document, but the fundamental differences were wrapped in the seemingly consensual language of this Document. In reality, the Final Document of the SSOD-I constituted a screen behind which the dichotomy of positions of the three political groups has been perpetuated until this time.[18]

The UN, instead of pragmatically coping with the dichotomy of positions, became a forum wherein a very determined majority took the initiative and imposed its approach. The SSOD-I changed the prior arrangements for, and courses of, negotiations and put decision-making in a new political context with significant implications for both the UN and the negotiating process of disarmament. As a result of modifications decided in the SSOD-I, the negotiating body was revitalized in the direction of the democratization of the discussion and the wider representation of states and concerns. The negotiating body ceased to be under the control of the superpowers as the institution of the United States-Soviet co-chair was abandoned and replaced by a presidency which rotated among member-states on a monthly basis. Also, the composition of the negotiating body (whose name changed in 1978 from CCD to Committee on Disarmament and again in 1984 to Conference on Disarmament) was expanded. This rendered it too unwieldy for fruitful negotiations as its composition reached the number of thirty-nine states.

The most notable change, however, was that the General Assembly was assigned a more powerful and regulating role than anything it had since 1960 when its role was limited simply to that of making recommendations. In effect, control over multilateral negotiations was returned to the UN with powers and authority more centralized on the General Assembly which, as a result of successive special sessions, has confirmed its supremacy by elaborating overall strategies, promoting new goals, and placing the organization and work of the multilateral body under its political authority.

Being directed to act in the mainstream of the global negotiations, the UN was placed in a new context which was the result of the attempt the Non-Aligned states made to enforce themselves as the prime agenda-setter for disarmament negotiations. The consequence was that the nature of the UN changed and its activities, quite unrealistically, were carried far from the images of an organization entrusted with the role of a potential conciliator or an inspired catalyst to a reinforcer and ratifier of the Non-Aligned policies.

This de facto transformation of the UN was based on an image of the UN that was at least as far removed from the reality as had been the image of the UN in the period of Cold War when the United States attempted to determine the agenda of negotiations and enlist the UN behind its disarmament policies with the view to force the other side to accept them. The importance of the UN, whose political ethos from 1978 and onwards has reflected the influence of the Non-Aligned approach, was grossly overestimated. The UN was used by the Non-Aligned states as a tool for accelerating, through disarmament, the pace of economic change in favour of them.

The attempt to use the UN as an instrument for dictating disarmament policy to the member-states of the UN, and especially the superpowers, was made through the launching of a strategy of action in the field of disarmament which was elaborated in the Final Document of the General Assembly's first special session on disarmament of 1978.[19] The Final Document constituted the fundamental political basis for the action-oriented UN to undertake to tackle the quixotic task of attempting to tame the superpowers and their allies. The negotiating practices which the Final Document established cannot be understood by merely reading its black letter. For deepened understanding one must examine how its implementation was sought in the subsequent negotiations. The Final Document is a detailed text which, after an introduction and declaration, envisions: a comprehensive strategy for action for disarmament culminating in general and complete disarmament as well as certain short-term measures, such as the conclusion of a comprehensive nuclear test ban treaty, which were part of this strategy but whose immediate negotiation would put the whole process in motion. Nuclear disarmament was the first priority, ranking in an order where other items followed, including chemical weapons, incendiary weapons, other weapons of mass destruction and conventional weapons.

According to the new strategy, nuclear disarmament, the primary short-term goal, was a sensitive issue which should be dealt with in the multilateral context because the principle of collective or common responsibility is paramount and governs all the aspects of disarmament activities.[20] Paragraph 28 of the Final Document contains an important statement and institutionalized completely the notion of one member-state one decisive and active participation in the negotiating process. This notion provided the conceptual foundations of the demands for democratization and universalization of the process of disarmament, for a global approach to the problem of disarmament. The latter part of Paragraph 28 recognizes that 'the nuclear-weapon states have the primary responsibility for nuclear disarmament'. This penultimate sentence acknowledges that, with 'other military significant states', the nuclear-weapon states share in 'halting and reversing the arms race'. Consequently, the final sentence concludes 'it is therefore important to secure their active participation'.

The role of the UN is acknowledged by Paragraph 27 as: 'In accordance with the Charter, the United Nations has a central role and primary responsibility in the sphere of disarmament'. A statement which seems to mirror more the demand of the Non-Aligned states for the central role to be accorded to the UN, and express less the demand of the Eastern and Western states for a central UN role that is supplemental, not primary. Implementation is less onerous, though as made explicit in the second part of Paragraph 27:

> In order to effectively discharge this role and facilitate and encourage all measures in this field, the United Nations should be kept appropriately informed of all steps in this field whether unilateral, bilateral, regional or multilateral, without prejudice to the progress of negotiations.

A role thus discharged by suitable official communications on stages reached in the process of negotiations. A role which does not seem to prevent the vital necessity of carrying out negotiations on all levels. One should, however, revert to the relevant part of Paragraph 28 of the Final Document:

> All the peoples of the world have a vital interest in the success of disarmament negotiations. Consequently, all states have the duty to contribute to efforts in the field of disarmament. All states have the right to participate in the disarmament negotiations. They have the right to participate on an equal footing in those multilateral disarmament negotiations which have a direct bearing on their national security.

Accordingly, the uncommitted states demanded that, like all the other issues of disarmament and arms limitation, nuclear disarmament 'is an international responsibility and therefore requires international, collective and multilateral efforts'.[21] Strong support was mobilized during and after the SSOD-I to keep the issue of disarmament in all its aspects within the exclusive margins of collective management involvement under the UN auspices and General Assembly's intervention.

The SSOD-I, quite unrealistically, set time limits for the implementation of the programme of action. Paragraph 44 of the Final Document explicitly provided that 'the present programme enumerates the specific measures of disarmament which should be implemented over the next few years'. A mandate was also given to the negotiating body in Geneva (CD) to complete the elaboration of such a programme in time for its adoption not later than the second special session on disarmament (SSOD-II) to be held in 1982. To further encourage the undertaking of intensive negotiations on such a programme of action, the Final Document provided that 'nothing shall preclude states from conducting negotiations on all priority items concurrently'.[22]

A comprehensive programme of action as envisioned by the Final Document is a complex matter of numerous parts. In reality, even nuclear disarmament by itself is a long-term objective which cannot be subjected or negotiated according to any predetermined timetable. One cannot learn to walk before crawling or to run before walking. The UN and the Non-Aligned states called for complex deep seated problems like the ending of the nuclear arms race and the achievement of general disarmament to be solved overnight. Experience has shown that the road to disarmament is difficult and complicated and that it calls for painstaking negotiations. The way the UN responded clearly revealed that the world organization under the political guidance of the Non-Aligned states attempted to solve all disarmament problems in a relatively short period and without sufficient regard to the contexts of world politics involved in the disarmament process. Working through an extensive and tight schedule of tasks, it was asserted that the UN business should be conducted at a hurried and hectic pace. The Non-Aligned states accentuated the fact that rapid advances in the sphere of disarmament might result in the diversion of substantial funds currently spent on armaments to develop assistance programmes. The achievement of disarmament was deemed extremely critical for the achievement of the collective objective of the Non-Aligned states, the NIEO. Immediate progress on disarmament would have a decisive impact on the other track, that of the promotion of their economic aims.

As it was formulated in the UN under a complicated programme of action and as its implementation was pursued in the aftermath of the SSOD-I, disarmament and especially nuclear disarmament was treated mechanistically and formalistically. The negotiating process of disarmament as a process of decision-making involving declaratory and deployment policies of national and international security was oversimplified. It was seen as a very expeditious process, as an intermediary stage from which the world community of the UN should depart with all possible dispatch to implement the aims of the NIEO.[23] In line with such a viewpoint, the Final Document of the SSOD-I, which devoted several paragraphs to emphasize 'the close relationship between disarmament and development',[24] explicitly proclaimed that such a course of action was appropriate because it would strengthen and consolidate the new international economic order. The new framework for international action in the field of disarmament was thus cut in the cloth of the Non-Aligned states. Disarmament in this context was seen as 'imperative for the realization of the goals of a NIEO'.[25]

What is of more significance is that disarmament in the realm of the UN was subordinated to the economic concerns of the Non-Aligned states. 'The centrality of the NIEO in the disarmament debate', as Beker observes, 'underscored the complexities of the politics of disarmament'[26] and resulted in estranging the course of negotiations from what is considered to be the real business of disarmament. What was demanded was quick action in all the fields of disarmament irrespective of the exigencies of context and the need to persuade the key-participants for a stable international security process. As a consequence, the political character of disarmament as an issue of power and other human value relations largely dependent on the ups and downs of international politics was completely undermined. The UN made light of the assumption that disarmament is bound up with large political and security choices, hard choices, affecting the states' strategies and policies, and that its achievement depends on a 'multitude of factors subject to unforeseeable change'.[27] Thus, the UN sought immediate agreements 'on abstract priorities determined without reference to their achievability'.[28] No effort was made to relate abstract propositions to the precise factual situations. Instead of emphasizing the factual elements in the decisional equation, the bases of principles and approaches are doubtful if they can contribute to the solution of all the problems of disarmament (e.g., nuclear disarmament).

By giving the Non-Aligned states the chance to expand the meaning of disarmament to reflect basic aims of a single group, the NIEO, the General Assembly highlighted the responsibility of the developed states of the North towards the underdeveloped states of the South. Thus, the UN increasingly pitted the Non-Aligned majority against the states the disarmament of which plays, according to the Non-Aligned claims, a key-role in the consolidation of the collective objective of NIEO. That explains why nuclear disarmament was given a first priority in the programme of action. Furthermore, like the Cold War period when each side wanted to talk about the other side's arms race, the tendency in the UN in the years after SSOD-I was to focus primarily on the nuclear aspects of disarmament in which the application of a global approach is questionable, and to brush aside those aspects, such as, conventional weapons and questions of limitation of arms transfers, in which the multilateral approach is more suitable. It is worthwhile to note that negotiating efforts to restrain the worldwide built-up of conventional weapons were given second order blessing in paragraph 45 of the Final Document. Unfortunately, to preserve their national and/or regional interests, many of these Non-Aligned states are major purchasers of conventional weapons and seem extremely hesitant to enter any disarmament negotiations in this field.

During and after the SSOD-I, the adoption of a comprehensive strategy with a detailed programme of action aimed to induce the world community to accept the collective conduct of negotiations in a context which would bring the universal membership of the UN into the picture and to make the UN directly relevant and functional. However, at the same time such a strategy made the disarmament issue in the UN quite irrelevant to the actual requirements of the disarmament process and therefore it was unworkable from the viewpoint of the superpowers. It may be concluded that the SSOD-I attempted unsuccessfully to turn the tide of negotiating efforts towards a comprehensive strategy through the instrumentality of the revitalized UN disarmament structures and the universality of the UN membership. The Eastern and Western states led by the superpowers signed the particular section of the Final Document which covered the programme of action, but only because the section was merely a declaration of intent, a call for negotiations put in a entirely new context. The erosion of consensus began to take a concrete shape as soon as the SSOD-I closed its doors and the CD attempted to get to the nuts and bolts of the programme of action drawn by the SSOD-I.

The CD, the multilateral negotiating body in Geneva, had from its inception worked on the basis of consensus, which, as a governing rule for taking decisions concerning its method of work, is tantamount to a veto right by any member.[29] Thus, the superpowers refused to embark on negotiations in a proposed working group dealing with nuclear disarmament per se, while the Non-Aligned states were critical of the fact that 'one group of states, in contradiction to its own commitment in the Final Document, has maintained that nuclear disarmament falls outside the purview of the Conference on Disarmament'.[30] The refusal of the superpowers to negotiate nuclear disarmament was deemed to be a real impediment to the application of the programme of action of the UN. As the Non-Aligned states argued, the desire of the superpowers to keep their members outside the process of nuclear disarmament negotiations 'is indeed the cause of the failure of all collective attempts' to carry out the UN programme of action.[31]

The negative attitude of the superpowers struck the Non-Aligned states with dismay. They saw the time for the convening of the SSOD-II approaching without any accomplishments in any part of the programme of action outlined in the Final Document. This made the Non-Aligned states feel the need to take further action to defend the Final Document of the SSOD-I to which the superpowers seemed to pay scant attention. However, their attempt to dictate to the superpowers that they should negotiate in the context of global disarmament negotiations suffered a further blow. Encouraged by their ministerial conferences, which were held in New Delhi[32] and Havana,[33] the Non-Aligned states called the CD into action to thrash out a comprehensive programme of disarmament to provide a solid basis for negotiation at the SSOD-II.[34] The newly crafted comprehensive programme of disarmament in essence constituted an altered and synoptic version of the comprehensive programme of action of the SSOD-I. It appeared to be a micrograph of SSOD-I. It had been elaborated in the seventies, as was seen in the previous chapter, but the superpowers had then refused to take it up for negotiation. It encompassed all the measures of which such a programme consisted in accordance with the order of priorities established in the Final Document of the SSOD-I. The primary concern of the Non-Aligned states for the elimination of nuclear weapons in advance of the completion of conventional disarmament was reflected in their proposal for the reworked comprehensive disarmament programme. The unrealistic ambitions of the Non-Aligned states was once again demonstrated as they proceeded with enthusiasm to try to negotiate nuclear disarmament in the context of a comprehensive plan while matters of practice and principle like verification remained basically unresolved due to the Soviet penchant for secrecy. The purpose of such a coherent scheme was the same as that envisaged in the programme of action in the Final Document: to lead to the goal of radical disarmament and then to a process which would address the economic concerns of the Non-Aligned states.

Hectic diplomacy continued to occupy the sessions of the CD before the convening of the SSOD-II for a breakthrough but in vain.[35] The CD's taking up of the reworked comprehensive disarmament programme witnessed the sharp contrast between the cool position of the superpowers during the SSOD-I and their subsequent practice in the negotiations. It was not only the fact that the interests of the superpowers was as best minimal, it was also that the CD submitted a draft of a comprehensive disarmament programme to the General Assembly for consideration at the SSOD-II which made things more dramatic than ever. Most of the part of the text on the comprehensive disarmament programme, which was a repetition of a large and substantive programme of action of the SSOD-I, was cluttered with brackets, thus indicating strong reservations and serious disagreements with the text of the Final Document of the SSOD-I itself.[36] Among the reserved provisions were those which deal with the role of the UN in the disarmament process, including all the key-provisions which provided for a universal approach to disarmament and certainly the pursuit of the NIEO through disarmament.[37] A few paragraphs of the draft comprehensive disarmament programme survived and were accepted without reservation, but they were among the less substantive ones. Thus, any initiative which might arise in the SSOD-II was substantially blocked.

By the time the General Assembly held its SSOD-II the differences between the three political groups remained undiminished and the participants showed no signs of mellowing. On the contrary, attitudes hardened during this special session. The Co-ordinating Bureau of the movement of the Non-Aligned states at the level of foreign ministers met on the eve of the SSOD-II and called upon their group to intensify its activities for 'the adoption of a comprehensive programme of disarmament' with the view to ensuring realization of the objective of general and complete disarmament.[38] This objective was heralded as essential by the Co-ordinating Bureau because it could enable the SSOD-II 'to give a new, sustained momentum to the attainment of the integral relationship between disarmament and international security and between disarmament and development'.[39]

There was much disappointment among the Non-Aligned states with the attitude of the major powers and especially the United States which, as Bennet pointed out, was 'unenthusiastic about global approaches to disarmament'[40] and made them circumvent the Final Document of SSOD-I, conformity with which was regarded by the group as a sort of sacred duty. In spite of the fact that the Final Document entrusted the CD with responsibility as the chief negotiating body and the General Assembly as merely a deliberative body,[41] the Non-Aligned group attempted in a dramatic manner to translate the deliberations of the 159 member General Assembly into effective negotiations for a comprehensive programme of disarmament.[42] They desperately tried to reach Mount Olympus in a single bound. The transformation of the SSOD-II, which was convened at a time when the rhetoric of the Cold War had been revived, into a forum for negotiation was in some way a counter-action to the superpowers' unwillingness to subscribe to global approaches to disarmament under UN auspices. As a consequence, the special session which was supposed to be an exceptionally important event lost its importance and became a ritual exercise. It led to disarray between the three political groups and in effect to a breakdown.[43] The UN membership found it difficult even to reach a consensus on a compromise text of a Final Document.[44] Strenuous diplomatic efforts were made by the Non-Aligned states to persuade the superpowers and especially the United States to accept a declaratory statement in the form of a resolution which merely reconfirmed the validity of the Final Document of the SSOD-I.[45] The reason the superpowers finally agreed to do so was the same one which had made them put their names to the Final Document of the SSOD-I, to avoid showing at least publicly that they were fallen away from the general trends prevailing in the proceedings of the SSOD-II.

By the time of the third special session on disarmament of the General Assembly (SSOD-III), in 1988, there had been no accomplishment in any part of the comprehensive programme of action of the UN. SSOD-III took place in a much improved political atmosphere as compared with the SSOD-II and was given an opportunity to rectify the drift and the political conflict within the UN. The main cause of this conflict continued to be the different perceptions which the states maintained over the role of the UN and which had forced the world organization to live in obscurity for the reason that such a disparity generated and perpetuated fundamental differences over the approach and scope, as well as the agenda, of negotiations.[46] Extraordinary positive developments in the field of international peace and security - the Treaty between the United States and the USSR on the elimination of their intermediate range and shorter range missiles (INF Treaty) had gone into effect before the opening of the SSOD-III, the boost given by the superpowers to the efforts for concluding a treaty on a 50 per cent cut in their strategic offensive arsenals, the conclusion in Geneva of the accords on the phased withdrawal of the Soviet forces from Afghanistan, and announcement of the cease-fire in the Iran-Iraq conflict - all provided a promising background for the SSOD-III and the actions the UN ought to take for a reconciliation of its membership.

The date for the convening of the SSOD-III had been fixed before all these developments began to take place and, in fact, did not allow adequate time for the UN community to digest the remarkable transformations which are taking place in international relations. The deadline for the convening of the SSOD-III should have been extended because it was too early for the astonishing world changes to have a catalytic function on the UN's work. However, SSOD-III mobilized by the bureaucratic machineries of the UN and the Non-Aligned states, proceeded quite prematurely to reassert the central position it attempts to have regarding the whole context of disarmament negotiations. Once again, disarmament received a setback as the UN failed in the universal approach to develop inclusive interests. The world community witnessed the sharp contrast between two processes: the one which develops at the present time outside the UN, where the two long-time adversaries, whose political co-operation according to the ideals held by the founders of the UN can give effect to the UN Charter, take radical steps bringing them closer to each other, the other is the activity in the realm of the UN which, as the proceedings of the SSOD-III clearly showed, remains a territory for cultivating political confrontation among its member-states. During the SSOD-III the UN membership was once again unable to reach a consensus on a Final Document. This session was more disappointing than the SSOD-II in terms of the unwillingness of important participants like the United States even to reaffirm the validity of the Final Document of the SSOD-I.[47]

However, the SSOD-III took an importance of it own because, due to the attitude two of the most powerful states adopted, the unspeakable was brought out into the open. This is that the UN was deluding itself, for more than a decade, with the false belief that states would co-operate within it to move forward disarmament negotiations. The appeal the INF Treaty had on the public, the fact that the SSOD-III failed to capture public attention as it was overshadowed by the pace of international events including the changes in Eastern Europe and the American presidential elections, and calls of individual states for more down-to earth approaches in the UN, prompted the United States to assert openly that the Final Document of the SSOD-I did not reflect, as the Non-Aligned states argued, a 'historic consensus'. The United States now admitted that the Final Document 'was treated as a compendium of universally accepted principles, while in reality there was a profound disparity of views on many of the disarmament issues addressed in the Final Document'.[48]

Both the United States and United Kingdom reacted negatively to a demand, which was made immediately after the SSOD-III ended, for strengthening the role of the UN which, according to UN Resolution 43/77 B, provides 'the most appropriate forum for all members to contribute effectively to the consideration and resolution of disarmament issues'.[49] The two states argued that this viewpoint which was expressed in the Resolution was totally misleading.[50] The Soviet Union voted for the Resolution in an effort to signify its changing attitude in world affairs and its intention to co-operate with the UN in the future rather than to endorse the existing framework for disarmament negotiations. However, the United States and United Kingdom refused to approve the text of the Resolution 43/77 B which, being drafted and tabled by the Non-Aligned states, proclaimed that the UN gave at the present time 'a new direction and impetus for disarmament efforts'.[51] Furthermore, by arguing that the Final Document of the SSOD-I had lost its relevance due to the changing circumstances, these states completely undermined the political basis of action the UN took after 1978.

Conclusions

The point of departure for any particular analysis of the UN's most recent involvement in the disarmament process is the lack of political reality that characterized the efforts on the part of the Non-Aligned group to place the UN at the centre of the global negotiating process. This proved to be unsuccessful because it ignored the different perceptions which the United States and the Soviet Union maintained as to the world structure for negotiating disarmament. Thus, the members of the UN continued to perceive the role of the UN in the negotiating process differently. Purporting to bring back the UN into the central position in the achievement of disarmament, the Non-Aligned group adopted and followed the unrealistic view that it could be done by the superimposition of their claims, which were connected with a strong belief in egalitarian principles, on the UN and the major powers. In reality, this lack of precision as to the role of the UN reached the surface during the SSOD-I where the three political groups failed to demonstrate a genuine desire to consolidate their claims. Instead, what emerged was the appearance of strong disagreements over, firstly, the use to which the UN machinery for disarmament negotiations should be put, secondly, the agenda and, finally, the form the institution-building of the particular disarmament machinery should take.

The contrast between the real facts of the international situation and the activity which took place in the realm of the UN under pressure from the Non-Aligned group could not have been be sharper. There was an excessive reliance on the decision-making process of the UN despite the strong opposition of the United States and the Soviet Union as well as their allies. The theoretical centre of decision-making was moved towards the UN and particularly the General Assembly and through it towards the states with unelected leaders which were the weakest and the smallest. The UN policy bears a close relationship to the expanding membership of the world organization during that period and became identified with the positions of the Non-Aligned states which were solely responsible for transforming the UN from what it ought to be, an inspired catalyst and facilitator, into a reinforcer of their special policies. As a result of this, the UN was used as an instrument for compelling the major powers to negotiate within a framework which was unacceptable to them. This was achieved through the adoption by the UN of a format for international action in the field of disarmament which had been tailored to suit to the Non-Aligned purposes. In this way the Non-Aligned states brought pressure to bear on and in effect to dictate disarmament policy to the major powers, thus forcing the UN to go far beyond the realities of its position in the international political system. Force of numbers of votes in the General Assembly did not add up to how to proceed with disarmament. Agreement of the major powers continued to be vital to disarmament discussions and the two superpowers were not voting on the same side, not yet that is.

The return of the UN to a more central role in dealing with disarmament was accompanied by the UN charting a course of action which, as it was enacted, resulted in estranging the course of the negotiations in the UN from the real business of disarmament. The problem of disarmament was shifted away from its political mooring of realities and was deeply mired in the arena of the politics of international economic relations between North and South. In this way, UN's disarmament machinery became irrelevant to the major powers which found this machinery an unsatisfactory basis through which to negotiate, and they were forced, once again, to show preference for the existing bilateral structures for dealing with the issue of disarmament.

Notes

1. UN Document A/AC.187/98, 2 February 1978, p. 2, Working paper submitted by USSR. None of the Eastern or Western states appealed for the strengthening of the role of the UN; see the following UN Documents: A/AC.187/35, 2 May 1977, United Kingdom; A/AC.187/13, 14 April 1977, Czechoslovakia.
2. The Eastern and Western states did not propose any concrete policy of action for the UN; see Report of the Preparatory Committee For the Special Session of the General Assembly Devoted to Disarmament, General Assembly, Official Records: Tenth Special Session, Supplement No 1 (A/S-10/I), vol. II, III, V and VI.
3. See, for example, USSR's position in UN Document A/AC.187/SR.14, pp. 2-4, cited in UN Document A/AC.187/76, 15 August 1977; United States' position in Document UN A/AC.187/17, 22 April 1977; Czechoslovakia's position in UN Document A/AC.187/13, 14 April 1977; United Kingdom's position in UN Document A/AC.187/35, 2 May 1977; France's position in UN Document A/AC.187/23, 27 April 1977.
4. UN Document A/AC.187/25, 26 April 1977, p. 3.
5. UN Document A/AC.187/55, 18 May 1977, Working Paper submitted by Sri Lanka on behalf of the Non-Aligned states, paras 7 and 13; see also UN Document A/AC.187/55/Add.I, 24 January 1978, para. 7; see also Report of the Preparatory Committee for the Special Session of the

General Assembly, Official Records, Tenth Special Session, Supplement No 1(A/S-10/I), Chapter IX, para. 4.

6. UN Document A/AC.187/5, 8 May 1977, paras 6 and 11, Working Paper submitted by the Non-Aligned group; see also M. A. Husain (1980), 'Third World and Disarmament, Shadow and Substance', *Third World Quarterly*, no 1, January, p. 97; see also Laurence Weiler (1978), 'Reflections of the Disarmament Session', *Bulletin of Atomic Scientists*, vol. 34, December, p. 9; see also Richard Jackson (1983), *The Non-Aligned, the UN and the Superpowers*, Praeger: New York, p. 172.

7. Document CD/PV. 336, 4 February 1986, p. 38, Mr. Lechuga, Cuba; for a similar view see Document CD/PV. 343, 27 February 1986, pp. 6-7, Mr. Velayati, Iran and Document CD/PV. 358, 22 April 1986, p. 23, Mr. Narayanan, India.

8. UN Document A/AC.187/77, 30 August 1977, Romania.

9. Ibid. See also UN Document General Assembly, Official Records, A/S10/PV. 4, 25 May 1978, p. 7.

10. UN Document A/AC.187/SR.7, p. 5, Finland, cited in UN Document A/AC.187/76, 15 August 1977, p. 21.

11. UN Document A/AC.187/SR.8, p. 4, Nepal, cited in UN Document A/AC.187/76, 15 August 1977, p. 59; for the Western position see UN Document A/AC.187/25, 26 April 1977, p. 2, Netherlands.

12. UN Document A/AC.187/SR. 7, p. 2, Austria, cited in UN Document A/AC.187/76, 15 August 1977, p.19.

13. UN Document A/AC.187/19, 26 April 1977, p. 2, Sweden; see also UN Document A/AC.187/28, 27 April 1977, pp. 2-4, Algeria.

14. Homer Jack (1977), 'The Special Session on Disarmament, The Non-Aligned Leadership', *Review of International Affairs*, vol. 28, 5-20 August, p. 16; see also Tariq Hyder (1978), 'Inchoate Aspirations for World Order Change', *International Security*, vol. 2, part 4, spring, p. 57.

15. Muchkund Dubey (1985), 'The Main Forces at Work', in Arthur Lall (ed.), *Multilateral Negotiations and Mediation*, Pergamon Press: New York, p. 172.

16. Charles Maynes (1983), 'UN Disarmament Efforts: Is there Life After the Second Special Session on Disarmament?' in Edward Luck (ed.), *Arms Control: The Multilateral Alternative,* New York University Press for UNA-USA: New York & London, p. 57.

17. Ibid.

18. Pakistan admitted that the consensus was superficial, in GAOR, A/S-10/PV.27, 6 July 1978, p. 98.

19. Final Document of the Tenth Special Session, adopted by the General Assembly in its Resolution S-10/2 of 30 June 1978. UNGA Resolution (S-X), cited in Appendix.

20. For the notion of common or collective responsibility see Document CD/PV. 336, 4 February 1986, pp. 20-21, Mr. Garcia Robles, Mexico; see also Document CD/PV. 334, 25 July 1985, p. 14, Mr. A. Karim, Bangladesh. Guidance for the interpretation of this notion can be found in the UNGA Resolutions and the recorded debates in the UN and CD. See for example UNGA Resolution 33/91, 16 December 1978 and 40/152 P, 1985; Document CD/PV. 222, 5 July 1983, p. 14, Mr. Mosjov, Yugoslavia; Document CD/PV. 249, 13 March 1984, p. 30, Mr. De Silva, Brazil; Document CD/PV. 339, 13 February 1986, p. 31, Mr. Q. Jiadong, China; Document CD/PV. 342, 25 February 1986, p. 28.

21. Document CD/PV. 249, 13 March 1984, p. 9, Mr. George, Nigeria.

22. Para. 46 of the Final Document of the Tenth Special Session, cited in Appendix.

23. UN Document A/AC.187/91, 26 January 1978, Working Paper submitted by Pakistan. Pakistan argued that 'the achievement of general and complete disarmament is essential to ensure universal peace and security and establish a New International Economic Order'.

24. See the preamble and paras 5, 12, 16, and esp. para. 35 of the Final Document of the Tenth Special Session, cited in Appendix.

25. UN Document A/AC.187/SR.7, p. 5, Finland, cited in UN Document A/AC.187/76, 15 August 1977, p. 21.

26. Avi Beker (1986), *Disarmament Without Order: The Politics of Disarmament at the United Nations,* Greenwood Press:Westport (Conn.) & London, pp. 108-109.

27. UN Document A/AC.187/17, 22 April 1977, p. 2, United States.

28. Ibid.

29. Document CD/PV. 226, 19 July 1983, p. 25, Mr. Garcia Robles, Mexico.

30. Document CD/PV. 358, 22 April 1986, p. 12, Mr. Narayanan, India.

31. Document CD/PV. 243, 21 February 1984, p. 11, Mr. Rouis, Algeria.

32. UN Document A/36/116, 6 March 1981, p. 21

33. UN Document A/37/333, S/15278, 16 July 1982, Annex, p. 32.

34. Document CD/283, 20 April 1982, Report of the Working group on Comprehensive Programme of Disarmament to the CD.

35. UN Document A/C.I/36/PV.12, 26 October 1981, pp. 22-23.

36. Document CD/PV. 237, 26 August 1983, p. 13, Mr. Cromantie, United Kingdom.

37. Special Report of the Committee on Disarmament, General Assembly,

Official Records, Supplement No 2(A/S-12/2) Appendix I, pp. 71-115.

38. UN Document A/37/333, S/15278, 16 July 1982, Annex, Appendix III, p. 79.

39. Ibid.

40. A. LeRoy Bennet (1983), *International Organizations*, Prentice Hall: Englewood Cliffs (New Jersey), p. 322.

41. Paras 113 and 120 of the Final Document of the Tenth Special Session, cited in Appendix.

42. Julie Dahlitz (1982), 'The Second Special Session of the General Assembly Devoted to Disarmament. An Account and Evaluation', *Disarmament: A Periodic Review by the United Nations*, vol. v, no 2, November, pp. 49-61, esp. p. 54.

43. United Nations (1983), *The United Nations Disarmament Yearbook, 1982*, United Nations: New York, pp. 15-65, esp. pp. 62-64.

44. A/S-12/32: Concluding Document of the Twelfth Special Session of the General Assembly, 10 July 1982, cited in ibid., pp. 497-508.

45. Ibid., p. 509.

46. See UN Document A/C.I/PV.41, 17 November 1988, Mr. Friedersdorf, United States.

47. United Nations (1989), *The United Nations Disarmament Yearbook, 1988*, United Nations: New York, p. 77.

48. Ibid., p. 81. For documentation concerning the SSOD-III see Report of the Preparatory Committee for the Third Special Session of the General Assembly Devoted to Disarmament, in General Assembly, Official Records, Fifteenth Special Session, Supplement No 1 (A/S-15).

49. A draft resolution submitted by 21 Non-Aligned states and entitled 'Third Special Session of the General Assembly devoted to Disarmament' fail to obtain the consent of the United States and United Kingdom. These two states justified their abstention from the voting process on the reason that the text of the draft resolution and especially paragraphs 3 and 4 were misleading. UNGA Resolution 43/77 B was adopted by 152 to none with 2 abstentions.

50. United Nations (1989), op.cit., pp. 81-82 and 89.

51. Ibid.

6 Conclusions and recommendations

The UN's effectiveness depends on the readiness of its member-states to work jointly for taking action in the field of disarmament. In the first years of negotiations in the UN, the major powers did not agree to make the UN the repository of atomic energy by bestowing it with far-reaching powers of control, development and inspection. The UN remained an organization without any intrinsic power to affect the process of nuclear disarmament on its own account. Therefore, it should have been the case that from the fifties until the present time the whole emphasis of its activities should have been turned towards the search for consensus among the UN on what precisely its authority ought to be. This should have been the forward-looking target for the world organization. In terms of the achievability or not of such consensus, one can proceed to evaluate the role the UN played, its successes, failures and shortcomings in its management and to identify negative and positive component parts of the UN's ability to address in an effective way the question of nuclear disarmament.

The search for consensus is conditional upon the ability of the UN to provide a forum for conciliation of the views of its membership. In the fifties, however, the UN was not in a position to play this role because it lived and grew in the most power-political character of international relations, the main characteristic of which was the direct political confrontation between East and West led by the two superpowers. The political environment has always been instrumental in determining the organisation's effectiveness, relevance and prestige, and this factor always deserves recognition in the analysis of the UN's performance. It may be fairly concluded that the UN's potential depends significantly on the degree of moderation or not which exists in the international milieu.

As the greater part of the normal life in the UN became consumed by its use as a means to wage the Cold War, so progress towards peaceful solutions and compromising attitudes in the purview of the UN was dulled. In light of the impossibility of a more powerful UN intervention in the question of nuclear disarmament, its role as a chamber for potential conciliation and as an agent for stimulating common action had to be demonstrated. However, the UN could not carry out two contradictory roles: to be a place of conciliation and peaceful co-existence and, at the same time, be an agency in the service of a particular majority group, the Western one, which systematically used the UN as a focal point against the Soviet Union in the name of international action. The UN was given a prime place in the exposition of the politics of conflict which prevailed during the Cold War. The 'Uniting for Peace' Resolution was just the example which testified to the UN's retreat from the great power unanimity principle which was the basic premise for action in the field of international security. The Cold War struggle as the super-issue of the fifties was the source of the superpowers' misguiding the UN into calling for comprehensive disarmament in the midst of the most intense hostility. Thus, the UN was saddled with an impossible task but its policy served the superpowers' predisposition for conducting propaganda warfare in relation to disarmament proposals. The superpowers used the world organization primarily as means of attacking each other and persuading the public that they were doing everything possible to lower the danger of mass destruction. An important inference which can be drawn is that the UN could not and cannot operate effectively in the context of a conflict between the superpowers in its environment.

The period of the sixties was quite different from that of the fifties. It proved in a positive way that the world organization depends for the successful promotion of its desire to deal with nuclear disarmament on the predisposition of the states and especially the superpowers for common action. The success of the UN in dealing with nuclear disarmament even in its arms control phase during the sixties was signified by a broad consensus of the main political groups of the UN.

A sharp downturn in the tensions which had dominated the world in the post-war era led to the establishment of a working relationship between the superpowers in the late fifties and this change in the world conditions was also reflected in the UN. The UN's membership was disposed to using a more rational approach to disarmament than before. A new approach which was an advance on previous positions to disarmament was visualized: the need for agreements on the implementation of limited objectives to disarmament as well as the build up of mutual confidence on the basis of which it would be feasible to proceed later to larger areas of disarmament. It was at this time that the UN began to develop a new picture and qualities of an impartial person standing between the superpowers and their two blocs. It became an arena for a real debate on, and realistic approaches to, the issue of nuclear disarmament which exceeded the narrow concerns of one bloc. Two significant interrelated factors actually contributed to this new role for the UN: the decline of the use of the UN as a monolithic instrument of US policy and the thrust onto the UN scene of new states from the so called Non-Aligned world which changed the correlation of the political forces in the UN in terms of number power.

Thus, a decentralised framework for disarmament negotiations came into existence in the beginning of sixties, the main feature of which was the establishment of a negotiating body, the ENDC (1962-1968), outside the UN but closely linked to it. The new framework for negotiations ensured, as the result of the UN conceding its primarily role to the Soviet Union and the US, leadership for the superpowers by virtue of which they jointly controlled the ENDC and consequently the path of the negotiations. The UN confined its role to that of making recommendations to the ENDC. It should be said, however, that the fact that the UN and especially the General Assembly were restricted to making only recommendations without attempting to dictate concrete policies of their own to the ENDC, facilitated the disarmament negotiations for the reason that it left negotiators with freedom of action in their search for common approaches to disarmament. Any attempt on the part of the UN to dictate concrete policy-action to the ENDC would have had the effect of prejudging the path of negotiations. In essence it would have prevented the ENDC from acting, as it really did, as a coherent whole, a facilitator which inspired international dialogue and action.

The broad consensus of this period reflected the wishes of the world community in terms of both the institutional format and the agenda for negotiations. The Non-Aligned states welcomed both. They agreed with the new institutional format because, firstly, they identified themselves as the laymen in the matters of negotiations and decided to leave it to the expertise of the major powers who would build up an institution under which they had the central management of the pace of negotiations; and secondly because, being just at the beginning of the historical process of organising themselves as a coherent group, the Non-Aligned states were only interested in ensuring their presence in the negotiations. Their determination to stand as a catalytic agent and conciliators between the superpowers and their consequential eagerness to show that they would not pursue their own goals, explains why the Non-Aligned states did not take issue with the superpowers either in the proposed limited approach to disarmament or on the agenda.

The building of international peace was perceived to be, according to the UN/ENDC, much more attainable and easier with the pursuit of arms control measures. It was clear that due to the 'premature political environment', the search for measures of physical disarmament was fraught with risks which could prevent the UN/ENDC from scoring the success it did. Viewed in this light, the UN/ENDC demonstrated its profound concern with the gradual construction of peace through their search for arms control measures, like the Partial Test Ban Treaty, the Outer Space Treaty, the Non-Proliferation Treaty and the Sea Bed Treaty. Taking the negotiations away from the 'dead centre' of grandiose plans for general and complete disarmament, the UN/ENDC took the most positive action in the field of political *detente*. It managed to break the Cold War barriers and reversed a situation which had long seemed likely to have no speedy outcome for peace. As such, it had far-reaching consequences. Peace and negotiations were put in a better perspective and the deep-rooted cause of accomplishments which took place subsequently in the field of arms control, like SALT I and II or the first real disarmament measure, the INF Treaty, should be traced back to the time the first conditions of political *detente* were created. On the basis of the results achieved in the sixties and their far-reaching consequences thereafter, one can infer that what the UN can at best do in circumstances of strained international relations is to concentrate on limited objectives of disarmament in order to promote perspectives of confidence among states. Although it may be difficult in the future for a return of the Cold War days which split the former allies of World War II into two opposing blocs, there will be situations built upon circumstances of tension and suspicion. In these circumstances the pursuit of arms control measures to build up perspectives of confidence will be the most useful approach and the only one whose success is within the bounds of possibility.

The hopes for a long-lasting consensus were short-lived. Different perceptions of the main political groups of the UN over its role in the world disarmament machinery arose sharply at the beginning of seventies and resulted in a swing of the UN's membership from the consensus it had achieved in the sixties. The negotiation and commitment of the overwhelming majority of the Non-Aligned states to the NPT, under an imbalance of obligations and responsibilities in comparison to the superpowers, made them acquire a lively sense of collective responsibility *vis-à-vis* disarmament and led them to form a group designed to exert pressure on the most powerful states to go for speedy nuclear disarmament. This was the most important reason why the camps of East and West institutionalized the disarmament and arms control dialogue through the bilateral institution of SALT-START and essentially in response to the UN limited responsibilities of a purely multilateral nature.

The surest reason, however, for the decline of the UN's influence on disarmament was the retreat of the Non-Aligned states from the role of mediators and conciliators which they had demonstrated in the past. The group changed from the original position it held in the sixties, when it acted as a bridge between the superpowers with an impartial approach to disarmament, to the evolution of a new international behaviour. The interrelated factors were equally responsible for the new international attitude the Non-Aligned states adopted: the huge increase of their numbers in the UN with the continued proliferation of new states and the gradual association of disarmament with their special goals which influenced them to approach disarmament with the aim of safeguarding their own interests and prestige. Most of the new states which came to the UN by virtue of the mass admission which occurred in the sixties carried with them a legacy of bitterness over their past colonial status as well as a host of problems mainly relating to their economic development. With the UN paying only intermittent attention to their economic problems, any subject which could promote development was regarded with interest and attempts were made to link such subjects with the efforts for the advancement of the economic position of the Non-Aligned states. One subject so treated was disarmament.

While the Non-Aligned states attempted to associate their own interests with disarmament, and this association of ideas was now pronounced in the the General Assembly in which the Non-Aligned states played the dominant role in decision-making, their interests could not pass into the disarmament negotiations where the course which was followed was unresponsive to linking of disarmament with the particular concerns of the Non-Aligned states. In essence the superpowers, taking advantage of their special status in the CCD (1969-1978) and of its autonomy from the UN, were circumventing that majority's decision at will. In consequence, the Non-Aligned states sought, in the name of democratization, the reform of the existing decentralized framework for disarmament negotiations and the complete subjection of the CCD to the UN. The basic aim was to make the UN's role predominant and central in the management of the negotiating process and to allow the General Assembly to draw up policies and create strategies of action in the field of disarmament. They sought thereby to firmly implant the group's access to the negotiating table where their problems could be taken into account and where, according to their perspectives, they could really influence decisions affecting their economies in the future.

With their predisposition to democratize the decision-making relating to disarmament, the Non-Aligned group initiated proceedings for restructuring the existing UN disarmament machinery against the wishes of the superpowers. The restructuring efforts took the form of a political struggle against the superpowers. Searching for a means of remodelling the negotiating machinery, the Non-Aligned states came inevitably into political confrontation with those states which they regarded as responsible for the existing UN disarmament framework of negotiations. The CCD which was supposed to be a body for negotiations was effectively marginalized by this severe political conflict. The conflict distorted practices followed in the negotiations which had so far proved quite satisfactory. Serious negotiations could not be established within the framework of the UN due to the fluidity of the situation. The politics of conflict became confused with the politics of peace which disarmament negotiations ought to serve. As the restructuring efforts turned out to be a challenge against the privileged position the superpowers enjoyed in the current decentralised framework of negotiations, they reinforced the superpowers' preference for the existing bilateral structure of SALT-START. The SALT institution, due to the conflict prevailing in the UN developed as a sort of institutional alternative to the world organization as evidenced by the lack of co-operation between the two forums.

What made the long term restructuring efforts of the Non-Aligned states critical for the UN's ability to address properly the issue of disarmament was the fact that the reconstruction they wanted to impose on the UN disarmament structures carried with it, and perpetuated, the differences between them and the other two major political groups of the UN, the East and the West. Restructuring was virtually a unilateral undertaking on the part of the Non-Aligned states against the decisions of the superpowers which did not acknowledge the 'control' of the UN but gave 'an important role' to it under the existing framework of negotiations, which allowed them to act beyond the direct guidance of the decision-making of the UN, in particular the General Assembly. The crisis which afflicted the UN was virtually an identity crisis, being rooted in the evolution of different perceptions of the UN's membership over its role in the global disarmament machinery and the degree of acceptance by member-states of a common decision framework of law and institutions and guiding international practices concerning disarmament negotiations. This crisis obstructed the world organization from coming up with a clear, attractive and affordable mission.

The first special session of the General Assembly devoted to disarmament (SSOD-I) was convened in 1978. One would expect that the SSOD-I, which was supposed to be an out of the ordinary occurrence, would focus political attention upon the veritable crisis facing the UN. The UN had to take action to resolve this crisis but it failed to do so because a very determined majority of the UN, the Non-Aligned states, being eager to impose their own position, became the master of the proceedings during the SSOD-I and made the UN's policy identify itself with their views. In fact the UN as a whole did not demonstrate any sort of differentiation from the Non-Aligned position. Indeed, it took, under the Non-Aligned group's pressure, a stand favouring that group's central position in disarmament matters. Thus, control over multilateral negotiations was totally shifted from the superpowers' responsibility to the General Assembly and through it towards the Non-Aligned states.

Without showing a sense of realism, the Non-Aligned states attempted to strengthen the powers of the UN and place it in the central position in the global negotiating process simply by relying on their numerical strength. Precisely because it is the quality rather than the quantity of support which the UN needed to become a more effective institution, the Non-Aligned strategy proved to be unsuccessful because it ignored the different perceptions of the superpowers as to the world structure for negotiations in which the UN does not occupy the central position. It can be said that the Non-Aligned states overestimated their importance relying excessively and unrealistically on the decision-making of the UN which is quite theoretical. The fact that the Non-Aligned policy stepped out of the world realities was further demonstrated by the attempt they made to use the UN as an instrument for forcing states and especially the major powers to disarm. Thus, the UN went far beyond the realities of its position in the international system which makes UN effectiveness dependent on the will of its most powerful states.

The Non-Aligned states clearly overestimated the importance of the UN when they transferred it from what it ought to be, namely an inspired catalyst and a potential conciliator and facilitator of disarmament negotiations, into a reinforcer of their policies which were intended to dictate that the major powers should negotiate within a framework which was unacceptable to them. This was done through the adoption by the UN of a format for international action in the field of disarmament which was not only unrealistic but also had been tailored to serve the specific interests of the Non-Aligned group. It claimed to facilitate the basic economic aims of the Non-Aligned states through demands for disarmament in all fields, nuclear disarmament was just a priority, which should take place under expeditious processes. Under such a claim, the political character of disarmament, including nuclear disarmament, which is an issue of power relations largely dependent on the ups and downs of international relations and primarily shaped by the major powers, lost its prominence. In consequence, disarmament was subordinated to the struggle of the Non-Aligned states for development and as such it reflected a North-South bias. This resulted in the estrangement of the debate in the UN from the real issues of disarmament as they were perceived to be in the real world outside the world organization. As the UN disarmament negotiations became increasingly irrelevant to the real problem of disarmament, the major powers turned their backs on the UN paying scant attention to its course of action and thus continuing to damage the UN's prestige up to the present time.

The lack of co-operation between states or groups of states, for reasons which were explained above, was largely responsible for the poor performance of the UN in the field of disarmament in the eighties. However, there are good reasons to believe that the 1990s may be better for the UN and its role in relation to disarmament. The astonishing scope as well as rate of world changes gives the UN the opportunity for the first time to operate under external conditions (both predispositional variables of peoples and environmental variables of the features of the larger community context) comparable to those which were deemed by the founders as essential for making the UN an effective instrument for the preservation of peace across the globe. A new global security situation is being shaped primarily by the revolutionary shifts in Eastern Europe which have brought an end to the ideologically charged contest which characterized relations between states as well as by the positive results in the field of disarmament, like the moves towards the scaling down of United States and Russian strategic nuclear arsenals and the agreed reductions in conventional weapons in Europe. This new security situation is bound to give the need for collective security and disarmament greater urgency. Will this new security situation pick up the potential it harbours to lead authoritative decision-makers to give the UN an enhanced place in the arenas of international life?

The changing international context has already affected the UN. There is an apparent tendency for the member-states and above all the major powers to act in concert to support the UN. A first practical step which has no precedent in the long life of the organization has already been taken towards strengthening its role. The major powers agreed to act under the authority of the UN following the aggression of Kuwait by Iraq. Action has been taken with unanimity to implement more than a dozen Security Council Resolutions and especially Resolution 678 (1990) which urged member-states 'to use all necessary means' with a view to drive Iraq out of Kuwait. The action which was taken to bring the invasion and occupation of Kuwait by Iraq to an end is rightly deemed to be the first act in the process of building a world order, arising from the ruins of the Cold War, both to be supported by the authority of the UN and to be based on full respect for international law.

The most urgent task for the UN at the present time is to initiate a dialogue involving its entire membership with the purpose of charting the future course of action of the UN with prospects of success and to exploit the momentum which currently exists in the international environment. The tendency which was shown especially during the Cold War to use the UN as an instrument for propaganda battles and making accusatory statements should become a thing of the past. The practice of making the UN take one or the other side's point of view or to rally the organization behind policies of the one or the other group, as happened in the fifties or the eighties, should immediately cease. The UN should be restored as an impartial forum to make its valuable contribution as a promoter of international dialogue on issues of disarmament and as a conciliator and facilitator of the disarmament negotiations.

The most recent work of the UN suggests that the endemic problem in the UN is the ambiguity of its role in disarmament due to the different perceptions the member-states have maintained. The use of the UN arena as a recourse depends on an awareness of common goals. As a matter of great urgency, the organization should work essentially for a special type of consensus in order to rectify the present situation. It is this consensus of the common interest of its membership that will enable progress to be made in the direction of the goals of the UN Charter. It presupposes rapprochement and, finally, agreement on a comprehensive world decision structure for negotiating disarmament wherein the UN may consistently play a role approved by the entire community.

It should be pointed out, that it might be better if the member-states would agree to restrict the role of the UN in those areas of disarmament and arms control where the multilateral approach is more suitable or necessary, rather than to attempt to incorporate within the UN negotiating bodies like the bilateral institution of START/INF. This would enable the UN to define the limits of its universal approach to disarmament within the overall framework of negotiations and would give the opportunity, for the first time, to co-operate with the other forums in order to promote the search for peace through arms reduction in a more effective way. It is the pronouncement of a clearcut continuity between the UN and other forums and their complementarity that one would like to see acknowledged more clearly.

There is a strong claim based on institutional, functional and political grounds that the UN could play a greater part by reconciling itself to a more restricted role rather than by attempting, as it unsuccessfully did in the past, to handle from a central position the burdensome range of all the disarmament issues including nuclear disarmament. From an institutional and functional point of view, the incorporation of other forums within the UN may cause difficulties and problems because of the universalization of principles and practices relating to disarmament which have been well established in the UN. From a political point of view, forums like the START institution or the Vienna talks on conventional forces in Europe have proved to be successful with significant breakthroughs and their functioning should continue uninterrupted in order to sustain and develop their momentum.

Tangible results in the field of nuclear disarmament provide strong evidence that the superpowers alone are moving forward the process of nuclear disarmament. By virtue of these developments the Final Document of the SSOD-I which put its main accent on nuclear disarmament by the superpowers has been rendered inoperative and is justifiably regarded by a part of the UN membership as outmoded. The next special session on disarmament, whenever it may be convened, should undertake to replace the Final Document of the SSOD-I by a new one. A new Final Document should focus the UN's action not only on the armaments of the superpowers but also on other issues of disarmament and arms limitation and arms control which are also of vital importance for the preservation of peace.

In the multilateral field absolute priority should be given to the negotiations for a world-wide comprehensive ban on chemical and biological weapons as well weapons that poison the environment for all. In the field of multilateral arms control, first priority should be the establishment of a more viable and stronger non-proliferation regime and measures to restrain international arms transfers. A first step which would pave the way for efforts to curb the transfer and to control the conventional arms race could be the setting up of a UN organ under the authority of the Security Council for registering arms deliveries and monitoring trends in the world arms trade. The Resolution which the General Assembly adopted on 9 December 1991 which requests states to record their imports and exports of certain major conventional weapon systems, and provide this information to the UN Secretary-General on an annual basis is a solid step in the right direction. Furthermore, the Conference on Disarmament in Geneva should consider converting the 1963

Partial Test Ban Treaty into a comprehensive test ban. However, the UN should avoid drawing up a time table of specific target dates for achieving measures of disarmament or arms control.

A considerable part of the current debate in the UN has turned to proposals for the establishment of an autonomous and integrated multilateral verification system within the UN. There are reasons to have serious reservations about this proposal. Verification under the UN's authority would be a co-operative exercise and would require, as a precondition, co-operative input by all states to place, in advance, their trust in the world organization. Furthermore, the cost for installing such a verification system may not be affordable in this period of financial restraints on the UN. What is considered to be realistically feasible, in the short run, is for the UN to supply service assistance for verification purposes on an ad hoc basis in the context of multilateral agreements on disarmament or arms control, if the parties so request. This would enable the UN gradually to gain experience and to develop some expertise. Following such a course and provided that the credibility gap of the states towards the UN can be narrowed, the Security Council could incrementally increase its involvement in the verification business for the stage to be reached where the UN will be entrusted with an autonomous mechanism for monitoring agreements.

It seems that the reconciliation of the views of the member-states of the UN is an imperative need if there is to be an upgrading of the role of the UN in the disarmament process. For so long as the member-states of the UN continue to disagree on the role of the UN, there cannot be the remotest possibility of them agreeing on a commonly accepted UN agenda for negotiation. With imagination and moderation on all sides, the UN has a chance to end its dismal record of failure and take advantage of the new international climate to play a significant role in future disarmament discussions. Whatever the outcome of the disarmament debate over the next few years, the agenda of the UN for the 1990s has already been set by the old ideologies that have been superseded by the more pragmatic policies of the last years of the twentieth century. An opportunity for the UN to fulfil its Charter obligations and play a significant role in the establishment of a new world order has become a real possibility at long last.

Appendix: The Final Document of the first special session on disarmament

The General Assembly,

Alarmed by the threat to the very survival of mankind posed by the existence of nuclear weapons and the continuing arms race, and recalling the devastation inflicted by all wars,

Convinced that disarmament and arms limitation, particularly in the nuclear field, are essential for the prevention of the danger of nuclear war and the strengthening of international peace and security and for the economic and social advancement of all peoples, thus facilitating the achievement of the new international economic order,

Having resolved to lay the foundations of an international disarmament strategy which, through co-ordinated and persevering efforts in which the United Nations should pay a more effective role, aims at general and complete disarmament under effective international control,

Adopts the following Final Document of this special session of the General Assembly devoted to disarmament:

I. INTRODUCTION

1. Attainment of the objective of security, which is an inseparable element

of peace, has always been one of the most profound aspirations of humanity. States have for a long time sought to maintain their security through the possession of arms. Admittedly, their survival has, in certain cases, effectively depended on whether they could count on appropriate means of defence. Yet the accumulation of weapons, particularly nuclear weapons, today constitutes much more a threat than a protection for the future of mankind. The time has therefore come to put an end to this situation, to abandon the use of force in international relations and to seek security in disarmament, that is to say, through a gradual but effective process beginning with a reduction in the present level of armaments. The ending of the arms race and the achievement of real disarmament are tasks of primary importance and urgency. To meet this historic challenge is in the political and economic interests of all the nations and peoples of the world as well as in the interests of ensuring their genuine security and peaceful future.

2. Unless its avenues are closed, the continued arms race means a growing threat to international peace and security and even to the very survival of mankind. The nuclear and conventional arms build-up threatens to stall the efforts aimed at reaching the goals of development, to become an obstacle on the road of achieving the new international order and to hinder the solution of other vital problems facing mankind.

3. Dynamic development of detente, encompassing all spheres of international relations in all regions of the world, with the participation of all countries, would create conditions conducive to the efforts of States to end the arms race, which has engulfed the world, thus reducing the danger of war. Progress on detente and progress on disarmament mutually complement and strengthen each other.

4. The Disarmament Decade solemnly declared in 1969 by the United Nations is coming to an end. Unfortunately, the objectives established on that occasion by the General Assembly appear to be as far away today as they were then, or even further because the arms race is not diminishing but increasing and outstrips by far the efforts to curb it. While it is true that some limited agreements have been reached, 'effective measures relating to the cessation of the nuclear arms race at an early date and to nuclear disarmament' continue to elude man's grasp. Yet the implementation of such measures is urgently required. There has not been either any real progress that might lead to the conclusion of a treaty on general and complete disarmament under effective international control. Furthermore, it has been possible to free any amount, however modest, of the enormous resources, both material and human, that are wasted on the unproductive and spiralling arms race, and which should be made available for the purpose of economic

and social development, especially since such a race 'places a great burden on both the developing and the developed countries'.

5. The Members of the United Nations are fully aware of the conviction of their peoples, that the question of general and complete disarmament is of utmost importance and that peace, security and economic and social development are indivisible and have therefore recognized that the corresponding obligations and responsibilities are universal.

6. Thus a powerful current of opinion has gradually formed, leading to the convening of what will go down in the annals of the United Nations as the first session of the General Assembly devoted to disarmament.

7. The outcome of this special session, whose deliberations have to a large extent been facilitated by the five sessions of the Preparatory Committee which preceded it, is the present Final Document. This introduction serves as a preface to the document which comprises also the following three sections: a Declaration, a Programme of Action and recommendations concerning the international machinery for disarmament negotiations.

8. While the final objective of the efforts of all States should continue to be general and complete disarmament under effective international control, the immediate goal is that of the elimination of the danger of a nuclear war and the implementation of measures to halt and reverse the arms race and clear the path towards lasting peace. Negotiations on the entire range of those issues should be based on the strict observance of the purposes and principles enshrined in the Charter of the United Nations, with full recognition of the role of the United Nations in the field of disarmament and reflecting the vital interest of all the peoples of the world in this sphere. The aim of the Declaration is to review and assess the existing situation, outline the objectives and the priority tasks and set forth fundamental principles for disarmament negotiations.

9. For disarmament, the aims and purposes of which the Declaration proclaims, to become a reality it was essential to agree on a series of specific disarmament measures, selected by common accord as those on which there is a consensus to the effect that their subsequent realization in the short term appears to be feasible. There is also a need to prepare through agreed procedures a comprehensive disarmament programme. That programme, passing through all the necessary stages, should lead to general and complete disarmament under effective international control. Procedures for watching over the fulfilment of the obligations thus assumed had also to be agreed upon. That is the purpose of the Programme of Action.

10. Although the decisive factor for achieving real measures of disarmament is the 'political will' of States, and especially of those possessing nuclear weapons,

a significant role can also be played by the effective functioning of an appropriate international machinery designed to deal with the problems of disarmament in its various aspects. Consequently, it would be necessary that the two kinds of organs required to that end, the deliberative and the negotiating organs, have the appropriate organization and procedures that would be most conducive to obtaining constructive results. The fourth and last section of the Final Document has been prepared with that end in view.

II. DECLARATION

11. Mankind today is confronted with an unprecedented threat of self-extinction arising from the massive and competitive accumulation of the most destructive weapons ever produced. Existing arsenals of nuclear weapons alone are more than sufficient to destroy all life on earth. Failure of efforts to halt and reverse the arms race, in particular the nuclear weapons, increases the danger of the proliferation of nuclear weapons. Yet the arms race continues. Military budgets are constantly growing, with enormous consumption of human and material resources. The increase in weapons, especially nuclear weapons, far from helping to strengthen international security, on the contrary weakens it. The vast stockpiles and tremendous build-up of arms and armed forces and the competition for qualitative refinement of weapons of all kinds to which scientific resources and technological advances are diverted, pose incalculable threats to peace. This situation both reflects and aggravates international tensions, sharpens conflicts in various regions of the world, hinders the process of detente, exacerbates the differences between opposing military alliances, jeopardizes the security of all States, heightens the sense of insecurity among all States, including the non-nuclear-weapon States, and increases the threat of nuclear war.

12. The arms race, particularly in its nuclear aspect, runs counter to efforts to achieve further relaxation of international tension, to establish international relations based on peaceful coexistence and trust between all States, and to develop broad international co-operation and understanding. The arms race impedes the realization of the purposes, and is incompatible with the principles, of the Charter of the United Nations, especially respect for sovereignty, refraining from the threat or use of force against the territorial integrity or political independence of any State, peaceful settlement of disputes and non-intervention and non-interference in the internal affairs of States. It also adversely affects the rights of peoples freely to determine their systems of social and economic development, and hinders the struggle for

self-determination and the elimination of colonial rule, racial or foreign domination or occupation. Indeed, the massive accumulation of armaments and the acquisition of armaments technology by racist regimes, as well as their possible acquisition of nuclear weapons, present a challenging and increasingly dangerous obstacle to a world community faced with the urgent need to disarm. It is, therefore, essential for purposes of disarmament to prevent any further acquisition of arms or arms technology by such regimes, especially through strict adherence by all States to relevant decisions of the Security Council.

13. Enduring international peace and security cannot be built on the accumulation of weaponry by military alliances nor be sustained by a precarious balance of deterrence or doctrines of strategic superiority. Genuine and lasting peace can only be created through the effective implementation of the security system provided for in the Charter of the United Nations and the speedy and substantial reduction of arms and armed forces, by international agreement and mutual example leading ultimately to general and complete disarmament under effective international control. At the same time, the causes of the arms race and threats to peace must be reduced and to this end effective action should be taken to eliminate tensions and settle disputes by peaceful means.

14. Since the process of disarmament affects the vital security interests of all States, they must all be actively concerned with and contribute to the measures of disarmament and arms limitations, which have an essential part to play in maintaining and strengthening international security. Therefore the role and responsibility of the United Nations in the sphere of disarmament, in accordance with its Charter, must be strengthened.

15. It is essential that not only Governments but also the peoples of the world recognize and understand the dangers in the present situation. In order that an international conscience may develop and that world public opinion may exercise a positive influence, the United Nations should increase the dissemination of information on the armaments race and disarmament with the full co-operation of member states.

16. In a world of finite resources there is a close relationship between expenditure on armaments and economic and social development. Military expenditures are reaching ever higher levels, the highest percentage of which can be attributed to the nuclear weapon States and most of their allies, with prospects of further expansion and the danger of further increase in the expenditures of other countries. The hundreds of billions of dollars spent annually on the manufacture or improvement of weapons are in sombre and dramatic contrast to the want and poverty in which two thirds of the world's population live. This colossal waste of resources is even more serious in that

it diverts to military purposes not only material but also technical and human resources which are urgently needed for development in all countries, particularly in the developing countries. Thus, the economic and social consequences of the arms race are so detrimental that its continuation is obviously incompatible with the implementation of the new international economic order based on justice, equity and co-operation. Consequently, resources released as a result of the implementation of disarmament measures should be used in a manner which will help to promote the well-being of all peoples and to improve the economic conditions of the developing countries.

17. Disarmament has thus become an imperative and most urgent task facing the international community. No real progress has been made so far in the crucial field of the reduction of armaments. However, certain positive changes in international relations in some areas of the world provide some encouragement. Agreements have been reached that have been important in limiting certain weapons or eliminating them altogether, as in the case of the Convention on the Prohibition of the Development, Production and Stockpiling of Bacteriological (Biological) and Toxin Weapons and on Their Destruction, and excluding particular areas from the arms race. The fact remains that these agreements relate only to measures of limited restraint while the arms race continues. These partial measures have done little to bring the world closer to the goal of general and complete disarmament. For more than a decade there have been no negotiations leading to a treaty on general and complete disarmament. The pressing need now is to translate into practical terms the provisions of this Final Document and to proceed along the road of binding and effective international agreements in the field of disarmament.

18. Removing the threat of a world war - a nuclear war - is the most acute and urgent task of the present day. Mankind is confronted with a choice: we must halt the arms race and proceed to disarmament or face annihilation.

19. This ultimate objective of the efforts of States in the disarmament process is general and complete disarmament under effective international control. The principal goals of disarmament are to ensure the survival of mankind and to eliminate the danger of war, in particular nuclear war, to ensure that war is no longer an instrument for settling international disputes and that the use and the threat of force are eliminated from international life, as provided for in the Charter of the United Nations. Progress towards this objective requires the conclusion and implementation of agreements on the cessation of the arms race and on genuine measures of disarmament taking into account the need of States to protect their security.

20. Among such measures, effective measures of nuclear disarmament and the prevention of nuclear war have the highest priority. To this end, it is

imperative to remove the threat of nuclear weapons, to halt and reverse the nuclear arms race until the total elimination of nuclear weapons and their delivery systems has been achieved, and to prevent the proliferation of nuclear weapons. At the same time, other measures designed to prevent the outbreak of nuclear war and to lessen the danger of the threat or use of nuclear weapons should be taken.

21. Along with these, agreements or other effective measures should be adopted to prohibit or prevent the development, production or use of other weapons of mass destruction. In this context, an agreement on elimination of all chemical weapons should be concluded as a matter of high priority.

22. Together with negotiations on nuclear disarmament measures, negotiations should be carried out on the balanced reduction of armed forces and of conventional armaments, based on the principle of undiminished security of the parties with a view to promoting or enhancing stability at a lower military level, taking into account the need of all States to protect their security. These negotiations should be conducted with particular emphasis on armed forces and conventional weapons of nuclear-weapon States and other military significant countries. There should also be negotiations on the limitation of international transfer of conventional weapons, based, in particular, on the same principle, and taking into account the inalienable right to self-determination and independence of peoples under colonial or foreign domination and the obligations of States to respect that right, in accordance with the Charter of the United Nations and the Declaration on Principles of International Law concerning Friendly Relations and Co-operation Among States, as well as the need of recipient States to protect their security.

23. Further international action should be taken to prohibit or restrict for humanitarian reasons the use of specific conventional weapons, including those which may be excessively injurious, cause unnecessary suffering or have indiscriminate effects.

24. Collateral measures in both the nuclear and conventional fields, together with other measures specifically designed to build confidence, should be undertaken in order to contribute to the creation of favourable conditions for the adoption of additional disarmament measures and to further relaxation of international tension.

25. Negotiations and measures in the field of disarmament shall be guided by the fundamental principles set forth below.

26. All States Members of the United Nations reaffirm their full commitment to the purposes of the Charter of the United Nations and their obligation strictly to observe its principles as well as other relevant and generally accepted principles of international law relating to the maintenance

of international peace ·and security. They stress the special importance of refraining from the threat or use of force against the sovereignty, territorial integrity or political independence of any State, or against peoples under colonial or foreign domination seeking to exercise their right to self-determination and to achieve independence, non-intervention in the internal affairs of other States; and the peaceful settlement of disputes, having regard to the inherent right of States to individual and collective self-defence in accordance with the Charter.

27. In accordance with the Charter, the United Nations has a central role and primary responsibility in the sphere of disarmament. In order effectively to discharge this role and facilitate and encourage all measures in this field, the United Nations should be kept appropriately informed of all steps in this field, whether unilateral, bilateral, regional or multilateral, without prejudice to the progress of negotiations.

28. All these peoples of the world have a vital interest in the success of disarmament negotiations. Consequently, all States have the duty to contribute to efforts in the field of disarmament. All States have the right to participate on the equal footing in those multilateral disarmament negotiations which have a direct bearing on their national security. While disarmament is the responsibility of all States, the nuclear-weapon States have the primary responsibility for nuclear disarmament, and, together with other military significant States for halting and reserving the arms race. It is therefore important to secure their active participation.

29. The adoption of disarmament measures should take place in such an equitable and balanced manner as to ensure the right of each State to security and that no individual State or group of States may obtain advantages over others at any stage. At each stage the objective should be undiminished security at the lowest possible level of armaments and military forces.

30. An acceptable balance of mutual responsibilities and obligations for nuclear and non-nuclear-weapon States should be strictly observed.

31. Disarmament and arms limitation agreements should provide for adequate measures of verification satisfactory to all parties concerned in order to create the necessary confidence and ensure that they are being observed by all parties. The form and modalities of the verification to be provided for in any special agreement depend upon and should be determined by the purposes, scope and nature of the agreement. Agreements should provide for the participation of parties directly or through the United Nations system in the verification process. Where appropriate, a combination of several methods of verification as well as other compliance procedures should be employed.

32. All States, and in particular nuclear weapon States, should consider various proposals designed to secure the avoidance of the use of nuclear weapons, and the prevention of nuclear war. In this context, while noting the declarations made by nuclear-weapon States, effective arrangements, as appropriate, to assure non-nuclear-weapon States against the use or the threat of use of nuclear weapons could strengthen the security of those States and international peace and security.

33. The establishment of nuclear-weapon-free zones on the basis of agreements or arrangements freely arrived at among the States of the zone concerned, and the full compliance with those agreements or arrangements, thus ensuring that the zones are genuinely free from nuclear weapons, and respect for such zones by nuclear-weapon States, constitute an important disarmament measure.

34. Disarmament, relaxation of international tension, respect for the right to self-determination and national independence, the peaceful settlement of disputes in accordance with the Charter of the United Nations and the strengthening of international peace and security are related to each other. Progress in any of these spheres has a beneficial effect on all of them; in turn, failure in one sphere has negative effects on others.

35. There is also a close relationship between disarmament and development. Progress in the former would help greatly to the realization of the latter. Therefore resources released as a result of the implementation of the disarmament measures should be devoted to economic and social development of all nations and contribute to the bridging of the economic gap between developed and developing countries.

36. Non-proliferation of nuclear weapons is a matter of universal concern. Measures of disarmament must be consistent with the inalienable right of all States, without discrimination, to develop, acquire and use nuclear technology, equipment and materials for the peaceful use of nuclear energy and to determine their peaceful nuclear programmes in accordance with their national priorities, needs and interests, bearing in mind the need to prevent the proliferation of nuclear weapons. International co-operation in the peaceful uses of nuclear energy should be conducted under agreed and appropriate international safeguards applied on a non-discriminatory basis.

37. Significant progress in disarmament, including nuclear disarmament, would be facilitated by parallel measures to strengthen the security of States and to improve in general the international situation.

38. Negotiations on partial measures of disarmament should be conducted concurrently with negotiations on more comprehensive measures and should be followed by negotiations leading to a treaty on general and complete

disarmament under effective international control.

39. Qualitative and quantitative disarmament measures are both important for halting the arms race. Efforts to that end must include negotiations on the limitation and cessation of the qualitative improvement of armaments, especially weapons of mass destruction and the development of new means of warfare so that ultimately scientific and technological achievements may be used solely for peaceful purposes.

40. Universality of disarmament agreements helps create confidence among States. When multilateral agreements in the field of disarmament are negotiated, every effort should be made to ensure that they are universally acceptable. The full compliance of all parties with the provisions contained in such agreements would also contribute to the attainment of that goal.

41. In order to create favourable conditions for success in the disarmament process, all States should strictly abide by the provisions of the Charter of the United Nations, refrain from actions which might adversely affect efforts in the field of disarmament, and display a constructive approach to negotiations and the political will to reach agreements. There are certain negotiations on disarmament under way at different levels, the early and successful completion of which could contribute to limiting the arms race. Unilateral measures of arms limitation or reduction could also contribute to the attainment of that goal.

42. Since prompt measures should be taken in order to halt and reverse the arms race, member states hereby declare that they will respect the above-stated objectives and principles and make every effort faithfully to carry out the Programme of Action set forth in section III below.

III. PROGRAMME OF ACTION

43. Progress towards the goal of general and complete disarmament can be achieved through the implementation of a programme of action on disarmament, in accordance with the goals and principles established in the Declaration on disarmament. The present Programme of Action contains priorities and measures in the field of disarmament that States should undertake as a matter of urgency with a view to halting and reversing the arms race and to giving the necessary impetus to efforts designed to achieve genuine disarmament leading to general and complete disarmament under effective international control.

44. The present Programme of Action enumerates the specific measures of disarmament which should be implemented over the next few years, as well as other measures and studies to prepare the way for future negotiations and

for progress toward general and complete disarmament.

45. Priorities in disarmament negotiations shall be: nuclear weapons; other weapons of mass destruction, including chemical weapons; conventional weapons, including any which may be deemed to be excessively injurious or to have indiscriminate effects; and reduction of armed forces.

46. Nothing should preclude Sates from conducting negotiations on all priority items concurrently.

47. Nuclear weapons pose the greatest danger to mankind and to the survival of civilization. It is essential to halt and reverse the nuclear arms race in all its aspects in order to avert the danger of war involving nuclear weapons. The ultimate goal in this context is the complete elimination of nuclear weapons.

48. In the task of achieving the goals of nuclear disarmament, all the nuclear-weapon States, in particular those among them which possess the most important nuclear arsenals, bear a special responsibility.

49. The process of nuclear disarmament should be carried out in such a way, and requires measures to ensure, that the security of all States is guaranteed at progressively lower levels of nuclear armaments, taking into account the relative qualitative and quantitative importance of the existing arsenals of the nuclear-weapon States and other States concerned.

50. The achievement of nuclear disarmament will require urgent negotiation of agreements at appropriate stages and with adequate measures of verification satisfactory to the States concerned for:

* cessation of the qualitative improvement and development of nuclear-weapons systems;

* cessation of the production of all types of nuclear weapons and their means of delivery, and the production of fissionable material for weapons purposes;

* a comprehensive phased programme with agreed time-frames, whenever feasible, for progressive and balanced reduction of stockpiles of nuclear weapons and their means of delivery, leading to their ultimate and complete elimination at the earliest possible time.

Consideration can be given in the course of the negotiations to mutual and agreed limitation or prohibition, without prejudice to the security of any State, of any types of nuclear armaments.

51. The cessation of nuclear-weapon testing by all States within the framework of an effective nuclear disarmament process would be in the interest of mankind. It would make a significant contribution to the above aim of ending the qualitative improvement of nuclear weapons and the development of new types of such weapons and of preventing the proliferation of nuclear weapons. In this context

the negotiations now in progress on a 'treaty prohibiting nuclear-weapon tests, and a protocol covering nuclear explosions for peaceful purposes, which would be an integral part of the treaty', should be concluded urgently and the result submitted for full consideration by the multilateral negotiating body with a view to the submission of a draft treaty to the General Assembly at the earliest possible date.

All efforts should be made by the negotiating parties to achieve an agreement which, following General Assembly endorsement, could attract the widest possible adherence.

In this context, various views were expressed by non-nuclear-weapon States that, pending the conclusion of this treaty, the world community would be encouraged if all the nuclear-weapon States refrained from testing nuclear weapons. In this connection, some nuclear-weapon States expressed different views.

52. The Union of Soviet Socialist Republics and the United States of America should conclude at the earliest possible date the agreement they have been pursuing for several years in the second series of the strategic arms limitation talks (SALT II). They are invited to transmit in good time the text of the agreement to the General Assembly. It should be followed promptly by further strategic arms limitation negotiations between the two parties, leading to agreed significant reductions of, and qualitative limitations on, strategic arms. It should constitute an important step in the direction of nuclear disarmament and ultimately of establishment of a world free of such weapons.

53. The process of nuclear disarmament described in the paragraph on this subject should be expedited by the urgent and vigorous pursuit to a successful conclusion of ongoing negotiations and the urgent initiation of further negotiations among the nuclear-weapon States.

54. Significant progress in nuclear disarmament would be facilitated both by parallel political or international legal measures to strengthen the security of States and by progress in the limitation and reduction of armed forces and conventional armaments of the nuclear-weapon States and other States in the regions concerned.

55. Real progress in the field of nuclear disarmament could create an atmosphere conducive to progress in conventional disarmament on a world-wide basis.

56. The most effective guarantee against the danger of nuclear war and the use of nuclear weapons is nuclear disarmament and the complete elimination of nuclear weapons.

57. Pending the achievement of this goal, for which negotiations should be

vigorously pursued, and bearing in mind the devastating results which nuclear war would have on belligerents and non-belligerents alike, the nuclear-weapon States have special responsibilities to undertake measures aimed at preventing the outbreak of nuclear war, and of the use of force in international relations, subject to the provisions of the Charter of the United Nations, including the use of nuclear weapons.

58. In this context, all States and in particular nuclear-weapon States should consider as soon as possible various proposals designed to secure the avoidance of the use of nuclear weapons, the prevention of nuclear war and related objectives, where possible through international agreement and thereby ensure that the survival of mankind is not endangered. All States should actively participate in efforts to bring about conditions in international relations among States in which a code of peaceful conduct of nations in international affairs could be agreed and which would preclude the use or threat of use of nuclear weapons.

59. In the same context, the nuclear weapon States are called upon to take steps to assure the non-nuclear-weapon States against the use or threat of use of nuclear weapons. The General Assembly notes the declarations made by the nuclear-weapon States and urges them to pursue efforts to conclude as appropriate effective arrangements to assure non-nuclear-weapon States against the use or threat of use of nuclear weapons.

60. The establishment of nuclear-free zones on the basis of arrangements freely arrived at among the States of the region concerned, constitutes an important disarmament measure.

61. The process of establishing such zones in different parts of the world should be encouraged with the ultimate objective of achieving a world entirely free of nuclear weapons. In the process of establishing such zones, the characteristics of each region should be taken into account. The States participating in such zones should undertake to comply fully with all the objectives, purposes and principles of the agreements or arrangements establishing the zones, thus ensuring that they are genuinely free from nuclear weapons.

62. With respect to such zones, the nuclear-weapon States in turn are called upon to give undertakings, the modalities of which are to be negotiated with the competent authority of each zone, in particular :

(a) to respect strictly the status of the nuclear-weapon-free zone;

(b) to refrain from the use or threat of use of nuclear weapons against the States of the zone.

63. In the light of existing conditions, and without prejudices to other measures which may be considered in other regions, the following measures

are especially desirable:

(a) Adoption by the States concerned of all relevant measures to ensure the full application of the Treaty for the Prohibition of Nuclear Weapons in Latin America (Treaty of Tlatelolco), taking into account the views expressed at the special session on the adherence to it.

(b) Signature and ratification of the Additional Protocols of the Treaty for the Prohibition of Nuclear Weapons in Latin America (Treaty of Tlatelolco) by the States entitled to become parties to those instruments which have not yet done so;

(c) In Africa, where the Organization of African Unity has affirmed a decision for the denuclearization of the region, the Security Council shall take appropriate effective steps whenever necessary to prevent the frustration of this objective;

(d) The serious consideration of the practical and urgent steps, as described in the paragraphs above, required for the implementation of the proposal to establish a nuclear-weapon-free zone in the Middle East in accordance with the relevant General Assembly resolutions where all parties directly concerned have expressed their support for the concept and where the danger of nuclear-weapon proliferation exists. The establishment of a nuclear-weapon-free zone in the Middle East would greatly enhance international peace and security. Pending the establishment of such a zone in the region, States of the region should solemnly declare that they will refrain on a reciprocal basis from producing, acquiring, or in any other way, possessing nuclear weapons and nuclear explosive devices, and from permitting the stationing of nuclear weapons on their territory by any third party and agree to place all their nuclear activities under International Atomic Energy Agency safeguards. Consideration should be given to a Security Council role in advancing the establishment of a Middle East nuclear-weapon-free zone;

(e) All States in the region of South Asia have expressed their determination of keeping their countries free of nuclear weapons. No action should be taken by them which might deviate from that objective. In this context, the question of establishing a nuclear-weapon-free zone in South Asia has been dealt with in several resolutions of the General Assembly which is keeping the subject under consideration.

64. The establishment of zones of peace in various regions of the world, under appropriate conditions, to be clearly defined and determined freely by the States concerned in the zone, taking into account the characteristics of the zone and the principles of the Charter of the United Nations, and in conformity with international law, can contribute to strengthening the security of States within such zones and to international peace and security as a whole.

In this regard, the General Assembly notes the proposals for the establishment of zones of peace, inter alia, in:

(a) South-East Asia where States in the region have expressed interest in the establishment of such a zone, in conformity with their views;

(b) Indian Ocean, taking into account the deliberations of the General Assembly and its relevant resolutions and the need to ensure the maintenance of peace and security in the region.

65. It is imperative as an integral part of the effort to halt and reverse the arms race, to prevent the proliferation of nuclear weapons. The goal of nuclear non-proliferation is on the one hand to prevent the emergence of any additional nuclear-weapon States beside the existing five nuclear-weapon States, and on the other progressively to reduce and eventually eliminate nuclear weapons altogether. This involves obligations and responsibilities on the part of both nuclear-weapon States and non-nuclear weapon States, the former undertaking to stop the nuclear-arms race and to achieve disarmament by urgent application of measures outlined in the relevant paragraphs of this Document, and all States undertaking to prevent the spread of nuclear weapons.

66. Effective measures can and should be taken at the national level and through international agreements to minimize the danger of the proliferation of nuclear weapons without jeopardizing energy supplies or the development of nuclear energy for peaceful purposes.Therefore, the nuclear-weapon States and the non-nuclear-weapon States should jointly take further steps to develop an international consensus of ways and means, on a universal and non-discriminatory basis, to prevent the proliferation of nuclear weapons.

67. Full implementation of all the provisions of existing instruments on non-proliferation, such as the Treaty on the Non-Proliferation of Nuclear Weapons and/or the Treaty for the Prohibition of Nuclear Weapons in Latin America (Treaty of Tlatelolco) by States parties to those instruments will be an important contribution to this end. Adherence to such instruments has increased in recent years and the hope has been expressed by the parties that this trend might continue.

68. Non-proliferation measures should not jeopardize the full exercise of the inalienable rights of all States to apply and develop their programmes for the peaceful uses of nuclear energy for economic and social development in conformity with their priorities, interests and needs. All States should also have access to, and be free to acquire technology, equipment and materials for peaceful uses of nuclear energy, taking into account the particular needs of the developing countries. International co-operation in this field should be under agreed and appropriate international safeguards applied through the

International Atomic Energy Agency on a non-discriminatory basis in order to prevent effectively proliferation of nuclear weapons.

69. Each country's choices and decisions in the field of the peaceful uses of nuclear energy should be respected without jeopardizing their respective fuel cycle policies or international co-operation, agreements, and contracts for the peaceful use of nuclear energy provided that agreed safeguard measures mentioned above are applied.

70. In accordance with the principles and provisions of Resolution 32/50, international co-operation for the promotion of the transfer and utilization of nuclear technology for economic and social development, especially in the developing countries, should be strengthened.

71. Efforts should be made to conclude the work of the International Nuclear Cycle Evaluation strictly in accordance with the objectives set out in the final communique of its Organizing Conference.

72. All States should adhere to the protocol for the Prohibition of the Use in War of Asphyxiating, Poisonous or Other Gases, and of Bacteriological Methods of Warfare.

73. All States which have not yet done so should consider adhering to the Convention on the Prohibition of the Development, Production and Stockpiling of Bacteriological (Biological) and Toxin Weapons and on Their Destruction.

74. States should also consider the possibility of adhering to multilateral agreements concluded so far in the disarmament field which are mentioned below in this section.

75. The complete and effective prohibition of the development, production and stockpiling of all chemical weapons and their destruction represent one of the most urgent measures of disarmament. Consequently, conclusion of a convention to this end, on which negotiations have been going on for several years, is one of the most urgent tasks of multilateral negotiations. After its conclusion, all States should contribute to ensuring the broadest possible application of the convention through its early signature and ratification.

76. A convention should be concluded prohibiting the development, production, stockpiling and use of radiological weapons.

77. In order to help prevent a qualitative arms race and so that scientific and technological achievements may ultimately be used solely for peaceful purposes, effective measures should be taken to avoid the danger and prevent the emergence of new types of weapons of mass destruction based on new scientific principles and achievements. Efforts should be appropriately pursued aiming at the prohibition of such new types and new systems of weapons of mass destruction.Specific agreements could be concluded on particular types of new

weapons of mass destruction which may be identified. This question should be kept under continuing review.

78. The Committee on Disarmament should keep under review the need for a further prohibition of military or any other hostile use of environmental modification techniques in order to eliminate the dangers to mankind from such use.

79. In order to promote the peaceful use and to avoid an arms race on the sea-bed and the ocean floor and the subsoil thereof, the Committee on Disarmament is requested - in consultation with the States parties to the Treaty on the Prohibition of the Emplacement of Nuclear Weapons and Other Weapons of Mass Destruction on the Sea-bed and the Ocean Floor and the Subsoil Thereof, and taking into account the proposals made during the 1977 Review Conference and any relevant technological developments - to proceed promptly with the consideration of further measures in the field of disarmament for the prevention of an arms race in that environment.

80. In order to prevent an arms race in outer space, further measures should be taken and appropriate international negotiations be held in accordance with the spirit of the Treaty on Principles Governing the Activities of States in the Exploration and Use of Outer Space including the Moon and Other Celestial Bodies.

81. Together with the negotiations on nuclear disarmament measures, the limitation and gradual reduction of armed forces and conventional weapons should be resolutely pursued within the framework of progress towards general and complete disarmament. States with the largest military arsenals have a special responsibility in pursuing the process of conventional armaments reductions.

82. In particular the achievement of a more stable situation in Europe at a lower level of military potential on the basis of approximate equality and parity, as well as on the basis of undiminished security of all States with full respect for security interests and independence of States outside military alliances, by agreement on mutual reductions and limitations would contribute to the strengthening of security in Europe and constitute a significant step towards enhancing international peace and security. Current efforts to this end should be continued most energetically.

83. Agreements or other measures should be resolutely pursued on a bilateral, regional and multilateral basis with the aim of strengthening peace and security at a lower level of forces, by the limitation and reduction of armed forces and of conventional weapons, taking into account the need of States to protect their security, bearing in mind the inherent right of self-defence embodied in the Charter of the United Nations and without prejudice

to the principle of equal rights and self-determination of peoples in accordance with the Charter, and the need to ensure balance at each stage an undiminished security of all States Such measures might include those in the following two paragraphs.

84. Bilateral, regional and multilateral consultations and conferences where appropriate conditions exist with the participation of all the countries concerned for the consideration of different aspects of conventional disarmament, such as the initiative envisaged in the Declaration of Ayacucho subscribed in 1974 by eight Latin American countries.

85. Consultations should be carried out among major arms supplier and recipient countries on the limitation of all types of international transfer of conventional weapons, based, in particular, on the principle of undiminished security of the parties with a view to promoting or enhancing stability at a lower military level, taking into account the need of all States to protect their security as well as the inalienable right to self-determination and independence of peoples under colonial or foreign domination and the obligations of States to respect that right, in accordance with the Charter of the United Nations and the Declaration on Principles of International Law concerning Friendly Relations and Co-operation Among States.

86. The 1979 United Nations Conference on Prohibitions or Restrictions of Use of Certain Conventional Weapons which may be Deemed to be Excessively Injurious or to have Indiscriminate Effects should seek agreement, in the light of humanitarian and military considerations, on the prohibition or restriction of use of certain conventional weapons including those which may cause unnecessary suffering or which may have indiscriminate effects. The conference should consider specific categories of such weapons, including those which were the subject-matter of previously conducted discussions.

87. All States are called upon to contribute towards carrying out this task.

88. The result of the Conference should be considered by all States and especially producer States, in regard to the question of the transfer of such weapons to other States.

89. Gradual reduction of military budgets on a mutually agreed basis, for example in absolute figures or in terms of percentage points, particularly by nuclear-weapon States and other militarily significant States would be a measure that would contribute to the curbing of the arms race, and would increase the possibilities of reallocation of resources now being used for military purposes to economic and social development, particularly for the benefit of the developing countries. The basis for implementing this measures will have to be agreed by all participating States and will require ways and means of its implementation acceptable to all of them, taking

account of the problems involved in assessing the relative significance of reductions as among different States and with due regard to the proposals of States on all the aspects of reduction of military budgets.

90. The General Assembly should continue to consider what concrete steps should be taken to facilitate the reduction of military budgets bearing in mind the relevant proposals and documents of the United Nations on this question.

91. In order to facilitate the conclusion and effective implementation of disarmament agreements and to create confidence, States should accept appropriate provisions for verification in such agreements.

92. In the context of international disarmament negotiations, the problem of verification should be further examined and adequate methods and procedures in this field be considered. Every effort should be made to develop appropriate methods and procedures which are non-discriminatory and which do not unduly interfere with the internal affairs of other States or jeopardize their economic and social development.

93. In order to facilitate the process of disarmament, it is necessary to take measures and pursue policies to strengthen international peace and security and to build confidence among States. Commitment to confidence-building measures could significantly contribute to preparing for further progress in disarmament. For this purpose, measures such as the following and other measures yet to be agreed, should be undertaken:

(1) The prevention of attacks which take place by accident, miscalculation or communications failure by taking steps to improve communications between Governments, particularly in areas of tension, by the establishment of 'hot lines' and other methods of reducing the risk of conflict.

(2) States assess the possible implications of their military research and development for existing agreements as well as for further efforts in the field of disarmament.

(3) The Secretary-General shall periodically submit reports to the General Assembly on the economic and social consequences of the arms race and its extremely harmful effects on world peace and security.

94. In view of the relationship between expenditure on armaments and economic and social development and the necessity to release real resources now being used for military purposes to economic and social development in the world, particularly for the benefit of the developing countries, the Secretary-General should, with the assistance of a group of qualified governmental experts appointed by him, initiate an expert study on the relationship between disarmament and development. The Secretary-General should submit an interim report on the subject to the General Assembly at its thirty-fourth

session and submit the final results to the Assembly at its thirty-sixth session for subsequent action.

95. The expert study should have the terms of reference contained in the report of the Ad Hoc Group on the Relationship between Disarmament and Development appointed by the Secretary-General in accordance with General Assembly resolution 32/88 A of 12 December 1977. It should investigate the three main areas listed in the report, bearing in mind the United Nations studies previously carried out. The study should be made in the context of how disarmament can contribute to the establishment of the new international economic order. The study should be forward-looking and policy-oriented and place special emphasis on both the desirability of a reallocation, following disarmament measures, of resources now being used for military purposes to economic and social development, particularly for the benefit of the developing countries and the substantive feasibility of such a reallocation. A principal aim should be to produce results that could effectively guide the formulation of practical measures to reallocate those resources at the local, national, regional and international levels.

96. Taking further steps in the field of disarmament and other measures aimed at promoting international peace and security would be facilitated by carrying out studies by the Secretary-General in this field with appropriate assistance from governmental or consultant experts.

97. The Secretary-General shall, with the assistance of consultant experts, appointed by him, continue the study of the interrelationship between disarmament and international security and submit it to the thirty-fourth session of the General Assembly, as requested in resolution A/RES/32/87/C.

98. The thirty-third and subsequent sessions of the General Assembly should determine the specific guide-lines for carrying out studies, taking into account the proposals already submitted including those made by individual countries at the special session, as well as other proposals which can be introduced later in this field. In doing so, the General Assembly would take into consideration a report on those matters prepared by the Secretary-General.

99. In order to mobilize world public opinion on behalf of disarmament, the specific measures set forth below, designed to increase the dissemination of information about the armaments race and the efforts to halt and reverse it, should be adopted:

100. Governmental and non-governmental information organs and those of the United Nations and its specialized agencies should give priority to the preparation and distribution of printed and audio-visual material relating to the danger represented by the armaments race as well as to the disarmaments

efforts and negotiations on specific disarmament measures.

101. In particular, publicity should be given to the final documents of the special session.

102. The General Assembly proclaims a week starting 24 October, the day of the foundation of the United Nations, as week devoted to fostering the objectives of disarmament.

103. To encourage study and research on disarmament, the United Nations Centre for Disarmament should intensify its activities in the presentation of information concerning the armaments race and disarmament. Also, the United Nations Education, Scientific and Cultural Organization (UNESCO), is urged to intensify its activities aimed at facilitating research and publications on disarmament, related to its fields of competence, especially in developing countries, and should disseminate the results of such research.

104. Throughout this process of disseminating information about the developments in the disarmament field of all countries, there should be increased participation by non-governmental organizations concerned with the matter, through closer liaison between them and United Nations.

105. Member states should be encouraged to ensure a better flow of information with regard to the various aspects of disarmament to avoid dissemination of false and tendentious information concerning armaments and to concentrate on the danger of escalation of the armaments race and on the need for general and complete disarmament under effective international control.

106. With a view to contributing to a greater understanding and awareness of the problems created by the armaments race and of the need for disarmament, Governments and governmental and non-governmental international organizations are urged to take steps to develop programmes of education for disarmament and peace studies at all levels.

107. The General Assembly welcomes the initiative of the United Nations Educational, Scientific and Cultural Organization in planning to hold a world congress on disarmament education and, in this connexion, urges that organization to step up its programme aimed at the development of disarmament education as a distinct field of study through the preparation, inter alia, of teachers' guides, textbooks, readers and audio-visual materials. Member states should take all possible measures to encourage the incorporation of such materials in the curricula of their educational institutes.

108. In order to promote expertise in disarmament in more member states, particularly in the developing countries, the General Assembly decides to establish a programme of fellowships on disarmament. The Secretary-General, taking into account the proposal submitted to the special session,

should prepare guidelines for the programme. He should also submit the financial requirements of 20 fellowships at the thirty-third regular session of the General Assembly, for inclusion in the regular budget of the United Nations bearing in mind the savings that can be made within the existing budgetary appropriations.

109. Implementation of these priorities should lead to general and complete disarmament under effective international control, which remains the ultimate goal of all efforts exerted in the field of disarmament. Negotiations on general and complete disarmament shall be conducted concurrently with the negotiations on partial measures of disarmament. With this purpose in mind, the Committee on Disarmament will undertake the elaboration of a comprehensive programme of disarmament encompassing all measures thought to be advisable in order to ensure that the goal of general and complete disarmament under effective international control becomes a reality in a world in which international peace and security prevail and in which the new international economic order is strengthened and consolidated. The comprehensive programme should contain appropriate procedures for ensuring that the General Assembly is kept fully informed of the progress of the negotiations including an appraisal of the situation when appropriate and, in particular, a continuing review of the implementation of the programme

110. Progress in disarmament should be accompanied by measures to strengthen institutions for maintaining peace and the settlement of international disputes by peaceful means. During and after the implementation of the programme of general and complete disarmament, there should be taken, in accordance with the principles of the United Nations Charter, the necessary measures to maintain international peace and security, including the obligation of States to place at the disposal of the United Nations agreed manpower necessary for an international peace force to be equipped with agreed types of armaments. Arrangements for the use of this force should ensure that the United Nations can effectively deter or suppress any threat or use of arms in violation of the purposes and principles of the United Nations.

111. General and complete disarmament under strict and effective international control shall permit States to have at their disposal only those non-nuclear forces, armaments, facilities and establishments as are agreed to be necessary to maintain internal order and protect the personal security of citizens and in order that States shall support and provide agreed manpower for a United Nations peace force.

112. In addition to the several questions dealt with in this Programme of Action, there are a few others of fundamental importance, on which, because

of the complexity of the issues involved and the short time at the disposal of the special session, it has proved impossible to reach satisfactory agreed conclusions. For those reasons they are treated only in very general terms and, in a few instances, even not treated at all in the Programme.

It should be stressed, however, that a number of concrete approaches to deal with such questions emerged from the exchange of views carried out in the General Assembly which will undoubtedly facilitate the continuation of the study and negotiation of the problems involved in the competent disarmament organs.

IV. MACHINERY

113. While disarmament, particularly in the nuclear field, has become a necessity for the survival of mankind and for the elimination of the danger of nuclear war, little progress has been made since the end of the Second World War. In addition to the need to exercise political will, the international machinery should be utilized more effectively and also improved to enable implementation of the Programme of Action and help the United Nations to fulfil its role in the field of disarmament.

In spite of the best efforts of the international community, adequate results have not been produced with the existing machinery. There is, therefore, an urgent need that existing disarmament machinery be revitalized and forums appropriately constituted for disarmament deliberations with a better representative character.

For maximum effectiveness, two kinds of bodies are required in the field of disarmament - deliberative and negotiating. All member states should be represented on the former, whereas the latter, for the sake of convenience, should have a relatively small membership.

114. The United Nations, in accordance with the Charter, has a central role and primary responsibilities in the sphere of disarmament. Accordingly, it should play a more active role in this field, and in order to discharge its functions effectively, the United Nations should facilitate and encourage all disarmament measures - unilateral, bilateral, regional or multilateral - and be kept duly informed through the General Assembly, or any other appropriate United Nations channel reaching all Members of the Organization, of all disarmament efforts outside its aegis without prejudice to the progress of negotiations.

115. The General Assembly has been and should remain the main deliberative organ of the United Nations in the field of disarmament and should make every effort to facilitate the implementation of disarmament

measures.

An item entitled 'Review of the implementation of the recommendations and decisions adopted by the General Assembly at its tenth special session' shall be included in the provisional agenda of the thirty-third and subsequent sessions of the General Assembly.

116. Draft multilateral disarmament conventions should be subjected to the normal procedures applicable in the law of treaties. Those submitted to the General Assembly for its commendation should be subject to full review by the Assembly.

117. The First Committee of the General Assembly should deal in the future only with questions of disarmament and related international security questions.

118. The General Assembly establishes, as successor to the Commission originally established by resolution 502 (VI), a Disarmament Commission composed of all Members of the United Nations.

The General Assembly decides that:

(a) The Disarmament Commission shall be a deliberative body, a subsidiary organ of the General Assembly, the function of which shall be to consider and make recommendations on various problems in the field of disarmament and to follow up the relevant decisions and recommendations of the special session devoted to disarmament. The Disarmament Commission should, inter alia, consider the elements of a comprehensive programme for disarmament to be submitted as recommendations to the General Assembly and , through it, to the negotiating body, the Committee on Disarmament;

(b) The Disarmament Commission shall function under the rules of procedure relating to the committees of the General Assembly with such modifications as the Commission may deem necessary and shall make every effort to ensure that, in so far as possible, decisions on substantive issues be adopted by consensus;

(c) The Disarmament Commission shall report annually to the General Assembly. It will submit for the consideration by the thirty-third session of the General Assembly a report on organizational matters. In 1979, the Disarmament Commission will meet for a period not exceeding four weeks, the dates to be decided at the thirty-third session of the General Assembly;

(d) The Secretary-General shall furnish such experts, staff and services as are necessary for the effective accomplishment of the Commission's functions.

119. A second special session of the General Assembly devoted to disarmament should be held on a date to be decided by the General Assembly at its thirty-third session.

120. The General Assembly is conscious of the work that has been done

by the international negotiating body that has been meeting since March 14, 1962 as well as the considerable and urgent work that remains to be accomplished in the field of disarmament.

The General Assembly is deeply aware of the continuing requirement for a single multilateral disarmament negotiating forum of limited size taking decisions on the basis of consensus. It attaches great importance to the participation of all the nuclear-weapon States in an appropriately constituted negotiating body: the Committee on Disarmament.

The General Assembly welcomes the agreement reached following appropriate consultations among the member states during the Special Session of the General Assembly Devoted to Disarmament will be open to the nuclear-weapon States, and 32 to 35 other States to be chosen in consultation with the President of the thirty-second session of the General Assembly; that the membership of the Committee on Disarmament will be reviewed at regular intervals; that the Committee on Disarmament will be convened in Geneva not later than January 1979 by the country whose name appears first in the alphabetical list of membership; and that the Committee on Disarmament will:

(a) Conduct its work by consensus;

(b) Adopt its own rules of procedure;

(c) Request the Secretary-General of the United Nations, following consultations with the Committee on Disarmament, to appoint the Secretary of the Committee, who shall also act as his personal representative, to assist the Committee and its Chairman in organizing the business and timetables of the Committee;

(d) Rotate the chairmanship of the Committee among all its members on a monthly basis;

(e) Adopt its own agenda taking into account the recommendations made to it by the General Assembly and the proposals presented by the members of the Committee;

(f) Submit a report to the General Assembly annually, or more frequently as appropriate, and provide its formal and other relevant documents to the member states of the United Nations on a regular basis;

(g) Make arrangements for interested States, not members of the Committee, to submit to the Committee written proposals or working documents on measures of disarmament that are the subject of negotiation in the Committee and to participate in the discussion of the subject matter of such proposals or working documents;

(h) Invite States not members of the Committee, upon their request, to express views in the Committee when the particular concerns of those States are under discussion;

(i) Open its plenary meetings to the public unless otherwise decided.

121. Bilateral and regional disarmament negotiations may also play an important role and could facilitate negotiations of multilateral agreements in the field of disarmament.

122. At the earliest appropriate time, a world disarmament conference should be convened with universal participation and with adequate preparation.

123. In order to enable the United Nations to continue to fulfil its role in the field of disarmament and to carry out the additional assigned to it by this special session, the United Nations Centre for Disarmament should be adequately strengthened and its research and information functions accordingly extended.

The Centre should also take account fully of the possibilities offered by United Nations specialized agencies and other institutions and programmes within the United Nations system with regard to studies and information on disarmament. The Centre should also increase contacts with non-governmental organizations and research institutions in view of the valuable role they play in the field of disarmament. This role could be encouraged also in other ways that may be considered as appropriate.

124. The Secretary-General is requested to set up an advisory board of eminent persons, selected on the basis of their personal expertise and taking into account the principle of equitable geographical representation, to advise him on various aspects of studies to be made under the auspices of the United Nations in the field of disarmament and arms limitation, including a programme of such studies.

125. The General Assembly notes with satisfaction that the active participation of the member states in the consideration of the agenda items of the special session and the proposals and suggestions submitted by them and reflected to a considerable extent in the Final Document have made a valuable contribution to the work of the special session and to its positive conclusion.

126. In adopting this Final Document, the States Members of the United Nations solemnly reaffirm their determination to work for general and complete disarmament and to make further collective efforts aimed at strengthening peace and international security; eliminating the threat of war, particularly nuclear war; implementing practical measures aimed at halting and reversing the arms race; strengthening the procedures for the peaceful settlement of disputes; and reducing military expenditures and utilizing the resources thus released in a manner which will help to promote the well-being of all peoples and to improve the economic conditions of the

developing countries.

127. The General Assembly expresses its satisfaction that the proposals submitted to its special session devoted to disarmament and the deliberations thereon have made it possible to reaffirm and define in its Final Document fundamental principles, goals, priorities and procedures for the implementation of the above purposes, either in the Declaration or the Programme of Action or in both. The Assembly also welcomes the important decisions agreed upon regarding the deliberative and negotiating machinery and is confident that these organs will discharge their functions in an effective manner.

128. Finally, it should be borne in mind that the number of States that participated in the general debate, as well as the high level of representation and the depth and scope of that debate, are unprecedented in the history of disarmament efforts. Several Heads of State or Government sent messages and expressed their good wishes for the success of the special session of the Assembly. Several high officials of specialized agencies and other institutions and programmes within the United Nations system and spokesmen of 25 non-governmental organizations and six research institutes also made valuable contributions to the proceedings of the session. It must be emphasized, more-over, that the special session marks not the end but rather the beginning of a new phase of the efforts of the United Nations in the field of disarmament.

129. The General Assembly is convinced that the discussions of the disarmament problems at the special session and its Final Document will attract the attention of all peoples, further mobilize world public opinion and provide a powerful impetus for the cause of disarmament.

Source: UN Document OPI/618-78-35909-July 1978-10 M (UN Office of Public Information).

Index

153, 157, 161, 172
Foreign Office, 5, 22, 25, 31, 34, 35, 38, 39, 41, 43, 45
France, 11, 31, 38, 39, 44, 62, 77, 120, 121, 128
Frye, 26
Gaglione, 30
general and complete disarmament (GCD), 73, 76, 77, 78, 101, 112, 113, 114, 152, 158
Georgetown meeting, 116, 119
Germany, 20
Ghana, 68
Goldblat, 88
good-faith clause, 99, 150
Gotlieb, 70
Hammarskjold, 43, 64
Hiroshima, 8
historic consensus, 160
Hitler, 7, 16
Howard, 25
Hydrogen bomb, 40, 55
incendiary weapons, 152
India, 68, 90, 126, 136
Indo-China crisis, 30
Indo-China war, 48
Indonesia, 68
inspection, 33, 34, 36, 38, 41, 80
International Atomic Development Agency (IADA), 13, 14
International Atomic Energy Agency, 16
International Control Authority, 16
Iran, 126
Iran-Iraq conflict, 159
Iraq, 174
Italy, 62
Jacobson, 66
Korea, 21
Korean war, 48

Kuwait, 174
Lall, 77
League of Nations, 7, 29, 144
Lima meeting, 133
limitation and reduction of armaments, 7
limited objectives of disarmament, 50
London and Paris Agreements of 1954, 43
Lusaka conference, 115, 116, 119
Mates, 73, 94
Maynes, 150
McLoy-Zorin Agreement of principles for disarmament, 70, 76
memorandum of eight, 81, 90
Mexico, 68, 74, 90, 120, 123, 124
Military Staff Committe, 8
Mojsov, 115
Moscow meeting, 9, 10, 11
Multilateral Nuclear Force (MNF), 85
National Security Council, 46
negative security assurances, 99
Netherlands, 147
New International Economic Order (NIEO), 117, 131, 132, 133, 148, 150, 154, 155
Nigeria, 68
Nitze, 150
Nogee, 32
Non-Aligned group, 64, 66, 83, 84, 87, 89, 92, 95, 105, 117, 123,124, 136, 147, 150, 171, 173
Non-Proliferation Treaty, 4, 78, 82, 86, 90, 103, 129, 150, 169, 170
North Atlantic Treaty Organization (NATO), 79, 85
nuclear disarmament, 2, 21, 23, 72, 89, 90, 100, 124, 129, 152, 154,